PAT CHAPMAN'S BALTI BIBLE

PAT
CHAPMAN'S
BALTI
BIBLE

PHOTOGRAPHY
BY
COLIN POOLE

Hodder & Stoughton

First published in 1998 by Hodder & Stoughton
A division of Hodder Headline PLC

10 9 8 7 6 5 4 3 2 1

A CIP catalogue record for this title is available from the British Library

ISBN: 0 340 72858 2

Colour origination by Ace Pre Press (Southampton)

Printed and bound in Great Britain by
Jarrold Book Printing, Thetford, Norfolk

Hodder and Stoughton
A division of Hodder Headline PLC
338 Euston Road
London NW1 3BH

Edited by Grapevine Publishing Services

Designed by Sara Kidd

Photography by Colin Poole

Jacket Photograph by Gerrit Buntrock

Food cooked and styled for photographs by Dominique and Pat Chapman

Props by Dominique Chapman

I would like to thank several well-known people in the Balti community, both in Birmingham and in Pakistan, who have always given me maximum co-operation in my quest for information. They are:

Mohamed Arif, and Rashid and Abid Mahmood of Adils Balti and Tandoori House, 148 Stoney Lane, Sparkbrook, Birmingham, B12

N. Pasha at K2 Balti House, 107 Alcester Road, Moseley, Birmingham, B13

Mr Gohil, Gohil Emporium (utensils, arts and crafts) 381 Straftford Road, Sparkhill, Birmingham B11

Mr Azad, Azad's Cash and Carry (Balti Supermarket) 154 Stoney Lane, Sparkbrook, Birmingham B12

Mr Dhirendhra Patel, Milan Sweet Centre, 191 Stoney Lane, Sparkbrook, Birmingham, B12, with branches at 93 Newhall Street, Birmingham B3 and 296S Abel Street, Milpitas, California, 95035.

Mr M. Anwar Sajid of the Pakistan Tourism Development Corporation, at Flashman's Hotel, Rawalpindi, and at K2 Motel, Skardu Baltistan.

And my special thanks to the Nazir brothers, and Chef Shafique, for giving me an excellent refresher training course at The Curry Club's 1998 Top UK Balti House, The Royal Naim, 417–419 Stratford Road, Sparkhill, Birmingham B11.

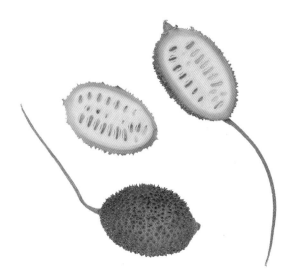

Balti Bible Menu

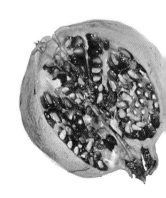

Side Orders

The Balti World

Keeping Balti

Glossary

The Curry Club

The Store Cupboard

Index

Foreword

It is six years since I wrote my first Balti book. Back then Balti was a little-known curry found only in the British Midlands. Mine was the first book on the subject, and it was not expected to sell well. Remarkably, it became a bestseller, and before long others followed suit, and at least 15 other Balti books have been published since. Even more remarkably, Balti spread around Britain and beyond in the space of just one year. Most of Britain's curry houses quickly added Balti to their menu, and there are several overseas Balti houses too, as far afield as Sydney. Every supermarket in Britain produced own-label Balti ready meals. Balti is by now so well established that even President Clinton tasted Balti when the G8 heads of state visited Birmingham for one of their regular meetings. If Balti is good enough for Clinton, Yeltsin and Chirac, what better time for me to update and supersede my original book with this generously illustrated Balti Bible?

But what of its title? A year ago, this book's sister volume *The Curry Bible* was published. I told in that book how its title came about. I hope you already own that book as well as this one, but just to summarise, the word 'Bible' in the title, chosen by my publisher, denotes an authoritative work. There are two stories I'd like to tell about Bibles.

Apart from selling great books like this one, many book shops excel in staging regular promotions involving author readings and book signings. If you happen to be a cookery writer, chances are you will find yourself doing, not readings, but cooking/tasting demonstrations at the bookshop. Dominique and I have done many such demos. Oh to be a poet! The logistics of a simple reading make the complexities of bookshop cooking akin to a space-shuttle mission. Not least, it requires us to bring with us everything but the kitchen sink, and it leads to many anecdotes. For example, at one large city bookshop, which had best remain nameless, we were placed for our demonstration by the large-format books and religious section. We had not even begun to cook, when a cleric with dog collar and purple bib, the local bishop we presumed, came up and asked us to be very careful not to stain 'God's works' (Bibles were behind us on the shelves). We assured him we'd do our best, but we always marvel at the courage of the store manager allowing us to create curry smells all over the branch in question! What is tantalising to some, is less so to others.

We probably have enough demo anecdotes to fill a book in its own right but there is just one more I must relate, before getting down to business. Dom and I were at a bookshop in Bradford, heart of one of Britain's thriving Pakistani curry communities. It was an evening do, with a seated audience for the demo, with wine and a curry-tasting. The audience of about 70 took their seats and sipped their wine, and a hush fell as the manager was about to introduce us. Just then there was a flurry at the back of the room, and a rather scruffily dressed woman bustled in, helped herself to some wine, and muttering all the while, took a seat. I began the demo by explaining about the book's title. The woman continued drinking and muttering throughout the event. At the end, I asked if anyone had any questions. After a number of

ntelligent queries from the members of the audience, the woman at the back piped up. 'Why did you call your book the Bible?' I explained. 'Don't you think it is an affront to Moslems?' she asked. As far as one could tell, she was not a Moslem, and I assured her the title had no religious connotations, and offended no one, but she became abusive, and in the end threw red wine all over some hapless customers, the manager and hundreds of pounds worth of book stock. She was ejected and banned for life from Waterstones in Bradford.

Fortunately, hers was the only adverse comment we've had on the subject of the title. So it is with pleasure that I offer you my second bible, *The Balti Bible*.

Pat Chapman

Introduction

Nowhere on earth uses more spices in its cooking than the lands we know as the subcontinent – Pakistan, Nepal, Bhutan, Bangladesh, Burma and Sri Lanka and, at its centre, India. The land mass of the subcontinent is bigger than Europe, its climate glacial to tropical. It contains the world's second largest population. However, its people have little in common, descending from many different races, with different cultures, languages and religions. All these countries are now independent states, some of which are hostile to each other, as one would expect of old adversaries, made no friendlier by successions of conquistadors.

With such a diverse racial background, it is not surprising that the food of the subcontinent, developed over thousands of years, varies from state to state and region to region. Some of the distinctions are subtle when measured from town to town, but the differences from the northern Himalayas to south India, and from the rugged mountains of north-western Pakistan to lush, flat, tropical Bangladesh in the east, are as vast as the land mass itself.

From time to time over the millennia, many of these states have been linked together by their various conquerors, only to split apart in violent conflict. Only Britain achieved an empire which included all these states. It was truly the jewel in the crown, not least for its food. Indeed the attempt to gain monopolies on spice crops was the driving force behind Britain's efforts to establish her world empire.

Sadly, at the time, the Raj virtually ignored the culinary attributes their jewel offered. Ironically it was not until the British left India, that Indian food became important to Britain. Now it is impossible to imagine Britain without it. Britain did leave many legacies in the subcontinent – one being the word curry. By definition, a mixture of spices thoroughly cooked with other main ingredients, such as meat, poultry, fish or vegetables is curry. There are numerous spices available, and no food tastes better than curried food.

Despite Britain's erstwhile connections with India, it was not until the 1960s that curry restaurants became established in significant numbers. Basing their menus around just two styles of traditional Indian cooking, Punjabi and Moghul meat and chicken dishes, they introduced Britain to savoury spicy dishes. Today Britain has a remarkable 7,500 Indian restaurants. London alone has 1,500 – more than Bombay, Calcutta, Delhi and Madras combined. And of course the food they offer is much more diverse than it was in those early days.

Balti is one type of curry. It has achieved a cult status in the West in a remarkably short space of time. Indeed, the very word Balti is as alien

the most of the peoples of the ubcontinent as was the 'curry' when hat word was coined long ago. Balti's rigins, as with all such food, go way ack. The northernmost part of the ubcontinent is Pakistan's Kashmir, a art of which is called Baltistan. The ood in this area evolved over enturies as one-pot dryish stews, ow-cooked over embers. Balti combines Moghul tastes with ne aromatic spices of Kashmir, and ne robustness of 'winter foods' found lands high in the mountains. The esults are very tasty indeed. Chilli eat is not in evidence. Spicing is ubtle with an emphasis on fresh arlic, ginger, coriander leaf and romatic spices including clove, cassia ark, cardamom, aniseed, fennel, and ummin. These spices are a type of aram masala – that aromatic mixture om Kashmir – which, when roasted, ives off a wonderful and unique roma and imparts a gorgeous dark rown colour to the curry.

As with most food from the ubcontinent, Balti is cooked in and aten from a two-handled bowl, nown as the karahi, *korai* or *kadai* – a ound-bottomed, wok-like, heavy cast-iron dish which has been used for cooking curries for as long as can be remembered. Somewhere along the line, the pan became known as the 'Balti pan'. Breads generally accompany a Balti dish, and are held in the right hand and used in place of cutlery to scoop up the food.

THE BRITISH BALTI

Britain's original Asian communities were Pakistanis and Indians from the Punjab and, as already noted, they and their food began to be established in the early 1960s. Their repertoire did not at that time include either Tandoori food or Balti. Tandoori, from a different area of Pakistan, quickly became a favourite amongst British diners in the 1970s and within a decade, every curry restaurant up and down the land offered tandoori dishes whether or not they possessed a tandoor.

It was at around this time that a new community arrived from Pakistan's Kashmir and settled in the run-down Sparkbrook area of Birmingham. Almost at once, a café opened with the express purpose of serving Kashmiri food to the Kashmiri community. The year was 1973, the café was incongruously called the Paris. It has long gone, its elderly owner, a Mr Ramzan, having retired and returned to his native Baltistan. But he has left behind a legacy, the scale of which he could never have envisaged in 1973.

All he did was simply to serve traditional food in the karahi without cutlery, without decor, and without alcohol. It was, however, delicious and above all, inexpensive, and before long a few brave local Brummies were hooked. The Paris was the forerunner of some 200 Balti houses now thriving in Birmingham, and numerous others worldwide.

There is no way Mr Ramzan could have foreseen that Balti would become an international cult within two decades. But was it he who coined the term Balti? And if he did was he referring to Baltistan or the Urdu word for karahi? As we see in The Balti World on pages 193–196, these glories are claimed by a second restaurateur who opened Adils in 1975.

Food journalist Russell Cronin, writing at the time for the *Independent*, told me that I had

invented the whole Balti thing and that there was no such place as Baltistan. Madhur Jaffrey led the Indian contingency and she vehemently insisted in 1995 that Balti did not exist, and she repeated her views in subsequently published food magazines. I promised to take her to Birmingham next time we met.

As it happened, we were to meet in Birmingham two years later, when she and I co-presented a BBC Television cookery programme. She planned to cook Pakoras. I was asked by producer Mary Klyne to cook Balti. I warned Mary that Madhur might not be impressed, and awaited recording day with trepidation. Amazingly, no adverse comment was received in the lead-up to the great day. And when I reached the studios, the reason became apparent. A large range of Balti pans had just been launched by wok-maker William Levene Ltd, and guess who had put her name to them? 'I designed them myself', Madhur proudly confided to me (justifiably so, because they are a very good range of pans). I did not have the courage to ask what had changed her mind about Balti, but she did say my TV Balti was

excellent, and asked me to take her to Birmingham's best Balti house!

Other Indians have told me in no uncertain terms that the whole business is nonsense. Reza Mohammed, owner of London's famous celebrated Star of India restaurant, for one. I was asked to appear in another BBC-TV series about Balti. The producer asked me to suggest a suitable Balti venue, and a contrasting true Indian venue, at which to film their *Good Food* programme. Having got Reza on national peak-time television, he then proceeded to pour scorn on the whole Balti concept. 'It doesn't exist,' he insisted. 'It's all rubbish. Balti just means a bucket in Hindi!' And to prove it, he produced his well-used floor mop bucket with one hand, while with the other, he fanned overheated presenter Pete Macarthy (such people can never stand the heat of the kitchen!), with a papadom.

Very funny Reza. But I've got news for you. I've got some chaps who tell me they can't wait to meet you. The lads from Mirpur and Pakistan's Kashmir, a.k.a. Baltistan, now operating the Balti houses in

Birmingham's Sparkbrook were not amused, and they invite you to come there to eat your words, and their food, if not your floor bucket. I'll com too. Indeed, I'll pay your rail fare there. Watch this space, folks!

I mentioned Indians earlier, and this is the point. There is no love lost between Pakistan and India; in fact, technically they are at war, and nowhere is more disputed than Kashmir, whose territory is divided between both countries with a nebulous border known as the 'cease fire zone'. Not all Indians deny the existence of Pakistani food. The India publisher Lustre Press published a book in 1995 entitled *Step by Step Indian Recipes – Balti*, which is described in the blurb as 'a variation of karahi cooking'. In its introduction the book, author unknown, says: 'Bal cuisine . . . a new way of cooking hot, spicy curries – is being popularised by Indian chefs in the West. Several Balti restaurants have opened in recent years to cater to the connoisseurs of Indian food.' At the end of the brief intro, the books does acknowledge Balti's roots: '... the cuisine originated in northern Pakistan, but has been

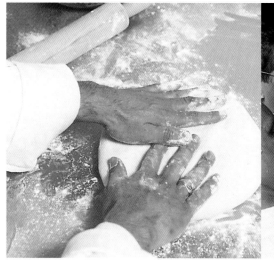 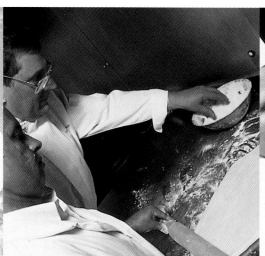 

fluenced deeply by the cuisine of
eighbouring India. The mélange of
dian and Pakistani cuisines is truly
spiring. The results are fascinating
cording to food enthusiasts.'

I'll buy that. In fact, Balti has a very
rong following of enthusiasts or
altimaniacs. Originally located just in
rmingham, such people discuss the
rtues of Brum's Balti houses,
omparing one chef or one venue with
other, in the way that wine masters
ompare vintages and vineyards. The
ssion for Balti today has extended
ell beyond Birmingham, and is now
uly worldwide. All curryholics will
entify with this enthusiasm.

I am one of them, and if you have
ad thus far, so are you, and this book
from me to you, whether you are a
teran curry cook or a Balti beginner.
is intended to be as definitive in its
wn way as the Curry Bible. It is, of
ourse, specifically devoted to just one
pe of curry – Balti – and its purpose
to look at every possible way of
oking it.

You can use this book to start from
ratch, knowing nothing about Balti,
indeed about curry. It will help you
ock your store cupboard, and make

up basic Balti mixes and apply all-
important cooking techniques, shown
in pictures, step-by-step. There are also
Ingredients Files, which examine every
ingredient needed to cook Balti
curries, many of which are illustrated
in colour.

The 'Balti World' feature takes us
into the Asian grocer and spice shop,
the Halal butcher, the sweet shop, and
the largest Asian pots and pans shop
in Britain. We also see outside and in
the Balti house.

For the recipes, I received hands-on
retraining from the experts themselves
at Britain's number one Balti House,
the Nazir brothers' Royal Naim in
Stratford Road, Sparkhill, Birmingham,
whose chefs took time to check me
out for going solo on the Balti pan.
Colin Poole's photographs show part
of that flame-throwing exhilarating
day in the kitchen. Following that
retraining session, I reviewed every
Balti recipe in my collection, and
revised them as required, and in this
book there are over 200, of which 140
are variations on the Balti theme.

The restaurateurs who started the
Balti craze going in Birmingham
quickly realised that they would need

to offer a whole range of familiar
favourites in the Balti style. I have
done the same, and you will find your
favourite curry, Balti style, for example
Balti Bhoona, Ceylon curry, Dhansak,
Dopiaza, Exotica Jalfrezie (or Jalfry),
Kashmiri, Keema, Kofta, Korma,
Madras, Malaya, Moglai, Pasanda,
Patia, Phal, Rhogan Josh, Tikka Masala
and Vindaloo. The main chapters
group the recipes together under type,
for example, Meat, Poultry, Fish and
Shellfish, Vegetables. There is also a
chapter on 'specials', and it is here that
you will find the amazing combination
dishes that make Balti unique, as well
as the truly authentic recipes collected
over the years during my visit to those
hauntingly beautiful areas of Baltistan,
Pakistan and Kashmir.

To ensure that you will be provided
with a complete multi-course meal
with all the trimmings, I have included
starters, rice, bread, chutneys, pickles
and desserts.

I hope you enjoy my Balti Bible. Now,
let's grab a pan and get cooking!

Workshop

THE BALTI PAN

The Balti Pan is to curry cooking what the wok is to Chinese. Both are very ancient implements made originally from heavy cast iron. Today they are pressed from chromium vanadium steel, making them thin but sturdy, with a rounded bottom that has been flattened to suit the modern stove top.

The wok probably came from China via a branch of the ancient Silk Route which passed across the Karakoram Pass and into Baltistan, down the Indus valley and in to the rest of India. It evolved from a pan with a long single handle into a slightly deeper, more rounded pan with two handles, and became one of the subcontinent's main cooking implements. Known all over India, Bangladesh and Pakistan as the karahi, or *kari, korai, kadai* or *kodoi*, the Balti pan is a circular, two-handled, hemispherical all-purpose pan used for stir-frying, simmering, frying and deep-frying. Sizes range from over a metre (3 feet) in diameter to just 8 cm (3.2 in).

In the north of the subcontinent, following tradition, the pan is used to cook in and serve straight to the table. It is this pan that is known as the Balti pan in the Midlands (the word 'Balti' means washing-up bucket in Hindi and Urdu). The 20 cm (8 in) diameter karahi, Balti pan or wok is ideal for roasting spices and for small portion items. The 30 cm (12 in) size is the all-purpose workhorse pan for stir-fries. This size takes up a lot of space on the stove, so that you can only use two at once. Smaller ones give you greater flexibility however, so my preferred combination is two large pans and two small.

Small karahis are available in iron and stainless steel. Silvered beaten copper and brass are also used to serve food, though they are not practical to cook in.

OBTAINING PANS

Your Balti meals can be cooked using conventional Western saucepans and frying pans – although I sincerely believe that much of the fun comes from the noisy clattering of a large chef's spoon in a Balti pan. Your guests can also join in the fun if you serve Balti in small Balti serving dishes, especially if your food goes sizzling from pan to table in the Balti dish (don't forget to use a wooden base unless you want to have burn marks all over your table).

All specialist equipment can be found at some Asian stores in this country, and by mail order.

PREPARING PANS

You will need to clean a new pan with an abrasive sink-cleaning cream to remove the plastic lacquer or machine oil applied by the manufacturers to prevent rust. This is not at all easy, but do it you must. After cleaning the pan, rinse it several times in hot water, then dry it by placing it on a heated ring on the stove for a minute or so. This dries it out for the next stage.

SEASONING PANS

Place about 3 or 4 tablespoons of cooking oil (old used cooking oil is acceptable) in the pan, heat it to smoking point, then swirl it around. Cool it. Empty the pan and wipe clean with kitchen paper. Repeat several times. It is dreadfully smoky, so it may be worth seasoning your pan outside if you can, say on a barbecue. The seasoning process starts the build-up of a protective film on the pan, which, over time creates a non-stick finish or patina, and is also said to improve the flavour of the food being cooked. Indeed the Chinese say of a cook, 'the blacker the wok, the better the cook'.

CLEANING PANS

Ideally, your pan should never be scoured since to do so would be to lose the blackening patina that has accumulated. It is true that a blackened pan looks the part, but (and I know this is almost sacrilegious), I honestly cannot tell the difference between using a new well-scoured pan and my old well-blackened (and I'm sure less hygienic) one. However, the best tool to use to clean the pan without scratching it or losing the patina is a Chinese wok brush. This has a firm round handle and a number of stout bamboo bristles. It cleans the pan effectively, but it then takes a fair bit of cleaning itself.

ANCILLARY ITEMS

The modern wok has a number of associated pieces of equipment which work just as well with the Balti karahi pan. It has a steel stand on which to place it when it is off the stove. It has a well-fitting domed lid. Also available are a wok spatula – a steel scraper whose blade is shaped to fit snugly to the curve of the wok, and two ladles – one perforated, the other not – designed for use with the wok.

OTHER EQUIPMENT

To cook the recipes in this book you will, of course, need a stove top (any type), a grill with tray and rack, and an oven and baking trays. In addition to your Balti pans and/or woks you may also find the heavy metal flattish tava useful for cooking chapattis and parathas (and omelettes and pancakes too). A nutmeg grater is really useful as can be a mortar and pestle if you just need to grind a few spices.

You will also need the following common kitchen utensils and tools to cook Balti:

- knives
- chopping boards
- mixing bowls – non metallic, large, medium and small
- a large sieve
- a large chef's spoon for stir-frying
- a large frying pan
- saucepans with lids – 3.5 litre (6 pint), 2.25 litre (4 pint), 1.3 litre (2¼ pint)
- a casserole pot with lid – 2.25–2.75 litre (4–5 pint) capacity
- a bamboo steamer, 20 cm (8 in) or a metal steamer,with perforated inner pan and a tight-fitting lid (a colander or strainer over a pan with a lid will substitute)
- a sprung-type mechanical vegetable chopper – this saves work and is very much cheaper than the electrical equivalent
- a barbecue – a great asset in the summer

ELECTRICAL TOOLS

For grinding spices, I recommend an electric coffee grinder (see page 41) or a spice mill attachment. To create the smooth texture needed in certain curry gravies, a blender or a purpose-designed hand blender is really useful. Food processors and blenders are not essential to the recipes in this book, but they are good tools, and will certainly help you with certain processes.

SLOW COOKER

A slow cooker is excellent for cooking many curries, especially meat. There are a number of electrically powered plug-in, lidded saucepans ideal for the busy working person. To make a stew, simply put in your ingredients (but remember to fry your masala first), switch on, go to work and when you come home the stew is ready. This is not unlike the original 'over the embers' slow cooking in Baltistan and is ideal for Balti meats.

MICROWAVE OVEN

This can be useful (but is not essential) for blanching vegetables and reheating food.

RICE COOKER

If you have one that's fine but if not, you'll find my method for cooking rice (see pages 180–181) gives you perfect results, and quicker.

SIZZLERS

Tandoori and kebab dishes can be served to the table, very hot, smoking and sizzling. This is a restaurant technique, and to do it you'll need to buy special heavy, cast-iron sizzlers. There are two types – a flat oval tray and a small, two-handled karahi dish. Each is made of cast iron and has a wooden base. They make an attractive presentation, but be careful not to burn yourself or your guests with the excruciatingly burning-hot dishes, nor to splutter hot oil over their clothes.

Using a sizzler:

1 Cook the food in a separate pan.
2 Just prior to serving, place the dry cast-iron dish directly on to the stove over a ring at its hottest. Allow the dish to get as hot as it can. It takes at least five minutes.
3 Turn off the heat (to prevent the oil from catching fire) and add a teaspoon or two of ghee or oil to the pan.
4 Carefully add ½ teaspoon of water or lime juice. Take care, because the hot oil and water will splutter and steam. Add the food at once. Do not overload.
5 Warn your guests, and using thickly padded gloves take the dish, still hissing, to the table, and place on table mats.

A-Z of Basic Ingredients

The Ingredients Files interspersed throughout this book study many of the major ingredients needed in Balti curry cooking. In the following pages the basic spices and garnishes are presented in alphabetical order with their Hindi/Urdu name in italics where appropriate. Page 204 provides a list of the ingredients you'll need in your store cupboard. To locate any particular ingredient or spice, please refer to the index.

Almond
Badam

Almonds are one of the most prevalently used nuts in northern Indian and Pakistani curries. They are used whole unpeeled or peeled (blanched) and raw or fried in certain rich curries. They make a great garnish, as do almond flakes, which can be raw or toasted. Ground almonds are used to thicken and flavour certain curry sauces.

Basil leaf
Tulsi

A really fragrant fresh herb, hardly used in Indian cooking. However, it makes a refreshing change used judiciously in Balti, where aromatics are paramount.

Bay Leaf
Tej Patta

Bay, or laurel leaf, is pointed and oval in shape, and grows to an average 7 cm (2³/₄ in) in length. It can be used fresh or dried. Fresh, it is glossy, smooth, quite fleshy, and dark green in colour, and has a more powerful flavour than dried, with a slightly bitter undertone. Dried it is paler, and quite brittle. The leaf grows on an evergreen tree or bush, found worldwide, and is familiar to most people in the West. Bay is used whole in aromatic curries, such as Korma and in Birianis. Ground bay is used in Balti masalas.

Cardamom
Ilaichi

Cardamom grows in south India, Sri Lanka, Thailand and Guatemala, on a herbaceous perennial plant, related to the ginger family, whose pods contain slightly sticky black seeds, their familiar flavour coming from the cineol in their oils. Cardamom is one of the most elegant, aromatic and expensive spices, and is one of India's most exported spices, earning the country considerable revenue, and the spice itself, the title 'the Queen of Spice'. There are three main cardamom types, all of which can be used whole or ground. Natural white cardamoms are much in demand for their flavour. They are of the same species as the green, with a similar flavour, rather more delicate than that of the brown. Green cardamoms, *chota laichi*, have a smooth, ribbed, pale green outer casing, about 1cm (½ in) long. The greener the cardamom, the fresher it is, though use of food dyes is not unknown to 'freshen-up' older specimens. They are used whole or ground, with or without their casing, in many savoury and sweet recipes. Brown (also called black) cardamoms, *bara elaichi*, have a rather hairy, husky, dark brown casing about 2 cm (⅞ in) long. Used in garam masala, kormas and pullaos, they are strong, astringent, and aromatic, though less so than the other species.

Cashew Nuts
Kaju

Whereas almonds are in used in certain northern Indian and Pakistani curries, cashews perform the same role in the south. They are used peeled (blanched) and raw or fried in certain curries. They make a great garnish as do almonds. Being soft, they make a good paste by grinding them down with water, and are used to thicken certain curry sauces.

Cassia Bark/Cinnamon
Dalchini

Cassia bark is the corky, outer bark of a tree, with a sweet fragrance, related to cinnamon. Indeed there is considerable confusion between the two, compounded by the many spice manufacturers who insist on labelling 'cassia bark' as 'cinnamon'. Cassia, shown top, originated in Burma, and is now also widely grown in the tropical forests of Indonesia and south China, hence its alternative name, Chinese cinnamon. Its tree is a large, evergreen, the leaves of which are also used as a spice. Branches are cut down, their bark is scraped off, and formed into reddish-brown quills about 1 metre (3 feet) long. These are fragile once dried, and by the time it is packed, cassia is usually in chips, averaging 5 cm (2 in) in length. Cassia's essential oil contains cinnamic aldehyde, giving it a sweet, clove-like, musky flavour. Cassia bark is usually much less fragrant, coarser, thicker and tougher than cinnamon, and it stands up to more robust cooking. It is also cheaper. It is used as an aromatic flavouring in subtle meat and poultry dishes, and as a major flavouring in Pullao Rice and Garam Masala. Although widely used in cooking, the bark should be removed before the dish is served.

Cinnamon, shown below, is native to Sri Lanka, and though it now also grows in the Seychelles, Brazil, the West Indies and Indonesia, the Sri Lankan variety is still regarded as the best. Cinnamon bark is used in the form of parchment-thin, tightly-rolled, pale brown quills of around 1 cm (½ inch) in diameter, by 10–12 cm (4–6 in) long. These quills are more aromatic than cassia, but also more delicate, and can break up in robust cooking. Little pieces of cinnamon have an unpleasant mouth-feel, so quills are best used for infusing drinks or as a flavouring in, for example, Pullao Rice. Ground cinnamon is used in some dishes, its sweetish aromatic flavour adding a haunting quality to food.

Chilli
Mirch

Chilli is the fleshy pod of the shrub-like bushes of the capsicum family. There are five species, and thousands of varieties. When people think of curry, 'heat' is the first thing that springs to mind, and it is the chilli that is the heat giver. Yet chilli is a relative newcomer to Indian cooking. It was 'discovered' by accident in the Americas, by explorers, of whom Columbus was the first. Indeed it was they who gave the chilli and allspice their confusing identical name of 'pepper' or *pimeñto* in Spanish. The chilli pepper soon caught on and was taken around the world to become adored by and grown in countries like India.

All varieties of chilli start out green and ripen through white, yellow or orange to red or purple, as we see in the pictures. They range in heat from zero (see Bell Peppers page 136) to incendiary, depending on the variety. In actual fact, in this context it would be more appropriate to refer to 'piquancy' than 'heat', meaning the burning sensation in the mouth caused by the alkaloid 'capsaicin', present to a greater or lesser degree, in both the flesh and seeds of all members of the capsicum family, irrespective of their colour (except bell peppers).

Capsaicin is related to caffeine, nicotine and morphine, which explains why the chilli is so popular around the world. Novices to chilli find it painful to taste, but the body compensates by releasing painkillers called endorphins. This allows the body to build up its capsaicin tolerance level, which becomes a mild addiction. As tolerance levels rise, chilli-lovers will agree that the capsaicin does not overwhelm other flavours but enhances them. The chilli level can be varied (up or down), as required, but must not be omitted altogether from the basic Balti mix since it acts as a catalyst to the other spices. Rich in Vitamin C, fresh chilli, like onion and garlic, actively helps to reduce blood pressure and cholesterol.

Depicted here are five chilli types readily available in the West.

Kenyan Red
Same as the African Snubs except in colour.

Dutch Green (similar to Serraños)
Rather a lot of pith and seeds, best discarded. Its modest 'heat' level, whilst more than enough for novices, will not satisfy the aficionado.

Scotch Bonnet (similar to Habañero)
The world's hottest; only very serious heat lovers (known in the US as chili-heads) should attempt to eat this variety.

African Snubs (similar to American Jalapeños)
The most commonly available chilli at the supermarket. Same as the Dutch Green only slightly hotter.

Indian Cayenne
The chilli most commonly used in curry/Balti cooking. Long, thin and quite hot with minimal pith and seeds, so it is not necessary to discard them.

Chilli Powder
Dried chilli is nearly always red, and is

available, whole, crushed, or ground to a fine powder.

Chive

Familiar, fine, long chive leaves are a member of the onion family. Although not traditionally used in Indian cooking, they make an excellent and easy garnish. Garlic chive is increasingly available. Interesting, especially as a garnish, with a more pungent flavour than the onion chive.

Citrus Fruit

Nimbu

The lemon originated in the Bay of Bengal and was taken in the 1300s to the Arabian Mediterranean for cultivation for trade. Limes originated slightly further east, probably in Thailand and the East Indies. There is a marked difference between the two in flavour. In fact, lemons are rarely found in India, but since we in the West have access to both, feel free to use either (or both). Kaffir or makrut are 'sweet' knobbly limes used particularly in Thai cooking. The shatkora, shown top right, is a larger member of the same family, used as a sweet/tart vegetable in Bengal.

Clove
Lavang

Clove is Britain's most familiar spice, having been used continuously since the Romans brought it here. We still use it in apple pies, and also to ease toothache because of its painkilling essential oil, eugenol. Clove grows on a smallish tropical evergreen tree, related to the myrtle family, which thrives near the sea. The clove itself is the unopened bud of the tree's flower. It is bright green at first, and must be picked just as it turns pink. If allowed to bloom, the flower is dark pink about 1 cm ($\frac{1}{2}$ in) in diameter. Dried clove is a dark red-brown, bulbous at one end (this is the bud, and is where the flavour is, so watch out for 'headless' cloves), with tapering stalks, about 1 cm ($\frac{1}{2}$ in) in length. The Romans thought they resembled nails – *clavus* being the Latin for 'clout' or 'nail'. Clove is the world's second most important spice, earning India alone around £20 million a year. It takes some 8–10,000 cloves to make up 1 kg ($2\frac{1}{2}$ lb).

Coconuts
Narial

The coconut is not native to Baltistan: the region is too cold for it to grow. But as a flavour, coconut is an excellent additive in certain Balti dishes.

Coconuts grow high up on palm trees in tropical climates. After harvesting, each huge nut is divested of its green case, revealing a pallid item, which, when sun-dried, becomes the familiar brown, hairy coconut. Once dried, it is opened to create an array of coconut products.

First, there is the liquid which should be present in all coconuts, and can be used in cooking (this is not coconut milk). From each half, coconut flesh is scraped out as chippings, which can be dried and desiccated. This can be substituted for fresh coconut, and is used by adding it dry to your cooking, or by simmering it in water and straining it to create coconut milk.

Fresh grated coconut can be mixed with water and strained to create coconut cream or milk, readily available canned. Coconut cream is the first straining (or pressing) and is thick, creamy and rich. The second and third pressings, using new water each time but the same flesh, produce coconut milk (the second

resembles milk, the third cloudy water). The best canned brands are produced from first pressings. Fresh grated flesh can also be freeze-dried and finely ground to create coconut milk powder, which when reconstituted with water creates rich coconut milk. It is convenient in this form, because it can be stored in a jar like a spice, for use bit by bit, unlike its canned counterpart which needs to be used once opened.

Coconut oil is extracted by a distillation process, and used for cooking. It is white when solid, and transparent when hot. The oil is also mixed with freshly ground flesh to make blocks of creamed coconut which must be kept under refrigeration. To use creamed coconut simply cut off the amount required and melt it in a little boiling water. If you try to fry it without water, it will burn.

No part of the coconut is wasted. The empty husks are used as containers, or for fuel and the hairs become coir, or coconut matting, well-known for its use in door mats.

Coriander Leaf and Seed
Dhania

Coriander is a member of the ubiquitous *Umbelliferae* family. It was native to India, but now grows worldwide, as an herbaceous annual plant. Its seed is used as an important spice; its rather bitter root is also used in much Thai and some Indian cooking. In terms of volume (but not value), coriander seed is the most important spice in Indian cookery. The country exports 80,000 tons a year, and uses more than that amount at home. Dried coriander seed imparts a sweetish flavour, with a hint of orange. There are many coriander species with minor variations in the appearance of their seeds. The seeds are used whole or ground, forming the largest single ingredient in most masalas, and are delicious roasted – try them as a garnish.

Indispensable to Indian cookery are coriander leaves, India's most widely used herb. They are mid-green and flat with jagged edges, resembling flat-bladed parsley (to differentiate between the two at the greengrocer's, crush a leaf in your fingers – only coriander has that musky smell). The flavour of coriander leaves bears absolutely no resemblance to that of the coriander seed. Not everyone enjoys the distinctive musky candle-waxy flavour of the leaves, also present in unripe seeds. Indeed, the word coriander derives from the Greek word *koris*, a bug, supposedly because its foetid smell resembles that of bed bugs! That's as may be, but once acquired, that taste is a must for curry lovers. Fresh, the leaves are used whole, chopped or ground. Soft stalks can also be used, but thicker stalks should be discarded.

Cummin
Jeera

Cummin (always spelt this way by the Raj, but 'cumin' elsewhere, after its Latin name *cuminum*), is an ancient spice, native to Syria and Egypt, and can be found intact and apparently still edible in the tombs of the Pharaohs, having been placed there some 4,000 years ago. Cummin was mentioned in the Old Testament, and was so important to the Romans, that it was used as a seasoning in place of salt, causing it to be very expensive. It also became synonymous with excess and greed, to the extent that the gluttonous Emperor Marcus Aurelius, was nicknamed 'Cuminus'.

Cummin grows on a smallish annual herb of the coriander (*Umbelliferae*) family. Its thin seeds are about 5 mm long. They are grey-brown to yellowy-green in colour, and have nine stripy longitudinal ridges and small stalks. Its oil, cuminaldehyde, gives it a distinctive, savoury taste with a slightly bitter overtone. Cummin predominates in Middle Eastern cooking, and has found a new role in the USA in Tex-Mex Chili-con-Carné.

Cummin has always played a major role in Indian cookery, its use in volume being second only to coriander's. Ground, it is a major component in curry powder and it is an important ingredient in masalas and curries. It is one of the five spices of panch phoran. Whole cummin seeds benefit greatly in taste from being 'roasted'.

Curry Leaf

Kari Phulia or Kurri Patta

Native to south-west Asia, the neem tree grows to about 6 metres (25 feet) in height, and 1 metre (3 feet) in diameter. It is especially prevalent in the foothills of the Himalayas, and south India. The tree is greatly adored in a smaller version as a garden ornamental. The young curry leaf from this tree is small, pale green and delicate, growing up to 4 cm (1½ in) in length. It is widely used whole in southern Indian cooking, and imparts a delicious flavour to dishes such as rasam, sambar, masala dosa and lemon rice. Despite its name, the leaf has a lemony fragrance, and no hint of 'curry'. This is because it is related to the lemon family. Ground curry leaf is used in many commercial curry powder blends. In addition, it is used as a tonic for stomach and kidney disorders. Fresh curry leaves are imported into the UK by air-freight from Kenya, but are hard to locate. Dry ones are readily available at Asian stores and make passable substitutes. If you enjoy south Indian food, they are a 'must-have' spice.

Fennel

Saunf, Sunf or Soonf

Fennel, a European native, is a hardy perennial, which grows to about 2 metres (6 feet) in height. Its leaf and bulb are relished in Europe, though not in India. There, it is the small pale greenish-yellow stripy seed that is important. It is slightly plumper and greener than cumin. Frequently confused in India with its near relative, the smaller aniseed, fennel seed is much more prevalent. Its similar, though slightly milder, flavour comes from the very distinctive essential oil, anethole (also present in aniseed and star anise). Fennel is comprised of 70 per cent anethole (compared with aniseed's 90 per cent), with a smaller amount of fenchone. This combination gives it its sweet and aromatic flavour, making it ideal for subtle dishes, garam masala, and paan mixtures. It is unique, in that it is the only spice to be common to the five-spice mixtures of both India (panch phoran) and China.

Fennel is grown all over north India but the Lucknow variety is the best quality. It is used medicinally as gripe water, and for eyesight, obesity and chest problems.

Fenugreek Leaf
Methi

Fenugreek is used in Indian cookery in two forms – the seed and the leaf. The latter is grey-green in colour and grows on a clover-like annual herb. Pronounced 'may-tee' in Hindi, fenugreek leaf derives from the Latin *foenum* (dried grass or hay); indeed the leaf is still used as cattle fodder.

The fresh leaf is popular in north Indian and Punjabi cookery, and in its dried form, it keeps like any other spice. A note of caution, however: after cropping, the leaves are dried in the sun on flat roofs. Consequently, it is imperative that you pick through them to remove grit and small stones. Unfortunately, you will also find a lot of tough stalks. These too should be discarded. Whilst doing this, you will notice how strongly the spice smells. It is a good idea to double pack it,

in an airtight container, within another airtight container. Use small amounts only. The leaf is rich in carotene, vitamin A, ascorbic acid, calcium and iron.

As well as the leaf, the fenugreek plant yields a 10–15 cm (4–6 in) long bean-like pod, which contains 10–20 miniature, hard, yellow ochre-brown, nugget-like, grooved seeds, each about 3 mm long. India produces over 20,000 tons of fenugreek seed a year, placing it in their top ten exported spices, the seed being a minor, but important ingredient in curry powder, and one of the five panch phoran spices. Though seeming to smell of curry, the seed is, in fact, quite bitter, its main oil being coumarin. Used whole, split or ground, in moderation, it is an important flavouring in masalas. Light roasting gives the seed an interesting depth, and

another way of using it is to soak it overnight (see Green Masala Paste, page 45). Incidentally, the fenugreek seed can also be sprouted, like mung beans, for beansprouts, when they have a light curry flavour.

Fenugreek has always been said to be good as a contraceptive and a hair tonic, and in Java it is used to counteract baldness. It lowers blood pressure, but it contains steroids. This may be why it was used by harem women to enlarge their chests!

Garlic
Lasan

Garlic has a history unparalleled by that of any other ingredient, probably originating in Turkistan and Siberia. The ancient Egyptians valued it highly, believing that a bulb of garlic represented the cosmos, and each clove a part of the solar system. It was fundamental to their diet, to the extent that 7 kg (15 lb) of garlic could buy one slave. Indeed an inscription on the great pyramid of Cheops states that the slaves were supplied garlic and radishes daily for health. History's first recorded industrial dispute took place 3,000 years before Christ, when these slaves mustered up the courage to go on strike because their garlic ration was cut. Garlic was found in Tutankhamen's tomb and it also had a large role to play in warding off the evil eye.

The Babylonians of 3000 BC considered garlic to have miraculous qualities, especially medicinally, as did the Greeks. In 460 BC Hippocrates extolled its virtues, as did Aristotle 80 years later, and Aristophanes believed it enhanced virility. The Phoenicians carried garlic in their Mediterranean trading ships and

he Talmudic dietary laws refer to its use. ohammed respected garlic: amongst her things he recommended its use to unteract the stings and bites of nomous snakes. Yet he warned that ey could have powerful aphrodisiac ualities, and he had a vision of Satan in e Garden of Eden with onion on the ound at his feet and garlic at his right. e know how the Europeans have vered garlic for centuries, but, hard to lieve, it took until the 1980s before rlic became widely available in Britain. arlic is indispensable to curry cooking. is best to buy one or more bulbs at a me, on each of which are clustered a umber of individual cloves. The skin is scarded and you should be left with a eamy, plump, firm clove. I prefer to op the cloves finely, but you can use a rlic crusher. You can also simply crush em under the flat side of a knife blade. purée garlic, use an electric food ocesser or a mortar and pestle. ndian restaurants often use large uantities of garlic powder in place of esh garlic which saves a lot of time. It

helps to capture that distinctive restaurant flavour, assisted no doubt by the sulphur dioxide and chemical stabilisers it contains. It also seems to cause dehydration. How often have you woken during the night with a raging thirst after eating an Indian restaurant curry? Fresh garlic does not seem to have that effect. If you do use garlic powder use 2 teaspoons for every clove specified in the recipe. Sometimes I like to use powder and sometimes fresh, and yet again a combination can be interesting.

An expensive (but good) product is garlic purée in tubes, and another I use

(as do many restaurants) is dehydrated garlic flakes. To use, soak in an equal volume of water for 3 minutes then mulch down in a food processor or blender. The taste is nearly as good as the fresh version, and the texture is indistinguishable.

If you and your friends like garlic, add more (a lot more if you like) to the recipes. If you are worried about what it might do to your career or social/love life, you can cut down on the recommended quantities. Do not, however, omit it altogether.

inger
drak

inger originated in India, and the best d juiciest still grows in south dia. Other ginger ows in Thailand, alaysia, Indo-hina and hina

itself. Ginger is a rhizome which grows underground to a considerable size. It provides an important flavour in Indian cooking, though it is not used in every dish. Externally, its beige-pink skin should have a bright sheen or lustre. When cut in half, the flesh should be

moist and creamy-lemon in colour, with no trace of blue (a sign of age). Ginger is also available dried and powdered, though with fresh ginger so readily available, powdered is not used in the recipes in this book.

Herbs

The French use the word *aromate* (aromatics) to describe any fragrant vegetable matter used for flavouring. Indian cooking uses few leafy herbs for this purpose, the most common being coriander and mint. Balti uses more of those than regular Indian cooking, being aromatic by definition, and we can be as adventurous as we wish with our choice of herbs for garnishing.

Mint

Podina

Mint grows prolifically as an herbaceous perennial, its bushy shrub growing up to a metre (3 feet) in height. The best variety for spicy cooking is spearmint, whose distinctive flavour comes from its volatile oil, consisting predominantly of menthol, with lesser amounts of carvone and limonene. Fresh mint is little used in Indian cooking, appearing here and there in chutneys and certain dishes, such as Podina Gosht and Balti. Dried mint is a useful store cupboard item.

Mustard Seed

Rai or Kalee Sarson

Mustard could be the world's oldest cultivated spice. Its branched annual plant is a member of the cabbage family. There are three varieties of mustard seed: brown, from India, with spherical seeds around 1 mm diameter, white (which is, in fact, yellow ochre in colour), and black, both around 2 mm in diameter and both native to the Mediterranean. Both white and black seeds are used to manufacture mustard and cress, and the familiar bright yellow powder or paste, although black is cropped less these days. The seeds are de-husked then milled. Flour is also added, and turmeric for colour. If you taste mustard powder, you find that it is not hot at first. Its heat develops when cold water is added. This causes a chemical reaction in which its components, including its volatile oil, isothiocyanate, react and develop a pungent heat. Indeed, mustard gets its name from the Latin, *mustum ardens*, meaning 'a burning must'.

The brown Indian mustard seed is not as pungent as the others. In fact, tasted raw, it is unappealing and bitter. Cooked, however, it becomes sweet and appetising, and is not as hot as you might expect. It is immensely popular in Bengal, where it is one of the five spices in panch phoran, and in southern India where it appears in many recipes roasted, or fried or as a garnish.

Nuts

The nuts important to curry cooking are almond, cashew and pistachio (see separate entries above and below). The small group of three items to the left are, top, chirongi nuts, then sunflower kernels, below right, and charoli nuts, to their left.

Onion

This ancient bulb originated in Central Asia and was much used by 3000 BC in Egypt and China alike. The onion, of which there are some 500 varieties, is related to the chive, garlic and leek. An onion consists of about 88 per cent water and 10 per cent carbohydrate. The 'heat' which makes onions so hard to prepare is caused by the onion's volatile oils called disulphides. The process of browning onion (illustrated on page 42) is enabled by the reduction of the huge water content, which allows the onion to be slowly fried without becoming incinerated. The browning and slight burning is caused by the carbohydrate turning to sugar and caramelising. The disulphides are neutralised, and the onion tastes savoury, yet sweet and delicious. Second to spices and along with garlic, this taste is the most important ingredient in curry cooking. It is the onion which, when cooked and puréed, gives the base for the creamy sauce so essential to most curries. Illustrated here are the best onion types for Balti and curry cooking – the pink onion is also very decorative for fresh chutneys and garnishing, as is the equally attractive white onion. The larger yellow one (also

called the 'Spanish' onion, but which grows all over Europe) is very mild, and with an average weight of around 225 g (8 oz), is easy to peel and prepare. The torpedo or red Italian onion is interesting for its shape.

Shallots are miniature relatives of onions, which probably originated in Israel. They were developed as bunches of bulbs in the Middle Ages by the French for gourmet purposes. Though fiddly to peel, they can be fun for dishes where

onions predominate, such as the Onion Bhaji or Pakora or Dopiaza Curry, and for garnishing. Three shallot types are illustrated here. Onion is an excellent source of vitamin C and provides 48 calories per 100 g (3½ oz).

Oils

Vegetable or butter ghee is commonly used in the cooking of the northern subcontinent, and in Balti cooking. It is popular for its flavour, and its high burning temperature, which enables the initial cooking of spices or garlic to be done without burning. Vegetable oil (usually made from rape seed) or corn oil (from maize), or ground nut oil (from peanut) are acceptable and less saturated than ghee, having the advantage of being neutral in flavour. Polyunsaturated oils (such as soya and sunflower oil) are also acceptable, although their burning temperature is much lower. Specialist oils used in different regions of the subcontinent include sesame oil, coconut oil (used in the south), and pure mustard oil (made from mustard seeds and used particularly in the north-east). EU regulations have recently compelled manufacturers to blend mustard oil with another oil because, say the bureaucrats, too much pure mustard oil is carcinogenic (although how much is too much is open to debate). Strongly flavoured oils, such as olive or walnut oil, are not used in Indian cooking, because they impart the wrong strong flavour into the spices.

Butter is rarely used because of its low burning temperature.

Paprika

Paprika is the Hungarian name for pepper. Chillies were first introduced here by Ottoman Turks in the 16th century. Over the centuries, a type of pepper was cultivated, especially in the Szeged and Kalocsa districts. At first paprika was deep red in colour and very pungent but over the years the pungency has been bred out of Hungarian paprika, so what we now expect is a tasty deep-red powder used for flavouring and colouring purposes, but not for heat. However, what we actually get may be wide of the mark: paprika may be mild or it may be hot. It can range in colour from rust to crimson, and it may have specified additions. The worst paprika can even be bitter. The reason for this is that, being a major crop, numerous other countries have become paprika

producers. Spain's paprika, called *nieñto para pimeñton*, is made from a different pepper from Hungary's, but ranks as second only to Hungary's in flavour and quality. As with everything else, expect to pay the most for the best, but be sure it is the best you're paying for. Once you've found your favourite brand stick with it.

Parsley

Flat-bladed parsley resembles coriander, but since it lacks its flavour, it is used as a garnish rather than in cooking.

Peanuts

Peanuts are used to a lesser extent in Indian cooking than almonds and cashews. They can act as a substitute for cashews. Here are redskin peanuts (above) and blanched polished peanuts (below).

Peppercorns

Kala Mirch

Pepper, India's major spice revenue earner for thousands of years, is justifiably called 'King of Spice'. The Romans brought it to England, where it was used as money. In the 13th century you could buy a sheep for a handful of pepper! Foreign ships entering London paid a levy of pepper, and it also paid debts, such as (peppercorn) rent. Until chilli was discovered in the 16th century, pepper was the main heat-giving agent in cooking, its heat coming from the alkaloid, piperine.

Peppercorns grow on a climbing vine, which thrives in monsoon forests. The vine flowers, then it produces berries, called spikes, in long clusters. Green peppercorns are immature when picked, and spikes are occasionally available in the UK. To obtain black peppercorns, the spikes are picked when they start changing colour to yellow. They are then sun-dried, and quickly become black and shrivelled. To harvest white pepper, the spikes are left on the vine until they turn red. The outer red skin is removed by soaking it off, revealing an inner white berry which is then dried. Pink pepper is obtained in the same way, from a specific variety of vine, and it is immediately air-dried, to prevent it turning white. The red peppercorn is not true pepper. It is from a South American shrub, whose reddish-brown berry is aromatic, and a little bitter, but not hot.

Pistachio nuts

Certain Indian recipes require pistachio nuts. Do not use the salted pistachios at all. Always use fresh shelled pistachio nuts, easily identified by their green colour.

Saffron

Saffron or Kesar

Saffron imparts unique colour, flavour and fragrance, to savoury and sweet dishes alike. Native to Greece, the saffron crocus is a different species from the springtime, purple-leaved, flowering garden plant. Throughout history, saffron has been used in medicine, dyeing, cosmetics and food. Once it was cropped in and around Saffron Walden in Essex. Today the main European saffron producing area is in the La Mancha district of Spain. Asian producers are in China (where it is called *safalan*), Kashmir (*kesar*) and Iran (*zafran*). It flowers there in October. The edible part is the golden stigma (a kind of stamen). Saffron is the world's most expensive spice, reflecting not just its scarcity, but the extraordinary labour-intensiveness required to harvest it. Only three stigma grow in each crocus flower, which must be picked on the very day the stigma is ready. The stigma are then carefully hand-plucked and dried, in La Mancha, by toasting them over very low heat, in Kashmir by sun-drying. Once dried a remarkable 70,000 individual crocuses, or 200,000 stigma are needed to produce 454 g (1 lb) of saffron worth over £1,000. This places its value not far behind that of gold (currently £3,600 per lb), which is why saffron is called 'liquid gold'. There is absolutely no substitute for saffron, and because of its price, many attempts are made to pass off imitation saffron.

The caveat is buy a reputable brand, and remember, there is no such thing as 'cheap' saffron. Beware the tasteless, cheap, similar-coloured, but feathery safflower (bastard saffron), and do not use turmeric, even when it is called Indian saffron.

Salt

Namak, Kala Namak or Saindhar

Salt is the most important taste additive, or seasoning, in the world, as well as the most ancient. It is an inorganic mineral, whose taste comes from sodium chloride, and it is essential to life. References to salt appear throughout history: it was so important to the Romans, that they paid their troops and officials part of their remuneration with salt, hence the word 'salary'. Indian food requires white salt, but unique to India is black salt (*kala namak*) from the Ganges district of central India. Ground, this salt is a pretty pink colour. Other mines give grey, or even blue salt. It has an acquired, distinctive taste.

Spring Onion

Spring onions are not used in traditional Indian cooking, but are excellent where a fresh taste is required such as in Jalfrezi, and for garnishing.

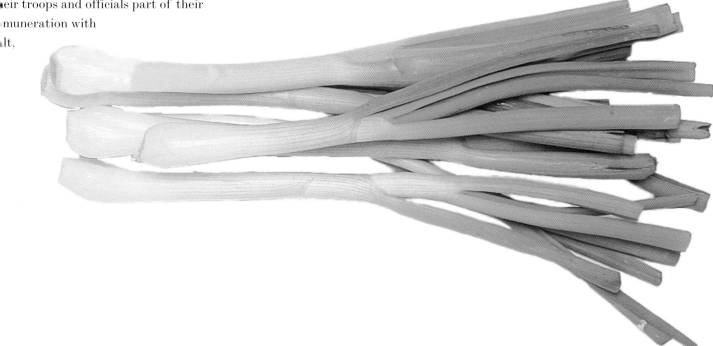

Tamarind
Imli

Tamarind, also known as the Indian date, is a major souring agent, particularly in southern Indian cooking. The tamarind tree bears pods of about 15–20 cm (6–8 in) long which become dark brown when ripe. These pods contain seeds and pulp, which are preserved indefinitely for use in cooking by compression into a rectangular block, weighing 300 g (10 oz) (see page 44).

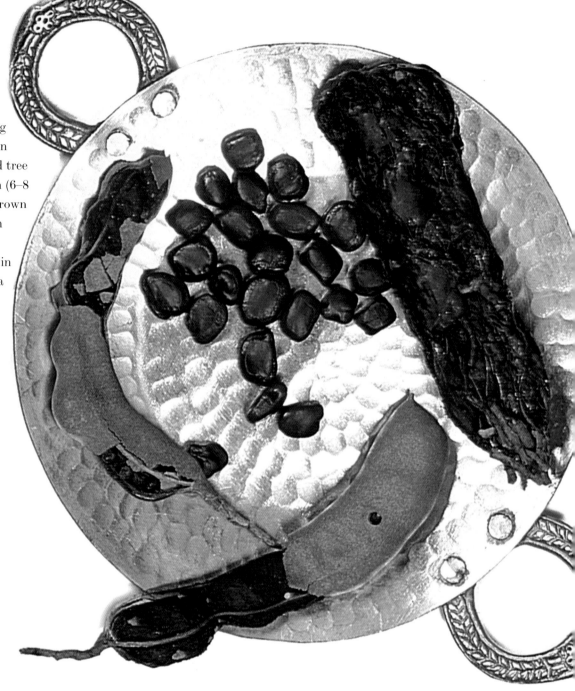

Turmeric
Huldi

Turmeric, like ginger, is a rhizome which grows underground. There are several varieties, of which two are depicted here. It can be used fresh in certain curries, and for pickles, and when halved its gorgeous vivid orange-yellow is a clue to the fact that turmeric is used to give curry its distinctive golden colour. To achieve the

...miliar powder, fresh turmeric is sun-
...ried until it is rock hard,
...hen it is ground.

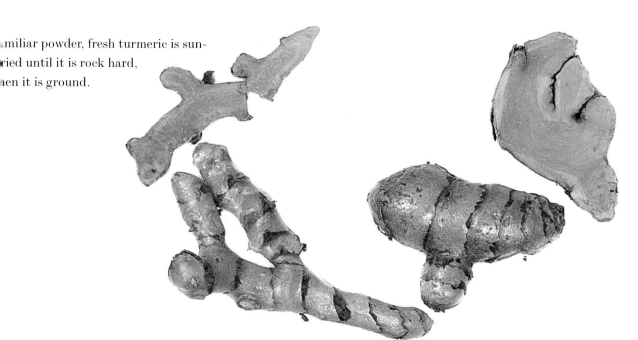

minor spices

...y minor, I mean spices which, though
...portant for their contribution of
...ique flavour and fragrance, are used in
...st a few recipes in this book.

...safoetida
...ing

...his spice is extracted from the carrot-
...aped rhizome of a giant perennial plant
... the fennel family, native to Kashmir.
...hen the rhizome is

mature enough, cuts are made in it to
yield a milky-white sap which slowly
oozes out and solidifies into a brown
resin-like substance. This is factory-
ground into a grey-brown or bright
greeny-lemon powder (depending on the
species). The Persian word *aza*, 'resin',
and Latin *foetidus*, 'stinking', indicates
that asafoetida has an obnoxious,
disagreeable odour, hence its other names

– 'devil's dung' and 'stinking gum'. This
is due to the presence of sulphur in its
composition, and, because of its smell, it
is a good idea to store it in its factory
packaging, inside a second airtight
container. Its use is confined to fish and
lentil dishes. Fortunately, its unpleasant
odour disappears once cooked, to give a
distinctive and pleasant fragrance and
sweetish taste.

Lovage
Ajwain or Ajowan
Lovage is an annual, herbaceous plant,
which grows up to 60 cm (2 feet) high,
with feathery leaves and pretty vermilion
flowers. It is a member of the prolific
Umbelliferae family, which also includes
aniseed, caraway, celery, coriander,
cummin, dill and fennel, all of which have
a characteristic taste due to the thymol
(in varying quantities) in their volatile
oil. This too is a spice with a confusing
nomenclature. In this case ajwain is
called 'carom' or, more commonly,
'lovage' (another relative), but it is not
the same as European lovage. Ajwain is

indigenous to Egypt, Afghanistan and
north India. Its seed, which is smaller
than its European counterpart, is a tiny
greyish sphere about 1½–2 mm in
diameter, with distinctive stripes. Its
taste is a little bitter, with a slightly
musky, but intense
flavour of thyme,
which is an
acquired taste. But
once acquired,
you'll enjoy this
minor spice in
Bombay mix,
snacks, and fish
dishes.

Mace and Nutmeg
Javitri and Jaifal

Mace is unique, because it grows inseparably with nutmeg. Their tree is a tall, tropical evergreen, which originally grew only on the tiny Indonesian island of Ambon, but is now also found in Sri Lanka, south India and Grenada, in the West Indies. Mace forms an arril or blade, which surrounds the inner seed, the nutmeg, with a tendril-like net. They are enclosed inside a pithy, inedible, bright green case (resembling a smooth horse-chestnut casing). When the green case is first opened, the mace is a delightful bright crimson or amber, through which peeps the shiny red-brown nutmeg. When cropped, mace is pliable and easy to separate from its nutmeg, and flatten, before drying it in the sun. As it dries, the nutmeg goes rather greyer in colour, and the mace often loses its red colour. Mace is very, aromatic and oily, its volatile oil being eugenol, though it has less of this than nutmeg.

Its use in Indian cooking is minimal. Its subtle flavour goes well with lighter fish, vegetables and sweet dishes. Nutmeg, with its very aromatic eugenol flavour, is excellent freshly grated over Indian desserts, and it is an ingredient of garam masala.

Dried Mango
Am Chur or Kachcha Am

This grey powdered spice is made by grinding sour, unripened, pitted, sun-dried mangoes. The resultant spice is exceedingly sour, but very distinctive. It is mostly used in chaats and some vegetable dishes.

Sesame Seed
Til

Sesame is a tropical, herbaceous, annual plant growing up to 2 metres (6 feet) in height, native to India and China, and elsewhere. Its capsules contain a large amount of tiny, buff, disc-shaped seeds, which grow to around 3 mm ($\frac{1}{8}$ in) in diameter. After polishing, they become creamy-white in colour. Sesame is very ancient, and a further contender to being the first cultivated spice. It was used to make a flour by the ancient Egyptians. It was also a main source of oil. To this day, it is still more popular in the Middle East than elsewhere. The manufacture of sesame cooking oil remains a major industry which suits the seed well, since it is already very oily, with 60 per cent of its content made up of oleic and linoleic volatile oils. Though sesame is a minor spice in Indian cooking, it is an importar export crop there. It has a somewhat neutral, nutty taste and it is used to texture delicate cooking, and in Indian bread and confectionery. It is also use as a garnish. As with many spices, sesame improves greatly with a little 'roasting'. As a cooking oil, the nutty flavour of sesame is delightful, but wasted in anything other than subtle dishes.

ar Anise
hasphal

ar anise grows on a small, evergreen
ee of the magnolia family, native to
ina, the Philippines and Indo-China. It
wers with single, yellow-green petals,
llowed by the seed, which develops
to a green star, the average size
which is around 2.5 cm
inch) in diameter. It has
ven or eight regularly spaced arms
ar points) radiating from the centre.
hen cropped, the still-closed star is
ied, after which it becomes red-brown
colour. At this stage, some of the
ms may slightly open, revealing one
eaming, pale brown seed. A whole
ecimen of star anise is arguably the
ettiest spice on earth, but it is fragile,
d the arms can easily break off in the
ckaging.
Although it has no relationship at all to
aniseed, star anise gets its name from the
fact that it smells and tastes of aniseed,
because it has the same volatile oil –
anethole – as aniseed. Star anise has been
used since ancient times in Japanese
cooking, and is one of the spices in
Chinese five-spice. Yet despite the
fact that clove, nutmeg and
mace were voluminously traded
from China, via the Spice Route, in
Roman times, there is no evidence
that star anise was sold to Rome,
Arabia or India, so there is no
traditional Indian use of the spice, even
in Moghul times. Equally, there is no
record of star anise use in Europe until
the 17th century, when the Dutch used it
to flavour their tea. Modern Indian
masterchefs have discovered the
attributes of star anise. It is astounding,
for example, used in Pullao Rice as much
for its shape as its colour.

ild Onion Seed or Nigella
alonji

minor spice, wild onion/nigella is a
tive of Asia and north India and a
ember of the *Ranunculus* family.
owing as an herbaceous annual, up to
cm (2 feet) high, it is also known as
ve-in-a-mist, with pale blue flowers. Its
ed, a matt-coal-black, irregular,
ntagonal nugget, is about 1.5–3 mm in
ze. Nigella has a distinctive, slightly
tter, intensely aromatic, delicious and
guely peppery taste. It
used whole in certain
rry recipes,
pecially in the
ngal area. It is
e of the
ve spices
panch
oran, and
essed into
an bread
ugh, it not
ly looks good, it
stes great.

Zeera Black Cummin Seed
Jeera or Kala Zeera or Shahi Jeera

Black cummin is a minor spice, and an
herbaceous plant of the *Umbelliferae*
family, which grows up to 45 cm (18 in) in
height. It yields dark brown seeds with
stripy, longitudinal, charcoal-
coloured ribs, ending in a
short, curved tail. The
seeds closely resemble
caraway, being about the same
3 mm (¹/s in) length, though
zeera seeds are darker and
narrower. White cummin,
on the other hand, is
much paler, fatter
and longer and, in
taste, less subtle and more
savoury, than zeera black
cummin, which has an
aromatic, astringent flavour,
with a hint of liquorice. Its
flavour comes from its oils which
contain limone and cyonene. Its
use is limited, but it is worth
having in stock for its great effect
in such dishes as Pullao Rice and certain
vegetable dishes.

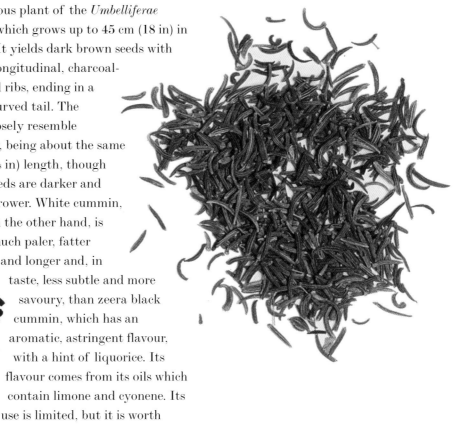

Nutritional Information

All food supplies the body with fuel or nutrients in the form of carbohydrates, fat, protein, minerals and vitamins.

Carbohydrates are composed mainly of starch which is a major energy source since the body converts it into sugar (glucose), also called blood sugar. Carbohydrates also contain dietary fibre, or roughage which is very important to the digestion process.

Proteins are one of the body's building blocks – they build and repair cells so that the body can grow and remain strong. High-protein foods include egg, meat, fish, dairy products, and legumes.

Vitamins are essential nutrients required in small amounts for general well-being – the word derives from the Latin *vita* meaning life. They are found in many foods, such as citrus fruits (vitamin C), green vegetables (vitamins A and K), carrots (vitamin A), wholemeal bread (vitamin B) and oily fish (vitamin D).

Minerals are inorganic substances needed by the body to build important molecules. Bulk minerals (including calcium, phosphorus, potassium and sodium) are needed to regulate heartbeat, water balance and nerve and muscle functioning. Trace elements (including iron) are needed in smaller amounts but are just as essential for good health.

Fat is present in oils, dairy products and nuts. Meat has varying amounts of fat, depending on the meat and the cut. Lamb and pork are fattier than beef. Much of the fat in meat is visible and can be discarded. Too much creates an excess of energy, which the body uses to create its own fat, leading to obesity. The body can in any case, create sufficient fat from carbohydrate and protein.

Neither does the body need an excess of sugar. Enough natural sugar (fructose) is generally available from fruit and vegetables. Sucrose is mostly man-made. It is a carbohydrate with an energy value of 394 calories per 100 g (3½ oz)

The body's energy requirements are expressed in calories. The kilocalorie or kilogram calorie (k cal), as it is correctly called, is 1,000 calories. One calorie or k cal is the unit of heat required to raise the temperature of a gram unit (1 g) of water the unit degree (1°C). All foods have a calorific value. Each person's calorific requirements vary according to their sex, age, height and activity level. A small, sedentary woman may only require 1,800 calories per day. A large, active man doing physical work will require at least twice that. Every 3,500 calories above a person's required intake will add 450 g (1 lb) of body weight. Given that a sugar lump is 10 calories, and that sugar is added to so many products, it is easy to see how weight problems occur.

Balti Masala Dry Spice Mix

The people of the subcontinent call any mixture of spices 'Masala'. Its simplistic name 'curry powder', has helped give Indian food a poor reputation and certain Indian foodies refuse ever to use it. However, there are recipes which can benefit from a pre-prepared, good quality, home-made mixture or masala mix and many of these are included in this book. It is easy to make and far better than factory-made powder. Firstly it is formulated by you, so, obvious though this sounds, you know exactly what is in it. You will have no stalks, no rubbish and no poor-quality spices. Secondly, you can adjust the formula to suit your own taste and requirements. Once made, the mix should be stored in an airtight, damp-free container away from natural light (the ultraviolet in sunlight 'fades' both the colour and the taste). It should be left to 'mature' for about a month, after which it should be used sooner rather than later (within six months; after that it will gradually lose its subtle flavours and become bitter). If you cannot weigh the following amounts precisely, a teaspoon is equal to about 5 g of spice.

makes about 255 g (9 oz)

40 g coriander
20 g cummin
20 g fenugreek
25 g gram flour (besan)
25 g garlic powder
20 g paprika
20 g turmeric
50 g garam masala (see page 41)
5 g bay leaf
5 g asafoetida
5 g ground ginger
5 g chilli powder
5 g English mustard
5 g black pepper
5 g cinnamon

1 Put all the Balti masala ingredients into a bowl.
2 Mix well.
3 Store in an airtight jar until required.

To make oil-based balti masala paste

You may prefer to make your own bottled paste with your dry mix. It must be fried to bring out the aromatic flavours, and remove the raw tastes, which spices are prone to if not cooked properly.

makes about 300 g (11 oz)

Use vinegar (any type) to make the paste
250 g (9 oz) balti masala dry mix
100 g (3½ oz) ghee or 100 ml (3 fl oz) vegetable oil

1 Add just enough vinegar to the dry mix to make a paste thick enough to drop sluggishly off the spoon.
2 Heat the ghee, then add the above paste, and stir continuously until after a few minutes its colour has gone much darker. To check it is fully cooked, leave the mixture to stand off the heat for a while. The ghee separates and 'floats'.
3 Wash and dry a suitably-sized lidded jar(s)
4 Fill the paste into the jar(s).
5 Inspect after a day. Top up with hot ghee or oil to cover the paste as needed. The paste will keep indefinitely.
Using 1 to 2 tablespoons of mix (depending on how spicy you want it), in the recipes for four in this book, it will

last you up to 10 to 20 Balti curries.
You can make the paste in 1 or more tablespoon amounts for a specific individual recipe. Just follow the method above, reducing the quantities of oil pro-rata. Use water if the paste is to be cooked into the recipe straight away, and not preserved.

Tandoori Masala Dry Mixture

You may like to make your own dry mix and bottled paste. It must be fried to bring out the aromatic flavours and to remove the raw tastes which may result if spices are not cooked properly. The paste will keep indefinitely.

makes about 250 g (9 oz) tandoori masala dry mix

40 g coriander
30 g cummin
40 g garlic powder
40 g paprika
20 g ginger powder
20 g mango powder
20 g dried mint
20 g beetroot powder
10 g anatto seed powder
10 g chilli powder
5 g red food colouring powder (optional)

Put all ingredients into a bowl and mix well.

Oil-based Tandoori Paste

makes about 300 g (10 oz)

2 tablespoons ghee or 100 ml (2 fl oz)
    vegetable oil
4 tablespoons tandoori masala dry mix

Heat the ghee then add the tandoori masala mix paste and stir continuously until after a few minutes its colour has gone much darker and the ghee separates and 'floats' when the mixture is left to stand off the heat for a while.

NOTE: You can fry all the 250 g (9 oz) tandoori masala dry mix and bottle it. Use vinegar instead of water to make the paste.

vinegar (any type)
250 g (9 oz) Balti masala dry mix
100 g (3½ oz) ghee or 100 ml (2 fl oz)
    vegetable oil

Follow the above method, stirring until the mixture darkens. Place the paste in a suitably sized lidded jar (or jars). Inspect after a day. Top up with hot ghee or oil to cover the paste as needed.

Using 1–2 tablespoons of paste per recipe (depending on how spicy you want it) this should stretch to between 10 and 20 Balti curries.

You can make the paste in quantities of 1 or more tablespoons for specific recipes following the method given above and reducing the quantities accordingly. Use water if the paste is to be cooked into the recipe straight away, and not preserved.

Balti Garam Masala

aram means 'hot' and masala a
ixture of spices'. Garam masala is an
cient Kashmiri invention and is a
ixture of aromatic whole spices which
e 'roasted' (cooked by dry-frying with
oil or liquid). The mixture is then
oled, ground and stored in airtight
rs. It may be used in various ways –
rinkled on finished dishes, added to
oghurt dips or added to certain curries,
wards the end of cooking, particularly
oghul curries from Kashmir and north
dia, such as Classic Korma and Roghan
sh. These retain the aromatic subtlety
garam masala's spices.
f Balti has one identifying feature, it is
aromatic tastes, and garam masala is
e key to achieving these. Its use in
lti cooking is unique because it can be
ed at the beginning of the cooking
ocess. There are as many recipes for
ram masala as there are cooks in the
dian subcontinent. This particular
cipe is for an authentic Kashmiri
ram masala, perfect for Balti, where
e emphasis is on aromatics rather than
at. As with the previous recipes you
ay wish to vary the quantities to suit
ur taste. Compare it with any factory-
ade garam masala of your choice and
u will always make it fresh from now
, I guarantee! As previously I have
ed approximate measures (heaped
oons) and more accurate measures in
etric only.

akes about 200 g (7 oz)

g (4½ tablespoons) coriander seeds
g (2½ tablespoons) white cummin seeds
g (5 teaspoons) aniseed
g (5 5 cm/2 inch pieces) cassia bark
g (1½ tablespoons) green cardamom
 seeds
g (1 tablespoon) cloves
g (4–6) bay leaves
g (1½ teaspoons) dried mint leaves

1 Mix all the ingredients except for the dried mint leaves together in your pan. Keeping it dry, stir the mixture continuously as it heats up.
2 Very soon the mixture will give off steam, rather than smoke. The process is called 'roasting'. The volatile oils, or aromas are now being released into the air. Stir for a few seconds more, then transfer the spices to a cold pan or bowl, to stop them cooking. The mixture must not burn; if it does, it will give your cooking a bitter, carbonised taste.

3 Allow the garam masala to cool completely. This will make it go more brittle so that it may be ground more easily. Also, if it is hot when you grind it in an electric grinder, the blades could overheat the spices and burn off the very volatile oil you are striving to capture.
4 Grind in batches, whether you are using a mortar and pestle or an electric grinder (here it is a coffee grinder).

5 Grind until all the clattering noises change to a softer sound, then grind on until the mixture is as fine as you want it, or as fine as the grinder will achieve.

6 Thoroughly mix all the ingredients together, including the dried mint leaves. Store in an airtight jar in a dark, dry place. It will last for many months, although like all ground spices it will gradually lose its fragrance until eventually it tastes of little or nothing. It is best to make garam masala freshly in batches even smaller than I've used here.

Balti Masala Gravy

Like the Indian restaurant, the Balti house has found a foolproof method which enables it to produce, very rapidly, any amount of different dishes, in its case 'formula' Baltis. Every day, meat, chicken and certain vegetables, are precooked then chilled, and a large stock pot of thick Balti Masala Gravy is made. The next part of the process is to fulfil customers' orders on a person-by-person, dish-by-dish basis using these main ingredients, pinches of appropriate spices, and a ladleful or two of the gravy.

I have modified restaurant techniques to produce four-portion dishes, by, for example, oven casseroling meat dishes, and stir-frying others. However, in order to recreate the smooth texture of restaurant curries, some recipes do need a Balti masala gravy. Here is enough to make twelve individual curries, each of which requires about 110 g (4 oz) of gravy. I keep saying 'about' because the exact gravy content can be varied according to taste. To save on time and washing up, you may wish to make several batches of this gravy at once.

makes about 1.3 kg (3 lb) Balti Masala Gravy

110 g (4 oz) ghee
150 g (5½ oz) garlic, finely chopped
110 g (4 oz) ginger (optional), finely chopped
1 kg (2 lb 4 oz) Spanish onions, chopped
600ml (1 pint) water
300 g (11 oz) cooked Balti masala paste

1 Heat the ghee and stir-fry the garlic and optional ginger for the minute or two it takes for it to go translucent (front wok). Lower the heat and add the onions bit by bit as they reduce in size in the wok, stir-frying as needed until they are browned and caramelised (rear wok).

2 Add the water, then mulch it down i a blender or hand blender until you achieve a smooth purée.

3 (Right wok) The Balti masala paste is added into the gravy. To preserve the finished gravy, fill 3 large yoghurt pots, pop on their lids and freeze. Each pot gives about 454 g (1 lb) or enough grav for one of my recipes for four people. Shown in the rear wok is onion tarka. This is onion which is fried on a very lo heat until it goes really brown and crispy.

Aromatic Salt

The recipes throughout this book call for aromatic salt. You can, of course, use ordinary salt, but aromatic salt adds a touch of 'magic' to your cooking. The light version, shown on the right, is complete in itself, but it can be further developed into a spicier version, shown top left. In each case, grind all the ingredients and store in an airtight jar.

Lightly Spiced Aromatic Salt

makes 100 g (3½ oz)

100 g (3½ oz) coarse sea salt
1 teaspoon allspice, freshly ground
1 teaspoon ground cinnamon

Spicier Aromatic Salt

makes 100 g (3½ oz)

1 quantity lightly spiced salt
1 teaspoon dried mint
½ teaspoon ground fenugreek
1 teaspoon ground almonds
½ teaspoon turmeric

Fragrant Stock

Certain Balti recipes need water added at some stage in their cooking. As with European dishes a light stock is most effective. In Balti dishes, this is known as 'Akhni' or 'Yakhni'. It adds fragrancy, is really easy to make and any surplus can be frozen in yoghurt pots so nothing is wasted.

makes about 700 ml (1¼ pints)

8–12 green cardamoms
8–12 cloves
4 or 6 bay leaves
6–8 pieces cassia bark
50 g dried onion flakes
1 tablespoon ghee
850 ml (1½ pints) water

1 Simply simmer all the ingredients for about 20 minutes, then strain, discarding the solids. The stock may then be frozen in small batches using disposable moulds, such as yoghurt pots.

NOTE: Using dried onion flakes (dehydrated onion) rather than fresh onion saves a lot of time.

Panch Phoran

Panch Phoran is a Bengali mixture of five (*panch*) whole aromatic seeds. There are several possible combinations, for example, celery, and/or caraway seeds can be substituted for cummin. Simply mix the spices together in equal parts (a teaspoon of each is plenty) and store in an airtight container.

white cummin seeds
fennel seeds
fenugreek seeds
black mustard seeds
wild onion seeds

Mango Hedgehog

serves 2

1 fresh ripe mango

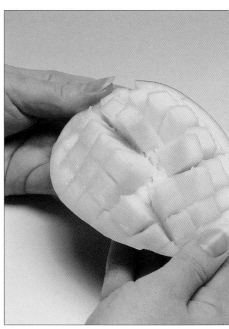

1 Stand the mango on its base and using a sharp knife, slice down it running the knife along the side of the stone. Repeat to the other side.

2 Place the mango halves on a plate, flesh side up. Score the flesh in straight lines, in a criss-cross pattern taking care not to cut down to the the skin.

3 Taking one half of the mango in bot hands, gently push the skin inwards an upwards, towards you. It is almost like turning it inside out.The inverted score flesh of the mango then resembles a hedgehog.
4 Repeat with the other half.

Tamarind Purée

Tamarind is a major souring agent, which gives a unique flavour to certain Indian cooking. There is no substitute. Vinegar or lemon/lime simply gives the wrong flavour. Very few dishes in this book use tamarind, and there is no short cut to making the real thing. But it is worth making up a batch and freezing it.

Makes about 450 g (1 lb)

300 g (10 oz) block compressed tamarind
1.3 litres (2¼ pints) water

1 Bring half the water to the simmer in a largeish saucepan. Break up the tamarind block into the hot water.
2 Simmer and occasionally stir for 10 minutes, pulping it well with the back of a spoon, then strain through a metal sieve, keeping the husks. The brown liquid should be quite thick, and there will be plenty of it.
3 Bring a second batch of fresh water to the simmer in the saucepan. Add the retained husks and repeat stage 2.
4 Mix the two batches together.
5 Use or freeze in yoghurt pot moulds as required.

Slow-cooking Garlic and Onions – Tarka

It is so important to get the first few minutes of cooking of every Balti curry correct, which is why I'm giving a very detailed method for it here. This precise initial stir-fry is required for Balti Jalfrezi (see pages 81, 93, 111, 142), one of the most popular Balti dishes. But exactly the same technique is used in virtually every Balti curry recipe in this book. The spices and ingredients may vary but the techniques do not, so it may be helpful to practise this recipe.

makes enough to start a 4-portion Balti recipe

2–3 tablespoons ghee or corn oil
3–6 garlic cloves, finely chopped
2.5 cm (1 inch) cube ginger, thinly sliced
110 g (4 oz) onion, thinly sliced
3 or 4 spring onions, bulbs and leaves, chopped
2–3 tablespoons Balti masala paste (see page 39)
1 tablespoon green masala paste (see right)
SPICES
1½ teaspoons cummin seeds
½ teaspoon lovage seeds
½ teaspoon coriander seeds

1 Heat the oil or ghee in your Balti pan over a high heat until it nearly smokes. Add the spices and stir-fry for about 20 seconds, keeping the seeds briskly on the move to prevent them from burning. Add the garlic and continue with the brisk stir-frying for a further 30 seconds. If using ginger, as we are here, add it now and continue the stir-fry for 30 more seconds.
2 Now add the onions and mix them in well. Lower the heat to the point where you can hear the mixture sizzle calmly. Stir from time to time to turn the mixture over. Cook like this until the onions go brown. At this stage it is

called the tarka. What is happening here is that the onion water content is being cooked out allowing the onions to become caramelised. Starch is turning to sugar. The process needs gentle heat and at least 12–15 minutes, maybe longer depending on the onion type and the heat level. The whole process is easy enough, but taking nearly 20 minutes it is somewhat slow. It is however crucial in achieving the Balti curry flavour. Curry pastes are added after the caramelisation has taken place.

You can, of course, make up a number of batches of tarka (onion only, or onion with garlic, or with ginger too), for the freezer. You can double up the quantity in the pan (but no more or it won't caramelise) and even do more than one pan at the same time. An hour or so of this work will yield a dozen or more batches and will save on kitchen smells, washing up and work time later.

NOTE: Remember the quantities stated above are for a 4-portion Balti curry, so freeze in containers which will yield the portion size or sizes you require. Yoghurt pots make great moulds for this.

Quick Method

If time is of the essence or you simply do not wish to spend 20–25 minutes browning onions as described in the previous recipe, here is a 3-minute method using quick dried or dehydrated chopped onion flakes. If the packet requires you to rehydrate the onions first, ignore that instruction. Simply add them to your stir-fry dry.

makes enough to start a 4-portion Balti recipe

4 tablespoons sunflower oil or butter ghee
1 teaspoon white cummin seeds
2 or 3 garlic cloves, finely chopped (or 2 or 3 teaspoons garlic purée)
2 teaspoons ginger, finely chopped
40 g (1½ oz) quick-dried sliced onions
100 ml (2 fl oz) cold water

1 Follow the first stage of the previous recipe.
2 Now add the dried onions, stir-frying briskly and continuously. They will absorb the available oil like a sponge, then they will start sizzling. Beware because they will start to go brown almost at once, and if allowed to they would blacken and burn. So we must, at this browning stage, instantly cool them down by pouring in the cold water and removing the pan from the heat.

Green Masala Paste

This is a kind of curry paste and it is green in colour because of the coriander and mint it contains. You can buy it factory made, but it does not have the delicious fresh taste of this recipe. Even if I have not specified the use of this paste, you can add a heaped teaspoon in place of, or as well as fresh coriander towards the end of cooking virtually any dish. It will keep in jars indefinitely if made correctly.

Makes about 250 g (9 oz)

1 teaspoon fenugreek seeds
6 cloves garlic, chopped
2 tablespoons ginger, chopped
30 g (1 oz) fresh mint leaves
60 g (2 oz) fresh coriander leaves
100 ml (4 fl oz) vinegar, any type
3 teaspoons salt
3 teaspoons turmeric
2 teaspoons chilli powder
½ teaspoon ground cloves
1 teaspoon ground cardamom seeds
150 ml (6 fl oz) vegetable oil

1 Soak the fenugreek seeds in water overnight. They will swell and acquire a jelly-like coating.
2 Strain the fenugreek seeds, discarding the water.
3 Mulch down all the ingredients, except the oil, in a blender or food processor, to make a purée.
4 To cook, follow the Balti Masala paste method on page 39.

Starters

It was French restaurateurs who perfected the notion that a meal was incomplete without a morsel or two before your main meal. The idea is to whet the appetite and prepare it for the delights to come. The concept of 'starters' is unknown in the Balti lands of Pakistan, and in much of the sub-continent of India. In many areas the complete meal is served at once and diners select what they want to eat with what. Sweet and savoury items thus sit side by side, which to Westerners gives a meal a new slant. We generally treat starters as savoury items in their own right. And there are a number of very tempting recipes from the subcontinent which make ideal starters. Of course they also make great snacks at any time.

A visitor to India cannot avoid meeting such delights, often served by street vendors. Papadoms and Bombay Mix are on offer piled up high on pavement stands. Kebabs and samosas, tikkas and tandooris, and all sorts of snacks, hot and cold are available. They translate well into starters, at the restaurant or cooked at home. Here are a number of starters which, when served in modest portions, make a great introduction to the Balti main course

My starter portion sizes are quite modest. But if you are a hearty eater, or if you wish to eat these starters as snacks or light meals in their own right you can simply increase the quantities accordingly.

pre-starter nibbles

People always feel hungry on arrival at a restaurant and crave little 'nibbles' to keep them going until their meal appears. These nibbles can easily be made at home using readily available packets of Bombay Mix, followed by papadoms and chutneys. Serve them with an apéritif.

◆ Bombay Mix

This is a pre-cooked packet snack – usually 100 g (3½ oz) – containing golden, savoury biscuity 'squiggles', spices and nuts. The 'squiggles' are made from a spicy lentil flour paste extruded through moulds and deep-fried. There are several other types of 'squiggle' called sev, ganthia, chevda and mooth, which together make up Bombay Mix – the most popular nibble of all.

Simply place the mix in a decorative serving bowl or bowls and place where people can help themselves. Once out of its airtight packaging, the mix, like biscuits, will go stale after a day or two.

◆ Papadoms

PAPADOMS (ALSO CALLED PAPADS) ARE THIN BRITTLE DISCS MADE IN SOUTH INDIA FROM LENTIL FLOUR AND OIL DOUGH. THEY ARE USUALLY SOLD IN PACKETS OR BOXES OF 12 OR 20 EACH. PAPADOMS COME IN MANY SIZES, FROM MINI TO LARGE, AND THEIR FLAVOURS VARY FROM PLAIN AND UNSPICED, TO THOSE SPICED WITH BLACK PEPPER, CUMMIN SEED, CHILLI, WHOLE LENTILS AND SO ON. THEY CAN BE COOKED IN THREE WAYS (DEEP-FRYING, GRILLING OR MICROWAVING), AND WILL KEEP, UNOPENED, UNTIL THEIR SELL-BY DATE. ALLOW 2 OR 3 PAPADOMS PER PERSON.

Deep-frying

This is the most popular method giving the best taste, but also containing the most calories

1 Preheat the oil to 170°C/340°F.
2 Deep-fry one papadom at a time in the hot oil for about 5 seconds. It will sizzle and expand at once.
3 Remove from the oil with tongs, shaking off the excess oil and place it on its end on kitchen paper to drain.
4 Repeat until you have cooked the required number of papadoms.
5 Allow to cool, but keep in a warm, damp-free place for a few hours until each is crispy and oil-free.

> ### CHEF'S TIP
> *To achieve dry non-greasy papadoms, fry them at least 6 hours before serving. They will go cold but not stale in that time. If you want them served warm, simply place them in a slightly warm oven for a few minutes, prior to serving.*

Grilling

1 Preheat the grill to medium-high.
2 Put two papadoms side by side on the rack on the grill tray.
3 Place the grill tray in the midway position under the heat.
4 The papadoms will cook within 10–1? seconds. They will bubble up and small areas will turn brown. Watch that there are no uncooked patches (especially at the edges). Equally watch that they do not burn; it all happens very quickly so a little practice may be needed.
Being oil-free, grilled papadoms can be served at once or stored in a warm place for a few hours until ready.

Microwaving

Papadoms can also be microwaved, although their flavour is not as good as when they are grilled. Most microwaves are power-rated at 650 watts. You'll need to experiment on the timing because micorwaves vary considerably

1 Place three papadoms side by side on the microwave tray.
2 Cook on full power for about 30 seconds to a minute.
3 Watch that the whole papadom has cooked. If not replace it and give it a few seconds longer.

Like grilling, this method gives rise to strong smells and also produces the least satisfactory taste of the three methods.

> ### CHEF'S TIP
> *The smell from this grilling operation can be a little strong so it is better done earlier rather than later.*

stuffed vegetables

ny vegetable which has a cavity is
itable for filling – peppers or chillies,
urgettes, mushrooms, aubergines,
ef tomatoes, potatoes, sweet potatoes
d yams can all be used. In most cases
u must scoop out the flesh to create a
vity, but be careful not to pierce
rough the vegetable. Any excess filling
n be frozen for future use, or cooked
to a curry.

◆ Stuffed Bell Peppers

RY TO USE DIFFERENT COLOURED PEPPERS AND
AKE SURE THEY ARE AS FRESH AS POSSIBLE. IF
OU LIKE HOT FLAVOURS YOU CAN SUBSTITUTE
RGE CHILLIES FOR BELL PEPPERS.

rves 4

–6 large peppers

Wash the peppers. Carefully cut off
eir tops (these can be used as lids).
  Carefully de-seed and de-pith the
sides.
  Pack the filling (see below) into the
mpty cavities, smoothing the top
urface into a rounded curve.
  Place the peppers on an oven tray and
ake in an oven preheated to
90°C/375°F/Gas 5 for 12–15 minutes.
  Serve hot on a bed of salad with
mon or lime wedges and chutneys.

ages 46–47: A selection of stuffed
egetables

◆ Vegetable Filling

makes enough to stuff 4–6 peppers

2–3 large potatoes, cooked and mashed
½ teaspoon salt
110 g (4 oz) frozen peas, thawed
½ teaspoon ground black pepper
1 teaspoon chilli powder (optional)
1 teaspoon ground coriander
½ teaspoon ground cummin
2 teaspoons dried fenugreek leaves

1 Mix together the ingredients. Allow
the mixture to cool completely before
using.

◆ Meat Filling

makes enough to stuff 4–6 peppers

300 g (10 oz) Balti Keema curry (see page
   66)
110 g (4 oz) frozen peas, thawed
1 or 2 chopped chillies (optional)
aromatic salt to taste (see page 43)
1 teaspoon garam masala (see page 41)
2 teaspoons dried fenugreek leaves

I Strain off any excess liquid from the
ingredients to ensure the filling will be
dry enough. Reserve liquid for another
use.
2 Mix all the ingredients together.
Allow the mixture to cool completely
before using.

◆ Sag Paneer Filling

makes enough to stuff 4–6 peppers

450 g (1 lb) spinach, fresh, frozen or canned
2–4 garlic cloves, finely chopped
110 g (4 oz) spring onions, finely chopped
1 tablespoon Balti masala paste (see page 39)
110 g (4 oz) crumbly paneer (see page 161)
   or cottage cheese
4 tablespoons fresh coriander, chopped
4 tablespoons fresh mint, chopped
1 tablespoon Balti garam masala (see
   page 41)
½ teaspoon aromatic salt (see page 43)
up to 4 green chillies, finely chopped
   (optional)

I Strain off any excess liquid from the
ingredients to ensure the filling will be
dry enough. Reserve liquid for another
use.
2 Finely chop or purée the spinach.
3 Mix together all the ingredients.
Allow the mixture to cool completely
before using.

◆ Rice Filling

makes enough to stuff 4–6 peppers

400 g (14 oz) rice – any type – cooked
150 g (5 oz) natural yoghurt
110 g (4 oz) spring onions, finely chopped
1 tablespoon Balti masala paste (see page 39)
4 tablespoons fresh coriander, chopped
1 tablespoon garam masala (see page 41)
½ teaspoon aromatic salt (see page 43)
up to 4 green chillies, finely chopped
   (optional)

1 Mix all the ingredients together.
Allow the mixture to cool completely
before using.

◆ Onion Bhaji

THE BHAJIA OR BHAJI COMPRISES SLICED OR CHOPPED INGREDEDIENTS MIXED INTO BATTER AND DEEP-FRIED. ONION BHAJI IS THE MOST POPULAR STARTER AT THE CURRY AND BALTI HOUSE.

makes 8–10 bhajis

225 g (8 oz) onion, chopped into fine
    2.5 cm (1 in) strips
vegetable oil for deep-frying
FOR THE BATTER
85 g (3 oz) gram flour
3 or 4 tablespoons natural yoghurt
1 tablespoon fresh or bottled lemon juice
1 teaspoon salt
1 teaspoon Balti masala dry mix or paste
    (see page 39)
2 teaspoons garam masala (see page 41)
2 teaspoons dried fenugreek leaves
1–2 teaspoons chilli powder

◆◆◆◆◆◆◆◆◆◆◆◆◆◆◆◆◆◆◆◆◆◆◆◆◆◆◆

1 Mix the batter ingredients together, adding sufficient water to achieve a thickish paste which will drop sluggishly off the spoon. Mix in the onion, then leave to stand for at least 10 minutes, during which time the mixture will fully absorb the moisture.
2 Meanwhile, heat the oil to 190°C/375°F. This temperature is below smoking point and will cause a drop of batter to splutter a bit, then float more or less at once.

3 Inspect the mixture. There must be no 'powder' left, and it must be well mixed. Scoop out an eighth of the mixture and place it carefully in the oil. Then repeat with the other seven portions, allowing about 15 seconds between each one so the oil will maintain its temperature.
4 Fry for about 10 minutes each, turning once. Remove from the oil in the order they went in, drain well and serve with salad garnishes, lemon wedges and chutneys. Alternatively, allow to cool, then freeze. Reheat in deep hot oil for about 2 minutes, but don't let them get too brown. Serve hot.

Variation Restaurant Method

1 Mix the batter as above but use less water to achieve a drier, mouldable texture. Add the onion and leave to stand, as above.
2 Heat the oil, as above.
3 Roll the mixture into smooth balls about 5 cm (2 in) in diameter. You will need to wash your hands frequently while doing this.
4 Deep-fry the bhajis for 2–3 minutes to set the batter firmly, then either remove them and allow them to cool for cooking later or continue cooking.
5 The part-cooked bhajis can be left spherical, or when cool enough they can be flattened into discs with the heel of your hand. When required, reheat the deep-frying oil and fry them for 5–7 minutes. Serve hot.

GARNISH

A sprinkling of green herbs on top of your Balti not only looks attractive, adding that professional touch, it also gives the dish a healthier appearance. Fresh coriander is the leaf most commonly used in Balti, but you can broaden horizons by using other herbs such as basil, dill, fennel leaf, mint, parsley, watercress, chives and garlic chives. Use pretty leaves whole or coarsely chopped, sprinkling them on the dish prior to serving.

◆ Kofta

KOFTAS ARE SMALL MOULDED BALLS OF GROUND MEAT, POULTRY, FISH OR VEGETABLES. NORMALLY KOFTAS APPEAR IN A CURRY GRAVY AS A MAIN COURSE DISH. WITHOUT THE GRAVY, THEY MAKE EXCELLENT STARTERS, SNACKS OR FINGER FOODS, ESPECIALLY WHEN SERVED WITH A CHUTNEY OR RAITA (SEE PAGES 188–189).

To make the koftas, please refer to the recipes on pages 68, 94, 115 and 148.

BALTI SALAD BED

I have mentioned that you may serve many of the previous starter recipes on a bed of salad. Pre-prepared mixed salad leaves, cleaned and hygienically packaged from the vegetable department provide you with a huge choice of salad vegetables, including lettuce, Chinese leaves, chives, white cabbage, parsley, rocket, radiccio, watercress, chicory leaves, endive or curly lettuce and carrot.
Mix your leaves together. Cover and chill in the fridge. Serve on plates (as a bed for the starter) or indeed to accompany your main course if you wish.

Koftas

The following four recipes are all Chaat (pronounced 'chart'), a general term meaning 'snack'. There is also a dish called chaat. They are based on curried chickpeas served either with diced chicken breast or diced potatoes, using canned kala chana – black chickpeas. They can be served hot, but they are also among India's few dishes which benefit from being served chilled with a salad and a lime wedge, plus some tasty chutneys. You can buy packets of ready-mixed chaat masala at Asian food stores. The distinctive feature of these mixes is that they contain tart mango powder and black salt, both an acquired taste.

◆ Three-bean Balti Stir-fry

THIS STIR-FRY HAS A LOVELY FRESH FLAVOUR AND USING CANNED BEANS AND CHICKPEAS AVOIDS ALL THE COMPLICATIONS OF SOAKING AND PREPARING DRIED ONES.

serves 4 as a starter or snack

100 g (3½ oz) canned chickpeas
100 g (3½ oz) canned red kidney beans
100 g (3½ oz) canned lobia beans
3 tablespoons sunflower or soy soil
3–4 garlic cloves, finely chopped
110 g (4 oz) onion, very finely chopped
1 tablespoon Balti masala paste (see page 39)
1 tablespoon tomato purée
1 tablespoon red, yellow or black bell pepper, chopped
1 or 2 fresh green chillies, chopped (optional)
4 or 5 cherry tomatoes, chopped
2 teaspoons Balti garam masala (see page 41)
1 tablespoon chopped fresh coriander leaves
½ teaspoon mango powder (optional)
black or aromatic salt to taste (see page 43)

◆◆◆◆◆◆◆◆◆◆◆◆◆◆◆◆◆◆◆◆◆◆◆◆◆◆◆◆◆◆◆◆◆◆◆◆◆

1 Heat the oil in your Balti pan or wok. Stir-fry the garlic for 30 seconds. Add the

Three-bean Balti Stir-fry with Potato

onion and stir-fry for a further 3 minutes or so.
2 Add the masala paste and stir-fry for a couple of minutes, adding just enough water to make it into a runny but cohesive paste.
3 Add the tomato purée, pepper and chillies. Lower the heat, add the canned items, and when it is simmering add the remaining ingredients, and simmer for another few minutes.
4 It should by now be neither too dry nor too moist. It can be served hot or cold on a bed of salad garnished with fresh coriander leaves and a lemon wedge or two.

Potato and Chickpea Balti Stir-fry

This is a variant of the Three-bean Balti Stir-fry recipe, above. For more generous servings simply add canned potatoes as required (the other ingredients remain the same, although you may wish to increase the amount of garam masala to taste). Serve hot or cold.

◆ Potato, Sweet Potato, Swede, Carrot Balti Stir-fry

A FURTHER VARIANT OF THE THREE-BEAN BALTI STIR-FRY RECIPE. THIS TIME PRE-COOKED POTATO, SWEET POTATO, SWEDE, AND CARROT TAKE THE PLACE OF THE THREE BEANS. THE OTHER INGREDIENTS REMAIN THE SAME.

serves 4

300 g (10 oz) mixture of potato, sweet potato, swede and carrot, precooked

◆◆◆◆◆◆◆◆◆◆◆◆◆◆◆◆◆◆◆◆◆◆◆◆◆◆◆◆◆◆◆◆◆◆◆◆◆

The method is nearly identical to that of the Three-bean Balti Stir-fry recipe, the only variation being to add the potato at the same time as the pepper. Cook for about 4 minutes then add the cooked lentils and proceed to the end of the recipe. Serve hot or cold.

◆ Balti Chicken and Pea Stir-fry

YET ANOTHER VARIANT OF THE THREE-BEAN BALTI STIR-FRY RECIPE. THIS TIME REPLACE THE CANNED ITEMS WITH CHICKEN AND PEAS. THE OTHER INGREDIENTS REMAIN THE SAME.

serves 4

200 g (7 oz) filleted and skinned chicken breast, chopped into bite-size pieces
110 g (4 oz) frozen peas, thawed

◆◆◆◆◆◆◆◆◆◆◆◆◆◆◆◆◆◆◆◆◆◆◆◆◆◆◆◆◆◆◆◆◆◆◆◆◆

The method is nearly identical to that of the Three-bean Balti Stir-fry recipe, the only variation being to add the chicken at the same time as the pepper. Cook for about 8 minutes then add the peas and proceed to the end of the recipe, ensuring that the chicken is fully cooked. Serve hot or cold.

◆ Balti Prawn Dhal Stir-fry

ANOTHER VARIANT OF THE THREE-BEAN BALTI STIR-FRY. THIS TIME SHELLED PRAWNS TAKE THE PLACE OF 150G CANNED BEANS/CHICKPEAS. THE OTHER INGREDIENTS REMAIN THE SAME.

serves 4

175 g (6½ oz) tub prawns in brine
200 g canned beans/chickpeas

◆◆◆◆◆◆◆◆◆◆◆◆◆◆◆◆◆◆◆◆◆◆◆◆◆◆◆◆◆◆◆◆◆◆◆◆◆

The method is nearly identical to that of the Three-bean Balti Stir-fry recipe, the only variation being to add the prawn at the same time as the pepper. Cook for about 4 minutes then add the canned beans/chickpeas and proceed to the end of the recipe.

◆ Tandoori Marinade

THE STANDARD, TANGY TASTY MARINADE.

makes 400 g (14 oz)

150 g (5 oz) plain yoghurt
2 tablespoons vegetable oil
2 tablespoons freshly squeezed lime juice
2–3 garlic cloves, finely chopped
2–3 fresh red chillies, finely chopped
2 tablespoons fresh coriander leaves, finely chopped
1 teaspoon white cummin seeds, roasted and ground
1 teaspoon Balti garam masala (see page 41)
2 tablespoons red tandoori paste (see below)
1 tablespoon tomato purée
½ teaspoon aromatic salt (see page 43)
about 125 ml (4 fl oz) milk

◆◆◆◆◆◆◆◆◆◆◆◆◆◆◆◆◆◆◆◆◆◆◆◆◆◆◆◆◆

1 Put all the ingredients, except the milk, into the blender and pulse.
2 Start drizzling in the milk until the purée is easy to pour, and as smooth as you can get it. As there are some variables in the ingredients you may need more or less milk than stated. Refrigerate until needed.
  To achieve the restaurant red or orange look, simply add ½ teaspoon of red and/or orange food colouring, but before you do, please read about it on page 181.

Tandoori Paste

The Tandoori Masala on page 40 makes 250 g (9 oz) dry mix. Using all 250 g, this can be made into a paste weighing 675 g (1½ lb) which can be bottled and stored indefinitely. (You can make smaller batches by reducing the ingredients this pro-rata – for example, a batch sufficient for the marinade below needs 30 g of dry mix, which is fried as in the recipe on page 40.)

◆ Chicken Tikka

serves 2 (as a starter)

10–12 chunky pieces skinned chicken breast, cut into 3.75 cm (1½ in) cubes
200 g (7 oz) tandoori marinade (see above)
2 bamboo or metal skewers

◆◆◆◆◆◆◆◆◆◆◆◆◆◆◆◆◆◆◆◆◆◆◆◆◆◆◆◆◆

1 Mix the chicken into the marinade in a non-metallic bowl. Cover and refrigerate for 24–60 hours.
2 To cook, divide the chicken between two skewers.
3 Preheat the grill to medium. Place the skewers on an oven rack above a foil-lined grill tray and place this in the midway position. Alternatively they can be barbecued.
4 Cook for 5 minutes, turn, then cook for a further 5 minutes.
5 Cut through one piece to ensure that it is fully cooked – it should be white right through with no hint of pink. If not, cook for a while longer. When fully cooked, raise the tray nearer to the heat and singe the pieces to achieve a blackening effect.

◆ Meat Tikka

serves 2 (as a starter)

200 g (7 oz) tandoori marinade (see above)
10–12 chunky pieces lean meat cut into 3.75 cm (1½ in) cubes
2 bamboo or metal skewers

◆◆◆◆◆◆◆◆◆◆◆◆◆◆◆◆◆◆◆◆◆◆◆◆◆◆◆◆◆

1 Mix the meat into the marinade in a non-metallic bowl. Cover and refrigerate for 24–60 hours.
2 To cook, preheat oven to 220°C/425°F/Gas 7. Line an oven tray with foil and place the oven rack above the tray.
3 Divide the meat between two skewers and place them on the oven rack, and cook for 15–20 minutes, depending on your oven. A degree of pinkness or rareness in the middle of the meat may

be preferred, and this is acceptable, except for pork which should be fully cooked – adjust cooking times accordingly.

◆ Tandoori Chicken

serves 2 (as a starter)

900 g (2 lb) double poussin (small chicken) or 2 large legs
3 tablespoons freshly squeezed lime juice
200 g (7 oz) red or green tandoori marinade (see above)
2 metal skewers

◆◆◆◆◆◆◆◆◆◆◆◆◆◆◆◆◆◆◆◆◆◆◆◆◆◆◆◆◆

1 Skin the chicken, and halve it. Clean inside and out. Legs simply need skinning. Then slash the flesh with short gashes. Rub in the lime juice. Leave it for about 30 minutes.
2 Mix the chicken into the marinade in a non-metallic bowl. Cover and refrigerate for 24–60 hours.
3 To cook, preheat the oven to 220°C/425°F/Gas 7. Shake off excess marinade (but reserve for basting) and place the chicken pieces on skewers and on an oven rack at the top of the oven. Be sure to put a foil-lined drip pan underneath.
4 Cook for about 10 minutes. Turn and baste the pieces with the excess marinade, and cook for a further 10–15 minutes, depending on your oven, or until the flesh is cooked right through. To check, prick the leg. If clear liquid runs out rather than cloudy, it is cooked. Then, to finish off, place it under the grill just long enough (a couple of minutes) to achieve a blackened effect.
5 Alternatively, if you are barbecuing, put the pieces of marinated chicken over the charcoal (not too near) and turn, baste and cook until ready.

A selection of Tikkas

◆ Liver Tikka Balti Stir-fry

THIS RECIPE WORKS EQUALLY WELL WITH KIDNEY OR HEART OR A MIXTURE OF OFFALS.

serves 4 (as a snack or starter)

225 g (8 oz) liver, cut into bite-sized pieces
4 tablespoons butter ghee
1 tablespoon tandoori paste (see page 40)
aromatic salt to taste (see page 43)

◆◆◆◆◆◆◆◆◆◆◆◆◆◆◆◆◆◆◆◆◆◆◆◆◆◆◆◆◆◆

1 Heat the ghee and the paste together.
2 When sizzling, add the liver.
3 Stir-fry until ready (about 8–10 minutes), adjusting the heat as necessary. Salt to taste and serve hot.

◆ Exotikka Balti Stir-fry

This is not to be confused with the Exotica dish on page 172, although being a combination dish there are similarities. This is a stir fry of various tikkas. It is particularly good for parties and barbecues. Simply make chicken, lamb and offal stir-fries. Prawns of any size can also be included, and stir-fried.

◆ Balti Lamb or Pork Chops

THE CHOPS ARE GRILLED (OR BARBECUED) UNTIL THEY ARE CRISPY AND DRY, YET SUCCULENT – SUITABLE FOR EATING AS 'FINGER FOOD' OR AS A STARTER. CHOOSE DAINTY CHOPS WITH A DELICATE BONE AND AMPLE MEAT RATHER THAN CHUNKY, BIG ONES.

serves 4

8 x 75–100 g (3–3½ oz) lamb or pork chops
200 g (7 oz) tandoori marinade (see page 54)

◆◆◆◆◆◆◆◆◆◆◆◆◆◆◆◆◆◆◆◆◆◆◆◆◆◆◆◆◆◆

1 Scrape back the meat from the top of the chop bone. It looks attractive and gives the diner a 'handle' to pick the chops up with.
2 Put the tandoori marinade into a non-metallic bowl, large enough to contain the chops. Add them, ensuring that they are well coated.
3 Cover and refrigerate for a minimum of 8 hours, maximum 24.
4 To cook, preheat the grill to medium-hot. Line the grill pan rack with foil (it makes for easier cleaning).
5 Generously recoat the chops with the marinade and place them on the foil. Put the grill pan midway under the heat and cook for about 6 minutes.
6 Remove. Turn the chops over. Put any remaining sauce on them.
7 Put back under the heat and cook for a further 5 minutes or so.

◆ Lamb Chop Kebab

serves 4

8 lamb chops, about 110 g (4 oz) each
aromatic salt (see page 43)
4 cloves garlic, crushed
1 teaspoon fresh ginger, finely chopped
110 g (4 oz) plain yoghurt
MASALA
2 teaspoons garam masala (see page 41)
1 teaspoon paprika
½ teaspoon chilli powder
⅛ teaspoon red food colouring powder (optional)

◆◆◆◆◆◆◆◆◆◆◆◆◆◆◆◆◆◆◆◆◆◆◆◆◆◆◆◆◆◆

1 Prick the chops with a fork, and sprinkle salt on them. Leave for a few minutes.
2 Using the blender, make a purée of the garlic, ginger, yoghurt and masala ingredients.
3 Rub the purée on to the chops and leave, covered in the fridge for up to 24 hours.
4 Cook under the grill or over charcoal, for 10–20 minutes, depending on the size and thickness of the chops, turning at least once.

NOTE: pork ribs can be substituted, though you would not find them at the curry house.

◆ Pakora

THE PAKORA USES THE SAME BATTER AS THE BHAJI BUT THE MAIN INGREDIENT IS KEPT WHOLE, NOT CHOPPED. THE BATTER LIGHTLY COATS THE VEGETABLES TO FORM A CRISP OUTER SHELL AFTER FRYING. GOOD VEGETABLES TO USE INCLUDE BABY SWEETCORN, BEANS, BELL PEPPER, BROCCOLI, CARROT, CAULIFLOWER, CELERIAC CHILLI, MARROW MOOLI, MUSHROOM, ONION RINGS AND PARSNIP. THIN STRIPS OF RAW CHICKEN BREAST OR PRAWNS WORK EQUALLY WELL.

full quantity of onion bhaji batter
225 g (8 oz) any of the raw vegetables listed above
vegetable oil for deep-frying

◆◆◆◆◆◆◆◆◆◆◆◆◆◆◆◆◆◆◆◆◆◆◆◆◆◆◆◆◆◆

1 Mix the batter ingredients, adding sufficient water to achieve a thickish paste which will drop sluggishly off the spoon. Let it stand for at least 10 minutes, during which time the mixture will absorb the moisture.
2 Add your chosen vegetables, mix in well and leave again for about 10 minutes to allow the vegetables to absorb the batter mixture.
3 Meanwhile, heat the oil to 190°C/375°F. This temperature is below smoking point and will cause a drop of batter to splutter a bit, then float more or less at once.
4 One by one, place the coated items carefully in the oil, allowing about 15 seconds between each one so the oil will maintain its temperature.
5 Fry for 10 minutes, turning once. Remove from the oil, drain well and serve with salad garnishes, lemon wedges and chutneys.

A selection of Pakora

Meat

Sheep and goats were domesticated over 10,000 years ago, pre-dating domesticated cattle and pigs by millennia. There are various species in the subcontinent, especially in the cooler areas, and they remain the main providers of meat, oil, leather and wool. Kid and lamb are rarely eaten there being considered a luxury. Even mature animals are expensive, so meat is nearly always combined with vegetables.

The wild pig was domesticated by the ancient Chinese by 6000 BC. It is still the most important meat in the Far East. Being a rooter, the pig does not thrive in arid desert conditions. It resorts to scavenging, and can become a carrier of parasites, which has led to its sometimes dubious reputation. Hindus rarely eat it, though pigs are reared in parts of India (Goa for example).

Cattle have been domesticated since about 6000 BC. They were brought to India by the dairy-farming Aryans in about 1500 BC. Hinduism evolved after that, and cattle scarcity led to their veneration. In today's India, woe betide anyone who hurts or kills a cow. They wander at will across main roads, private gardens, public parks, railways and markets. I well remember seeing an aged buffalo standing next to a vegetable stall near Mysore, swishing its tail across the adjoining knick-knack stall. While both the stall owners were preoccupied with damage limitation at the rear end, the front end was chomping away at assorted fruit and vegetables. When the stall owner finally cottoned on, the beast was shooed away.

Hindus will not eat beef or veal. Muslims are not averse to beef, and in Bangladesh, it is reared for the table, although the carcasses are much smaller and the meat tougher and much more expensive than that in the West.

◆ Balti Afghani Meat Curry

A DELICIOUS HERBY MEAT CURRY AUGMENTED WITH ROOT VEGETABLES AND NUTS IN THE AFGHAN/BALTI STYLE.

serves 4

450 g (1 lb) meat (lean leg of lamb, or pork, or stewing steak), weighed after discarding unwanted matter and diced into 3 cm (1¼ in) cubes
2–3 tablespoons ghee or vegetable oil
175 g (6 oz) onion, very finely chopped
1 or more red chilli, chopped
175 g (6 oz) leeks, chopped into discs
175 g (6 oz) carrots, chopped lengthways
175 g (6 oz) parsnips, chopped lengthways
200 ml (7 fl oz) fragrant stock (see page 43) or water
20 whole almonds, peeled
8–12 walnuts
1 tablespoon Balti garam masala (see page 41)
1 tablespoon fresh coriander leaves, very finely chopped
aromatic salt to taste (see page 43)
SPICES
1 teaspoon green cardamom seeds
2 teaspoons cummin seeds
3 or 4 pieces cassia bark
1 teaspoon cloves

◆◆◆◆◆◆◆◆◆◆◆◆◆◆◆◆◆◆◆◆◆◆◆◆◆◆◆◆◆◆◆

1 Heat the ghee or oil in your Balti pan or wok on high heat. Stir-fry the spices for 20 seconds.
2 Add the onion and reducing the heat, stir-fry for about 10 minutes, allowing it to become translucent and begin to brown.
3 Add the meat, and stir-fry briskly, to seal it, for about 5 minutes.
4 Place all the stir-fried ingredients in a large lidded casserole dish of 2.25–2.75 litre capacity (4–5 pints) and add the chilli, leek, carrot and parsnip. Cover and place in an oven preheated to 190°C/375°F/Gas 5.
5 Cook for about 20 minutes. Inspect

and stir, adding about half of the stock or water.
6 Cook for 20 more minutes. Test for tenderness. It should still have a bite, but not be quite ready. It may need a while more cooking. Add the remaining stock or water.
7 Simmer for another 10–15 minutes then test again.
8 When it is as you like it, stir in the nuts, garam masala, fresh coriander leaves and salt to taste. Let it simmer for 5–10 minutes more, then serve with bread or plain rice and dhal, or with another curry.

CHEF'S TIP

Beef may require a little less cooking time than lamb. Veal almost certainly will. Mutton and Goat will require a little more time, as will Venison and Pork.

▶ THE INGREDIENTS FILE

In the English-speaking lands, we are still predominantly carnivorous, despite often passionate leanings towards vegetarianism. The facts are that meat can be high in saturated fat and in cholesterol and in extremely rare cases, can transmit disease. On the plus side meat is a rich source of protein and vitamin B12. It also supplies niacin, riboflavin and iron. Sensible rearing and butchery on the part of the professionals and equally sensible buying and cooking on the part of the consumer, enables those who enjoy meat to continue to do so. Always buy from a reputable butcher or supermarket, and keep meat chilled or frozen until required.

The meat in the West is much juicier and more tender than that of the subcontinent. There, to counter toughness they use tenderisers, and slow-cooking techniques in pots over embers. Generally, an hour or so in a casserole pot in an efficient oven suffices.

Always work with a total raw weigh of around 675 g (½ lb) of meat or meat plus other ingredients to serve four.

In the following pages, the best mea cuts for Balti and curry cooking are examined.

Previous pages: Balti Afghani Meat Curry

Lamb

...amb is a young sheep under a year ...d. Quite small whole lambs are a ...aditional feast dish in the curry ...nds, though only for the really ...ealthy. Generally, in the West lamb ...not consumed until the animal is several months old, when its carcass weighs about 18 kg (40 lb). The largest lamb carcass can weigh up to 25 kg (55 lb). Raw best lean lamb is 106 calories per 100 g (3½ oz).

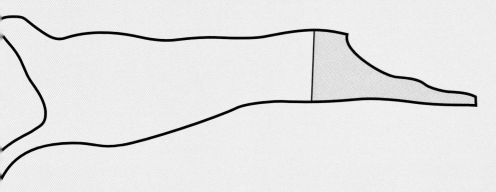

...he lamb carcass, showing the area providing the best meat

Lamb Steak

...he best part of the boned lamb leg, ...e top, yields boneless leg steaks. The ...eat is very lean, but expensive, ...hough it will be virtually gristle and ...new free. Each steak weighs ...10–225 g (4–8 oz). These can be beaten ...r pasanda, or minced for high quality ...eema or ground (in the food processor) ...r kebab meat. This is expensive. It ...an also be diced. 'Kebab quality' is a ...utcher's term for cubes cut only from ...e leg. Such meat is ideal for cooking ...the tandoor as lamb tikka, or ...hashlik/hassina kebabs, or it can be ...urried.

The cut of lamb meat normally used for currying is diced lamb stewing steak. This is cut from any combination of meat other than the leg, and is generally fattier than leg meat with more unwanted matter. The butcher should not permit more than 20 per cent visible fat,and unless you specify otherwise, the cubes will be no smaller than 13 mm (½ in), and no bigger than 32 mm (1¼ in).

Leg of Lamb

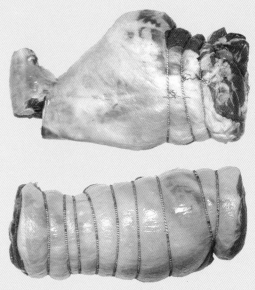

The very best, most expensive part of the lamb is the leg. This is available on the bone (used in the English-speaking world for the celebrated roast lamb) or in one piece, with the bone removed ('boned'). Your butcher can do this for you, though it will cost more, or you can you do it yourself. The leg is used to create the speciality dish Raan, also called Kurzi Lamb, a recipe for which appears in the companion volume to this book, *Pat Chapman's Curry Bible*.

Mutton

Sheep meat is known as mutton when its carcass weighs 25 kg (55 lb) or more (a mutton carcass can weigh up to 39 kg/90 lb). Mutton is not generally available at the high-street butcher, except by special request. Mutton has a stronger, more distinctive flavour than lamb, and is less tender too, becoming tougher as the animal ages. Generally, this is acceptable in curry cooking, providing more time is allowed. The cuts are the same as for lamb.

beef

America is synonymous with steak and 'cowboys' while Australia breeds plentiful beef, of exceptionally good quality. British beef has recently taken a beating, despite its being generally of superb quality – Aberdeen Angus being a prime example.

A beef carcass weighs up to 363 kg (800 lb). Raw best lean beef is 122 calories per 100 g (3½ oz).

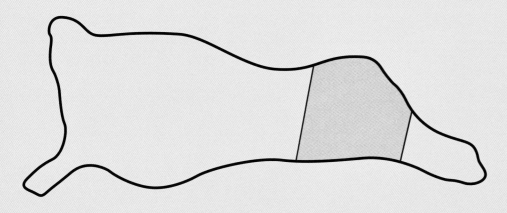

The beef carcass, showing the area providing the best meat

FILLET

Tenderest of all beef is the long fillet, cut from under the sirloin. Ask the butcher to supply it 'larder trimmed' i you want all unwanted matter removed, when it will weigh between 1.5 and 2.3 kg (3½–5 lb). He'll weigh it first and charge for the gross weight, plus maybe a bit more for his time.

Fillet steak meat (rump, loin, sirloin and long fillet) can be beaten for pasanda, or minced for high quality keema or ground (in the food processo for kebab meat. It can also be diced. Such meat is ideal for cooking in the tandoor as lamb tikka, or shashlik/hassina kebabs, or it can be curried, albeit less satisfactory for this purpose, curiously, because it lacks fat though the virtual absence of unwanted matter offsets even its expense.

TOPSIDE

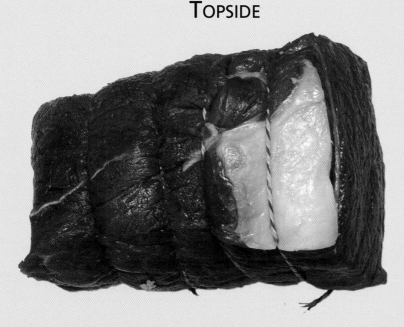

A leg of beef (or top piece) weighs up to 50 kg (110 lb). It is from here that the boned roasting cuts come; these are – topside, top rump and silver side.

The rear top back of the carcass provides the tenderest meat in the form of boned (fillet) steaks – rump, loin, sirloin, each weighing up to 2.7 kg (6 lb).

CHEAPER CUTS

Chuck steak is a cheaper cut, available butcher-diced, and with no more than 20 per cent visible fat permitted. Cheaper still is pie meat (diced; also called stewing steak) in which 25 per cent visible fat is permitted. Both thes cuts come from the front end of the carcass, and both are ideal for currying

kid and goat

id is a young goat under a year old.
id and goat are available from
ecialist butchers.

Goat meat is tougher than mutton,
d the carcass is smaller. It has a
ronger flavour, but in other respects
e cuts of meat and its qualities are
e same as those described for lamb
d mutton.

veal

he best meat comes from the topside
f the leg (see beef). The fatless
oneless meat from this is called the
ushion, from which escalopes are cut.
eaten, they make great pasanda
rries. Alternatively, the cushion can
e diced for currying. Butcher-diced
eal is equally suitable, and cheaper. It
fattier though, with a visible fat
ntent of 20 per cent.

◆ Basic Balti Meat Curry

THIS IS THE 'STANDARD' BENCHMARK BALTI CURRY, BY WHICH ALL MEAT BALTIS ARE MEASURED. IT COMPRISES TENDER, BITE-SIZED CUBES OF MEAT IN A GOLDEN-BROWN, PLEASANTLY FLAVOURED, SPICY GRAVY, NEITHER TOO HOT NOR TOO MILD.

serves 4

675 g (1½ lb) meat (lean leg of lamb or
    pork, or stewing steak), weighed after
    discarding unwanted matter and diced
    into 3 cm (1¼ in) cubes
2–3 tablespoons ghee or corn oil
3–6 garlic cloves, finely chopped
225 g (8 oz) onion, very finely chopped
3–4 tablespoons Balti masala paste
    (see page 39)
200 ml (7 fl oz) fragrant stock (see page 43)
    or water
1 tablespoon Balti garam masala
    (see page 41)
1 tablespoon fresh coriander leaves, very
    finely chopped
aromatic salt to taste (see page 43)

◆◆◆◆◆◆◆◆◆◆◆◆◆◆◆◆◆◆◆◆◆◆◆◆◆◆◆◆◆◆◆

1 Heat the ghee or oil in your Balti pan or wok on high heat. Stir-fry the garlic for 30 seconds.
2 Add the onion and reducing the heat, stir-fry for about 10 minutes, allowing it to become translucent and begin to brown.
3 Add the Balti masala paste, and stir-fry to the simmer. Add the meat, and stir-fry it briskly, to seal it, for about 5 minutes.
4 Add all the fried ingredients to a large lidded casserole dish of 2.25–2.75 litre capacity (4–5 pints), and place it in an oven preheated to 190°C/375°F/Gas 5.
5 Cook for about 20 minutes. Inspect and stir, adding about half of the stock or water.
6 Cook for 20 more minutes. Test for tenderness. It should still have a bite, but not be quite ready. It may need a while more cooking. Add the remaining stock or water.

7 Simmer for another 10–15 minutes then test again.
8 When it is as you like it, stir in the garam masala, fresh coriander leaves and salt to taste. Let it simmer for 5 or 10 minutes more, then serve.

NOTE: You can use 320–450 g (11 oz–1 lb) Balti masala gravy (see page 00) in place of the onion and Balti masala paste. But keep half the ghee and all the garlic. Follow stage 1, add the gravy, and when simmering, go to stage 8.

◆ Balti Madras

MADRAS IS THE AFFICIONADO'S HOT DISH – HOT BUT NOT SEARING – CONTAINING INTERESTING FLAVOURINGS IN THE FORM OF TOMATO, LEMON AND ALMOND, ALONG WITH A CERTAIN AMOUNT OF CHILLI.

serves 4

675 g (1½ lb) meat (lean leg of lamb, or pork, or stewing steak), weighed after discarding unwanted matter and diced into 3 cm (1¼ in) cubes
2–3 tablespoons ghee or vegetable oil
5 or 6 garlic cloves, finely chopped
225 g (8 oz) onion, very finely chopped
1–2 tablespoons Balti masala paste (see page 39)
200 ml (7 fl oz) fragrant stock (see page 43) or water
6 oz (175 g) canned tomatoes, strained
2 tablespoons tomato ketchup
2 tablespoons ground almonds
1 tablespoon Balti garam masala (see page 41)
1 tablespoon fresh coriander leaves, very finely chopped
2 tablespoons lemon juice
aromatic salt to taste (see page 43)
SPICES
2–4 teaspoons chilli powder
1 teaspoon cummin powder

◆◆◆◆◆◆◆◆◆◆◆◆◆◆◆◆◆◆◆◆◆◆◆◆◆◆◆◆◆◆◆◆

1 Heat the ghee or oil in your Balti pan or wok on high heat. Stir-fry the garlic and spices for 30 seconds.
2 Add the onion, and, reducing the heat, stir-fry for about 10 minutes, allowing it to become translucent and begin to brown.
3 Add the Balti masala paste, and stir-fry to the simmer. Add the meat, and stir-fry briskly to seal, for about 5 minutes.
4 Place all the stir-fried ingredients in a large lidded casserole dish of 2.25–2.75 litre capacity (4–5 pints). Cover and place in the oven preheated to 190°C/375°F/Gas 5.
5 Cook for about 20 minutes. Inspect and stir, adding about half of the stock or water.

6 Cook for 20 more minutes. Test for tenderness. It should still have a bite, but not be quite ready. It may need a while more cooking. Add the remaining stock or water, the tomatoes, ketchup and ground almonds.
7 Simmer for 10–15 minutes more then test again.
8 When it is as you like it, stir in the garam masala, fresh coriander leaves, lemon juice and salt to taste. Give it a final 5 or 10 minutes simmering, then serve.

◆ Balti Methi Gosht

METHI (PRONOUNCED MAY-TEE) IS FENUGREEK LEAF OR SEED WHICH CREATES A VERY SAVOURY BALTI CURRY. FRESH FENUGREEK LEAF IS ALWAYS AVAILABLE FROM ASIAN GROCERS.

serves 4

675 g (1½ lb) meat (lean leg of lamb or pork, or stewing steak), weighed after discarding unwanted matter and diced into 3 cm (1¼ in) cubes
2–3 tablespoons ghee or corn oil
3–6 garlic cloves, finely chopped
225 g (8 oz) onion, very finely chopped
3–4 tablespoons Balti masala paste (see page 39)
200 ml (7fl oz) fragrant stock (see page 43) or water
1 tablespoon dried fenugreek leaf, ground (see Chef's Tip right)
OR 4 tablespoons fresh fenugreek leaf, de-stalked and chopped
1 tablespoon Balti garam masala (see page 41)
110 g (4 oz) rocket leaf, chopped
1 tablespoon fresh coriander leaves, very finely chopped
aromatic salt to taste (see page 43)
SPICES
1 teaspoon white cummin seeds
½ teaspoon black onion seeds
½ teaspoon fenugreek seeds

◆◆◆◆◆◆◆◆◆◆◆◆◆◆◆◆◆◆◆◆◆◆◆◆◆◆◆◆◆◆◆◆

1 Heat the ghee or oil in your Balti pan or wok on high heat. Stir-fry the spices for about 20 seconds, then add the garlic. Continue stir-frying for a further 30 seconds.
2 Add the onion, and, reducing the heat, stir-fry for about 10 minutes, allowing it to become translucent and begin to brown.
3 Add the Balti masala paste, and stir-fry to the simmer. Add the meat, and stir-fry it briskly, to seal it, for about 5 minutes.
4 Place all the stir-fried ingredients in large lidded casserole dish of 2.25–2.75 litre capacity (4–5 pints). Cover and place in the oven preheated to 190°C/375°F/Gas 5.
5 Cook for about 20 minutes. Inspect and stir, adding about half of the stock or water.
6 Cook for 20 more minutes. Test for tenderness. It should still have a bite, but not be quite ready. It may need a while more cooking. Add the remaining stock or water and the fenugreek leaf.
7 Simmer for 10–15 minutes more then test again.
8 When it is as you like it, stir in the garam masala, rocket leaf, fresh coriander leaves and salt to taste. Give a final 5 or 10 minutes simmering, then serve.

CHEF'S TIP
In the Punjab, fenugreek leaf is plucked from the trees and dried on the roofs of the villagers' houses. It sometimes contains grit and stalks so inspection is advisable. It is available in boxed packs of 50 or 100 g (50 g goes a long way). Grinding makes it more effective; grind it in a coffee or spice grinder for best results and store in an airtight jar.

pork

s with all meat, pork should only be urchased from reputable sources – ever buy it 'on the cheap'. Keep raw ork refrigerated (or frozen) and ways cook it properly. Rare pork is acceptable; it must be well cooked so that its internal temperature reaches 77°C/170°F for at least 20 minutes. Pig is rarely eaten before it reaches nine months old. Before that age it is uneconomical. The exception to this is suckling pig which should be no more than 8 weeks old, the carcass (with head) weighing 4.5–9 kg (10–20 lb). An adult carcass without the head weighs between 55 and 68 kg (120–150 lb). Raw best lean pork is 166 calories per 100 g (3½ oz).

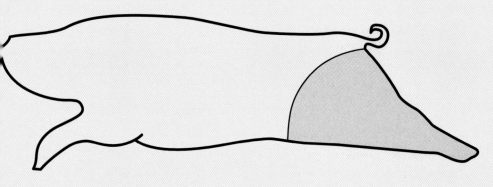

e pork carcass, showing the area providing the best meat

BONELESS LEG

LOIN STEAK

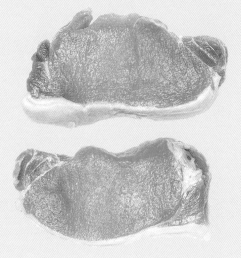

DICED LEG, DICED CHEAPER CUTS

Butcher-diced pork is cut from any suitable meat, other than the best cuts (above) and is relatively cheap. The cubes are normally between 13 mm and 32 mm (½–1¼ in), though you can specify the size you require. Visible fat must not exceed 20 per cent.

he best, leanest, tenderest meat comes om the leg. Silverside boned joint eat, leg steaks and escalopes are cut om the leg.

Fillet tenderloin steaks are also cut from boneless middle (hogmeat).

◆ Balti Kashmiri Meat

FOR THOSE WHO LOVE THE CONTRASTS OF SAVOURY CURRY AND INTERESTINGLY TEXTURED LOTUS ROOTS AND SWEET FRUITS SUCH AS LYCHEES.

serves 4

675 g (1½ lb) meat (lean leg of lamb, or pork,or stewing steak), weighed after discarding unwanted matter and diced into 3 cm (1¼ in) cubes
2–3 tablespoons ghee or corn oil
3–6 garlic cloves, finely chopped
110 g (4 oz) onion, very finely chopped
4–6 spring onions, bulbs and leaves, finely chopped
2 tablespoons Balti masala paste (see page 39)
200 ml (7 fl oz) fragrant stock (see page 43) or water
85 g (3 oz) lotus roots
110 g (4 oz) canned lychees, strained
2 tablespoons juice from the above
1 tablespoon dark muscovado sugar (optional)
1 teaspoon Balti garam masala (see page 41)
1 tablespoon fresh coriander leaves, very finely chopped
1 tablespoon fresh basil leaves, very finely chopped
aromatic salt to taste (see page 43)
GARNISH
fresh coriander leaves

◆◆◆◆◆◆◆◆◆◆◆◆◆◆◆◆◆◆◆◆◆◆◆◆◆◆◆◆◆◆

1 Heat the ghee or oil in your Balti pan or wok on high heat. Stir-fry the garlic for 30 seconds.
2 Add both the onion types, and reducing the heat, stir-fry for about 10 minutes, allowing them to become translucent and begin to brown.
3 Add the Balti masala paste, and stir-fry to the simmer. Add the meat, and stir-fry it briskly to seal, for about 5 minutes.
4 Place all the stir-fried ingredients in a large lidded casserole dish of 2.25–2.75 litre capacity (4–5 pints). Cover and place in an oven preheated to 190°C/375°F/Gas 5.
5 Cook for about 20 minutes. Inspect and stir, adding about half of the stock or water.
6 Cook for 20 more minutes. Test for tenderness. It should still have a bite, but not be quite ready. It may need a while more cooking. Add the remaining stock or water and the lotus roots, lychees, juice and sugar (if using).
7 Simmer for 10–15 minutes more then test again.
8 When it is as you like it, stir in the garam masala, fresh leaves and add salt to taste. Let it simmer for a final 5–10 minutes, then garnish and serve.

◆ Balti Keema

SIMPLE MINCED BEEF (OR INDEED ANY MINCED MEAT – LAMB, PORK, VENISON) MAKES THE MOST DELICIOUS BALTI DISH. MINCE IS ALMOST INDESTRUCTIBLE IN THE COOKING PROCESS, SO IT SIMPLY CANNOT BE OVERCOOKED. THIS IS THEREFORE A GREAT DISH FOR THE BEGINNER.

serves 4

675 g (1½ lb) minced meat
2 tablespoons ghee or corn oil
4–6 garlic cloves, finely chopped
225 g (8 oz) onion, finely chopped
3–4 tablespoons Balti masala paste (see page 39)
1 tablespoon tomato purée
500 ml (16 fl oz) fragrant stock (see page 43) or water
1 tablespoon Balti garam masala (see page 41)
1 tablespoon fresh coriander leaves, chopped
aromatic salt to taste (see page 43)

◆◆◆◆◆◆◆◆◆◆◆◆◆◆◆◆◆◆◆◆◆◆◆◆◆◆◆◆◆◆◆◆

1 Put the mince into the Balti pan or wok, and stir-fry in a teaspoonful of oil for about 10 minutes. This seals it and brings out any liquids, which should be strained off and reserved. Put the meat into a large lidded casserole dish of 2.25–2.75 litre capacity (4–5 pints).
2 Heat the ghee or oil in your Balti pan or wok on high heat. Stir-fry the garlic for 30 seconds.
3 Add the onion and reducing the heat, stir-fry for about 10 minutes, allowing it to become translucent and begin to brown.
4 Add the masala paste and the tomato purée. Raise the heat and bring to a brisk sizzle, stir-frying as needed for about 2 or 3 minutes.
5 Add the stir-fried items to the casserole dish, cover and place in the oven preheated to 190°C/375°F/Gas 5.
6 Cook for about 20 minutes. Inspect and stir, adding about half of the stock or water.
7 Cook for 20 more minutes. Test for tenderness. It should still have a bite, but not be quite ready. It may need a while more cooking. Add the remaining stock or water.
8 Simmer for another 10–15 minutes, then test again.
9 When it is as you like it, stir in the garam masala, fresh coriander leaves and salt to taste. Let it simmer for a final 5–10 minutes, then serve.

VARIATIONS
Balti Tandoori Keema
This variation of Balti Keema is truly delicious, combining Balti and Tandoori tastes. Ingredients as for Balti Keema with the addition of:
1 teaspoon cummin seeds
½ teaspoon aniseed
1 tablespoon tandoori paste (see page 40)
3 oz (75 g) Greek yoghurt

At stage 2, fry the seeds for 10 seconds then add the garlic. Add the tandoori paste at stage 4 in place of the Balti masala paste. Add the yoghurt little by little with the liquid in stage 6.

Balti Keema Mattar
Ingredients as for Balti Keema with the addition of up to 250 g (9 oz) frozen peas, thawed. Add the peas at stage 7.

Balti Kashmiri Meat

◆ Balti Korma

THIS BALTI KORMA IS TRADITIONALLY VERY MILD AND CREAMY, USING COCONUT AND CREAM.

serves 4

675 g (1½ lb) meat (lean leg of lamb, or pork, or stewing steak), weighed after discarding unwanted matter and diced into 3 cm (1¼ in) cubes
2–3 tablespoons ghee or vegetable oil
2–3 garlic cloves, finely chopped
225 g (8 oz) onion, very finely chopped
3–4 tablespoons Balti masala paste (see page 39)
150 ml (5 fl oz) fragrant stock (see page 43) or water
4 fl oz (100 ml) double (thick) cream
100 g (3½ oz) creamed coconut, chopped
1 teaspoon sugar
1 tablespoon Balti garam masala (see page 41)
20 whole almonds, peeled
1 tablespoon fresh coriander leaves, very finely chopped
aromatic salt to taste (see page 43)
GARNISH
fresh coriander leaves
SPICES
4 bay leaves
5 cm (2 in) cassia bark
4–6 green cardamoms
4–6 cloves

◆◆◆◆◆◆◆◆◆◆◆◆◆◆◆◆◆◆◆◆◆◆◆◆◆◆◆◆◆◆◆◆

1 Heat the ghee or oil in your Balti pan or wok on high heat. Stir-fry the spices for 30 seconds then add and stir-fry the garlic for a further 30 seconds.
2 Add the onion, and reducing the heat, stir-fry for about 10 minutes, allowing it to become translucent and begin to brown.
3 Add the Balti masala paste and stir-fry to the simmer. Add the meat, and stir-fry briskly to seal for about 5 minutes.
4 Place the stir-fried ingredients in a large casserole dish of 2.25–2.75 litre capacity (4–5 pints). Cover and place in the oven preheated to 190°C/375°F/Gas 5.
5 Cook for 20 minutes. Inspect and stir, adding about half of the stock or water.

6 Cook for 20 more minutes. Test for tenderness. It should still have a bite, but not be quite ready. It may need a while more cooking. Add the remaining stock or water, plus the cream and coconut.
7 Simmer for 10–15 minutes more then test again.
8 When it is as you like it, stir in the sugar, garam masala, almonds, fresh coriander leaves and salt to taste. Let it simmer for a final 5–10 minutes, then garnish and serve.

◆ Balti Kofta Curry

KOFTAS – SMALL GROUND MEATBALLS – ORIGINATED IN THE MIDDLE EAST AND WERE PROBABLY TAKEN TO PAKISTAN BY THE ANCIENT PERSIANS. THEY ARE SPICY AND DELICIOUS WHEN FLOATED IN TOMATO-FLAVOURED GRAVY, AND EASY TO MAKE USING THIS FOOLPROOF METHOD.

serves 4

FOR THE KOFTAS
560 g (1¼ lb) meat (lean leg of lamb, or pork, or stewing steak), weighed after discarding unwanted matter
3–6 garlic cloves, chopped
2 tablespoons dehydrated onion flakes
1 tablespoon fresh coriander leaf, chopped
1 tablespoon Balti dry masala powder (see page 39)
1 teaspoon Balti garam masala (see page 41)
½ teaspoon salt
FOR THE BALTI KOFTA CURRY GRAVY
1 tablespoon ghee or vegetable oil
2–3 garlic cloves, finely chopped
300 g (10½ oz) Balti masala gravy (see page 42)
1 tablespoon tomato purée
175 g (6 oz) canned tomatoes, strained, juice reserved
1 teaspoon white granulated sugar
½ teaspoon dried fenugreek leaf
1 tablespoon fresh coriander leaves, very finely chopped
1 tablespoon fresh basil leaves, very finely chopped
aromatic salt to taste (see page 43)

◆◆◆◆◆◆◆◆◆◆◆◆◆◆◆◆◆◆◆◆◆◆◆◆◆◆◆◆◆◆◆◆

TO MAKE THE KOFTAS
1 Coarsely chop the meat into chunks about 5 cm (2 in) square. Run it through a food processor (in several batches so as not to overload the machine) or through a mincer, to achieve a coarse mince.
2 In a bowl, add in the remaining kofta ingredients, then, again in several batches, run it through the machine until you achieve a finely textured paste.
3 Mix the paste thoroughly then divide it into four equal parts. From each part, roll 6 small balls (koftas) making a total of 24 koftas.
4 Preheat the oven to 190°C/375°F/Gas
5 Place the 24 koftas on an oven tray and bake them for 15 minutes.

TO MAKE THE BALTI KOFTA CURRY GRAVY
1 Heat the ghee or oil in the Balti pan or wok, and stir-fry the garlic for 30 seconds.
2 Add the Balti masala gravy, tomato purée, canned tomatoes, sugar and fenugreek leaf, and bring to the simmer.
3 Add the cooked koftas, with any juices they may have made, and stir-fry for about 3 minutes.
4 Add the remaining ingredients. Simmer for a few more minutes, adding the reserved tomato juice to keep things mobile.

Balti Kofta Curry

other cuts

OFFAL

Offal is the off-cuts or 'off-fall' from the carcass. Heart, liver and kidney are the most popular items of offal. Others include tongue, brain, lung (lights), spleen (milt), pancreas (sweet breads), feet (trotters) and tail (ox and pig). The stomach (tripe) is from cattle only. Offal is a valuable provider of protein, minerals and vitamins. It is ideal for stir-frying and it goes well with Balti spices. It can be substituted for, or used with meat in any of the recipes in this chapter.

Lamb's kidney

Lamb's liver

Pig's liver

Pig's kidney

Lamb's heart

MINCE

Butcher's mince usually contains cuts of cheaper meat, but not head meat or offal, and it must not exceed 25 per cent fat. Lean meat is similar, but the visual fat content must not exceed 15 per cent. The coarseness of the mince can be varied from fine upwards. The butcher will, of course, mince better-quality meat to order, or you can do it yourself using a hand mincer or an electric attachment.

MEAT ON THE BONE

Meat will almost always be cooked 'on the bone' in the subcontinent, including the Balti area of Pakistan, because it is universally accepted that you get juicier, tastier results, especially when sucking on the bones. If you wish to eat it like this, you can use a combination of diced steak, and leg meat on the bone (cut into small boned pieces). This is not a British butcher's cut, but most will do it if you explain what you want. Extend the minimum cooking time by at least 10 to 15 minutes, otherwise follow the recipes.

◆ Balti Dhansak

NE OF THE ALL-TIME BALTI FAVOURITES – THE
ALTI BASE IS THICKENED WITH CREAMY COOKED
NTILS (DHAL PURÉE).

rves 4

75 g (1½ lb) meat (lean leg of lamb, or
   pork, or stewing steak), weighed after
   discarding unwanted matter and diced
   into 3 cm (1¼ in) cubes
tablespoons ghee or vegetable oil
-6 garlic cloves, finely chopped
-3 fresh green chillies, finely chopped
25 g (8 oz) onion, very finely chopped
-3 tablespoons Balti masala paste
   (see page 39)
00 ml (7 fl oz) fragrant stock (see page 43)
   or water
00 g (3½ oz) masoor dhal, cooked
00 g (7 oz) canned ratatouille, mashed
tablespoons brinjal pickle
tablespoon white granulated sugar
teaspoons vinegar, any type
teaspoons Balti garam masala (see page 41)
tablespoon fresh coriander leaves, very
nely chopped
romatic salt to taste (see page 43)
ARNISH
esh coriander leaves
PICES
teaspoon cummin seeds
teaspoon fenugreek seeds

◆◆◆◆◆◆◆◆◆◆◆◆◆◆◆◆◆◆◆◆◆◆◆◆◆◆

Heat the ghee or oil in your Balti pan
r wok on high heat. Stir-fry the spices,
arlic and chillies for 30 seconds.
   Add the onion and reducing the heat,
ir-fry for about 10 minutes, allowing it
 become translucent and begin to
rown.
   Add the Balti masala paste, and stir-
y to the simmer. Add the meat and
ir-fry it briskly, to seal it, for about
 minutes.
   Place all the stir-fried ingredients in a
rge lidded casserole dish of 2.25–2.75
tre capacity (4–5 pints). Cover and place
 an oven preheated to 190°C/375°F/
as 5.
   Cook for about 20 minutes. Inspect

and stir, adding about half of the stock
or water, plus the masoor dhal,
ratatouille, brinjal pickle, sugar and
vinegar.
6 Cook for 20 more minutes. Test for
tenderness. It should still have a bite, but
not be quite ready. It may need a while
more cooking. Add the remaining stock
or water.
7 Simmer for another 10–15 minutes
then test again.
8 When it is as you like it, stir in the
garam masala, fresh coriander leaves
and salt to taste. Let it simmer for 5–10
more minutes, then garnish and serve.

◆ Balti Bhoona Gosht

serves 4

675 g (1½ lb) meat (lean leg of lamb, or
   pork, or stewing steak), weighed after
   discarding unwanted matter and diced
   into 3 cm (1¼ in) cubes
1 teaspoon turmeric
3–6 garlic cloves, finely chopped
225 g (8 oz) onion, very finely chopped
3–4 tablespoons Balti masala paste (see
   page 39)
350 ml (7 fl oz) fragrant stock (see page 43)
   or water
2 tablespoons natural yoghurt
1 tablespoon Balti garam masala (see
   page 41)
1 tablespoon fresh coriander leaves, very
   finely chopped
aromatic salt to taste (see page 43)

◆◆◆◆◆◆◆◆◆◆◆◆◆◆◆◆◆◆◆◆◆◆◆◆◆◆

1 Heat the ghee or oil in your Balti pan
or wok on high heat. Stir-fry the
turmeric and garlic for 30 seconds.
2 Add the onion and, reducing the
heat, stir-fry for about 10 minutes,
allowing it to become translucent and
begin to brown.
3 Add the Balti masala paste, and stir-
fry to the simmer. Add the meat, and
stir-fry it briskly, to seal it, for about 5
minutes.

4 Place all the stir-fried ingredients in a
large lidded casserole dish of 2.25–2.75
litre capacity (4–5 pints). Cover and place
in an oven preheated to 190°C/375°F/
Gas 5.
5 Cook for about 20 minutes. Inspect
and stir, adding just enough stock or
water (if needed) to keep things mobile.
6 Cook for another 20 minutes. Test for
tenderness. It should still have a bite, but
not be quite ready. It may need a while
more cooking. Add the remaining stock
or water.
7 Simmer again for 10–15 minutes, then
test again.
8 When it is as you like it, stir in the
yoghurt, garam masala, fresh coriander
leaves and salt to taste. Let it simmer for
5–10 more minutes, then serve.

> *Remember, Balti is usually eaten as a
> combination of ingredients. All the
> meat recipes in this chapter can be
> treated as 'combination' recipes by
> adding any other ingredients, for
> example, chicken, seafood and/or
> vegetables.*
> *Always achieve a total weight of
> around 675 g (1½ lb) of your main
> ingredients to serve four.*

◆ Balti Rhogan Josh Gosht

THE AUTHENTIC RHOGAN JOSH ORIGINATED IN KASHMIR AT THE TIME OF THE MOGHUL EMPERORS. LITERALLY MEANING COOKED IN GHEE IN RED GRAVY, IT USES AROMATIC WHOLE SPICES. THE BALTI HOUSE INCORPORATES RED PEPPER FOR COLOUR; I'VE ALSO ADDED BEETROOT (OPTIONAL) TO ACHIEVE A GORGEOUS DEEP HUE.

serves 4

675 g (1½ lb) meat (lean leg of lamb, or pork, or stewing steak), weighed after discarding unwanted matter and diced into 3 cm (1¼ in) cubes
2–3 tablespoons ghee or corn oil
3–6 garlic cloves, finely chopped
225 g (8 oz) onion, very finely chopped
4–6 spring onions, bulbs and leaves, finely chopped
2 tablespoons Balti masala paste (see page 39)
1 teaspoon tandoori paste
200 ml (7 fl oz) fragrant stock (see page 43) or water
1 tablespoon tomato purée
2 tablespoons ground almonds
1 red pepper, cut into diamonds
2 oz (50 g) fresh beetroot, peeled and shredded
1 tablespoon Balti garam masala (see page 41)
1 tablespoon fresh coriander leaves, very finely chopped
1 tablespoon fresh basil leaves, very finely chopped
aromatic salt to taste (see page 43)
GARNISH
fresh coriander leaves
SPICES
6 cloves
2 bay leaves
5 cm (2 in) piece cassia bark
2 brown cardamoms
4 green cardamoms
½ teaspoon black cummin seeds
½ teaspoon paprika

◆◆◆◆◆◆◆◆◆◆◆◆◆◆◆◆◆◆◆◆◆◆◆◆◆◆◆◆◆◆◆

1 Heat the ghee or oil in your Balti pan or wok on high heat. Stir-fry the spices and garlic for 30 seconds.
2 Add both types of the onion, and, reducing the heat, stir-fry for about 10 minutes, allowing it to become translucent and begin to brown.
3 Add the Balti masala and tandoori pastes, and stir-fry to the simmer. Add the meat, and stir-fry briskly to seal it, for about 5 minutes.
4 Place all the stir-fried ingredients in a large lidded casserole dish of 2.25–2.75 litre capacity (4–5 pints). Cover and place in the oven preheated to 190°C/375°F/ Gas 5.
5 Cook for about 20 minutes. Inspect and stir, adding about half of the stock or water.
6 Cook for 20 more minutes. Test for tenderness. It should still have a bite, but not be quite ready. It may need a while more cooking. Add the remaining stock or water and the tomato purée, ground almonds, red pepper and beetroot.
7 Simmer for 10–15 minutes more then test again.
8 When it is as you like it, stir in the garam masala, fresh leaves and salt to taste. Let it simmer for a final 5–10 minutes, then serve.

CHEF'S TIP
To cut a pepper into diamonds: cut the top off the pepper (where the stalk used to be) and the bottom. Stand the pepper on one end and cut down through the flesh. Open it out and pare off and discard the pith and seeds. You should now have a more or less rectangular shape which you can easily cut into equal-sized diamonds, strips, squares or rectangles.

game

Game is defined as wild animals and birds that are hunted. The word derives from the French *gibecer* – to hunt. Nowadays there is considerable public antipathy towards hunting. We should perhaps remember, however, that until quite recently, hunting was an important way to obtain meat for the table. Most game today is bred specifically for eating and in their 'wild' state they enjoy a better standard of living than some of their factory-reared counterparts. Game is divided into two categories – non-flighted and flighted. In this chapter we briefly look at non-flighted game. In pre-Victorian time the hedgehog and dormouse were considered 'fair game' along with the fox and badger, but tastes have changed since then.
Only specialist butchers (and most supermarkets) are licensed to sell game and they will readily supply venison, hare, rabbit and even the more specialised wild boar.

HARE

The hare has been resident in Britain for 100,000 years. The hare carcass is smaller than domesticated rabbit's, its flesh darker and its taste 'gamier'. A two- to four-month-old hare is called a leveret and its carcass weighs around 1.5 kg (3 lb). A one-year-old's carcass weighs 2.5–3 kg (5½–6½ lb) and older animals weigh up to 6 kg (13 lb).

The yearling is considered best for flavour. The meat (rabbit or hare) should be jointed into six pieces – four legs and two saddle halves. Cooked on the bone at this weight it will yield enough meat for 2–3 servings. Cooking time is 15–20 minutes per 450 g (1 lb).

WILD BOAR

ncestor of the domestic pig, the wild
ar once thrived in England's forests,
t has long since been hunted out of
xistence. In Europe, France and
ermany in particular, and in wealthy
dia, it still prevails and is very
opular. The meat is available from
ecialist butchers. Young wild boar
ound 6 months old (called marcassin)
very tender. Normally the animal has
be between one and four years old to
suitable for the table. Cuts of meat
e specified as for pork. Wild boar is
aner than domesticated pigs, and
aller. There is consequently less meat
ailable from each respective cut.

VENISON

Venison is the meat of a deer up to
2½ years in age, specially bred for the
table. Fresh venison is seasonal,
but the freezer makes it available all
year round.

Venison must be hung by the butcher
to maximise tenderness and flavour. It
is ideal for marination and spicy
applications.

Four types of venison are available:
Reindeer – the largest of all, and
   mostly imported from Scandinavia
Red deer – large carcass, strong
   flavours
Fallow deer – smaller carcasses,
   best flavour
Roe deer – paler flesh and least gamey
   flavour

Venison is dark red and, as with most
meat, the best cuts are from the haunch
and saddle (rear leg and top back) and
good-quality steak cuts can be obtained
from there. Cheaper cuts come from the
loin, shoulder and neck. With venison
more than other meats it is advisable to
remove all fat because its taste after
cooking is quite bitter. Venison curries
well and is worth trying. Specify the

type of venison you want and give your
butcher ample time to obtain it. He will
fillet and 'larder trim' the cut of your
choice to your requirements.

DICED VENISON

Diced venison is cut from the butcher's
choice of meat. The cubes are normally
12–32 mm (½–1¼ in), though you can
specify the size you require. Visible fat
must not exceed 20 per cent. Cooking
time will vary depending on the type of
venison and the cut, but in general the
times are the same as those for mutton.

RABBIT

he first rabbits came from Morocco
d were introduced to Britain by the
ormans. There are two types of
bbit available – wild or domesticated.
he meat of the wild animal is darker
d stronger in flavour. Rabbit
rcasses should be skinned just prior
use and can weigh between 1.1 and
kg (2½–20 lb). Best for flavour are
ur-month-old rabbit carcasses
eighing around 2.3 kg (5 lb). The meat
eld will be no more than one-quarter
the carcass weight.

◆ Balti Rezala

A RICH CREAMY CURRY, ORIGINALLY FROM
BANGLADESH, BUT NOT A MILD ONE – WATCH
THOSE CHILLIES, TEMPERED AS THEY MAY BE BY
RAISINS.

serves 4

675 g (1½ lb) meat (lean leg of lamb, or
  pork, or stewing steak), weighed after
  discarding unwanted matter and diced
  into 3 cm (1¼ in) cubes
3–4 tablespoons ghee or corn oil
10 garlic cloves, very finely chopped
225 g (8 oz) onion, very finely chopped
3–4 tablespoons Balti masala paste (see
  page 39)
3 or 4 fresh green chillies, sliced lengthways
410 g (1 lb) canned evaporated milk
20–30 strands saffron (optional)
1 tablespoon raisins (optional)
2 teaspoons white granulated sugar
2 tablespoons pistachio nuts, chopped
1 tablespoon ground almonds
1 tablespoon Balti garam masala (see
  page 41)
1 tablespoon fresh coriander leaves, very
  finely chopped
1 tablespoon rose water (optional)
aromatic salt to taste (see page 43)
SPICES
1 teaspoon turmeric
12 green cardamoms, crushed
3–4 5 cm (2 in) pieces cassia bark
2 teaspoons panch phoran (see page 43)

◆◆◆◆◆◆◆◆◆◆◆◆◆◆◆◆◆◆◆◆◆◆◆◆◆◆◆◆◆◆

1 Heat the ghee or oil in your Balti pan
or wok on high heat. Stir-fry the spices
and the garlic for 30 seconds.
2 Add the onion and reducing the heat,
stir-fry for about 10 minutes, allowing it
to become translucent and begin to
brown.
3 Add the Balti masala paste and the
chillies, and stir-fry to the simmer. Add
the meat and stir-fry it briskly, to seal it,
for about 5 minutes.
4 Place the stir-fried ingredients in a large
lidded casserole dish of 2.25–2.75 litre
capacity (4–5 pints). Cover and place in an
oven preheated to 190°C/375°F/Gas 5.

5 Cook for about 20 minutes. Inspect
and stir, adding about half of the
evaporated milk.
6 Cook for 20 more minutes. Test for
tenderness. It should still have a bite, but
not be quite ready. Add the remaining
evaporated milk plus the saffron and
raisins (if using), sugar, pistachio nuts,
and ground almonds.
7 Simmer for 10–15 minutes more then
test again.
8 When it is as you like it, stir in the
garam masala, fresh coriander leaves,
rose water (if using) and salt to taste.
Give it a final 5 or 10 minutes simmering,
then serve.

◆ Balti Phal

PHAL IS SERIOUSLY HOT, AND MUST NOT BE EATEN
BY THE UNINITIATED. SERIOUS CHILLI-HEADS WILL
ENJOY THE 'EXTRA-HOT' CHILLI POWDER AND MAY
TOP UP WITH SCOTCH BONNET OR HABAÑERO
CHILLIES, THE HOTTEST AVAILABLE.

serves 4

675 g (1½ lb) meat (lean leg of lamb, or
  pork, or stewing steak), weighed after
  discarding unwanted matter and diced
  into 3 cm (1¼ in) cubes
2–3 tablespoons ghee or corn oil
4 or more teaspoons 'extra-hot' chilli
  powder
3–6 garlic cloves, finely chopped
225 g (8 oz) onion, very finely chopped
3–4 tablespoons Balti masala paste (see
  page 39)
200 ml (7 fl oz) fragrant stock (see page 43)
  or water
6 oz (175 g) tomato, chopped
4–8 fresh red and/or green chillies, whole or
  chopped
1 tablespoon vinegar, any type
1 tablespoon Balti garam masala (see
  page 41)
1 tablespoon fresh coriander leaves, very
  finely chopped
aromatic salt to taste (see page 43)
GARNISH
fresh coriander leaves

◆◆◆◆◆◆◆◆◆◆◆◆◆◆◆◆◆◆◆◆◆◆◆◆◆◆◆◆◆◆

1 Heat the ghee or oil in your Balti pan
or wok on high heat. Stir-fry the chilli
powder and garlic for 30 seconds.
2 Add the onion, and, reducing the
heat, stir-fry for about 10 minutes,
allowing it to become translucent and
begin to brown.
3 Add the Balti masala paste, and stir-
fry to the simmer. Add the meat, and
stir-fry briskly to seal, for about 5
minutes.
4 Place all the stir-fried ingredients in a
large lidded casserole dish of 2.25–2.75
litre capacity (4–5 pints). Cover and place
in the oven preheated to 190°C/375°F/
Gas 5.
5 Cook for about 20 minutes. Inspect
and stir, adding about half of the stock
or water.
6 Cook for 20 more minutes. Test for
tenderness. It should still have a bite, but
not be quite ready. It may need a while
more cooking. Add the remaining stock
or water, the tomato, fresh chillies and
the vinegar.
7 Simmer for 10–15 minutes more then
test again.
8 When it is as you like it, stir in the
garam masala, fresh coriander leaves
and salt to taste. Let it simmer for a final
5–10 minutes, then garnish and serve.

Balti Phal

Balti Sag Gosht

IS COMBINATION OF TASTES – MEAT AND
NACH (SAG) WITH SAVOURY SPICES CREATES
OTHER TYPICALLY AUTHENTIC REGIONAL DISH.
LICIOUS – AND ONE OF THE MOST EFFECTIVE
ES OF SPINACH.

rves 4

0 g (1¼ lb) meat (lean leg of lamb, or
 pork, or stewing steak), weighed after
 discarding unwanted matter and diced
 into 3 cm (1¼ in) cubes
3 tablespoons ghee or corn oil
6 garlic cloves, finely chopped
5 g (8 oz) onion, very finely chopped
4 tablespoons Balti masala paste (see
 page 39)
0 ml (7fl oz) fragrant stock (see page 43)
 or water
0 g (1 lb) fresh baby spinach leaves
tablespoon Balti garam masala (see
 page 41)
tablespoons fresh coriander leaves, very
 finely chopped
omatic salt to taste (see page 43)
CES
easpoons white cummin seeds
easpoon black mustard seeds

◆◆◆◆◆◆◆◆◆◆◆◆◆◆◆◆◆◆◆◆◆◆◆◆

Heat the ghee or oil in your Balti pan
 wok on high heat. Stir-fry the spices
r 20 seconds then add the garlic and
ntinue stir-frying for 30 seconds.
 Add the onion, and, reducing the
at, stir-fry for about 10 minutes,
owing it to become translucent and
gin to brown.
 Add the Balti masala paste and stir-fry
 the simmer. Add the meat, and stir-fry
iskly to seal it for about 5 minutes.
 Place the stir-fried ingredients in a
ge lidded casserole dish of 2.25–2.75
re capacity (4–5 pints). Cover and place
the oven preheated to 190°C/375°F/
s 5.
Cook for about 20 minutes. Inspect
d stir, adding about half of the stock
water.

Iti Sag Gosht

6 Cook for 20 more minutes. Test for
tenderness. It should still have a bite, but
not be quite ready. It may need a while
more cooking. Add the remaining stock
or water and the spinach.
7 Simmer for 10–15 minutes more then
test again.
8 When it is as you like it, stir in the
garam masala, fresh coriander leaves
and salt to taste. Let it simmer for a final
5–10 minutes, then serve.

◆ Balti Elaichi

CARDAMOMS (ELAICHI) MAKE THIS DISH VERY
FRAGRANT WITH BOTH BROWN AND GREEN
VARIETIES BEING USED. ALTHOUGH ANY MEAT
WORKS WELL WITH THIS DISH, WHITE MEAT (SUCH
AS VEAL OR PORK) IS ESPECIALLY GOOD.

serves 4

675 g (1½ lb) meat (lean leg of lamb, or
 pork, or stewing steak), weighed after
 discarding unwanted matter and diced
 into 3 cm (1¼ in) cubes
2–3 tablespoons ghee or corn oil
3–6 garlic cloves, sliced
200 g (7 oz) onion, cut into long strips
12–16 green cardamoms
4 brown cardamoms
1 teaspoon allspice
¼ teaspoon caraway seeds
425 ml (¾ pint) fragrant stock (see page 43)
1 green pepper, cut into small squares
5 cm (2 in) piece of cucumber, cut into strips
3 tablespoons fresh coriander leaves,
 chopped
1 tablespoon fresh mint leaves, finely
 chopped
2 teaspoons garam masala (see page 41)
aromatic salt to taste (see page 43)

◆◆◆◆◆◆◆◆◆◆◆◆◆◆◆◆◆◆◆◆◆◆◆◆◆◆◆

1 Preheat the oven to 190°/375°F /
Gas 5.
2 Heat the ghee or oil in your Balti pan
or wok on high heat. Stir-fry the garlic
for 30 seconds.
3 Add the onion and reducing the heat,
stir-fry for 10 minutes, allowing it to
become translucent and begin to brown.

4 Place the stir-fried ingredients in a
large lidded casserole dish of 2.25–2.75
litre capacity (4–5 pints) with the meat,
cardamoms, allspice and caraway seeds.
Cover and place in the preheated oven.
5 Cook for about 20 minutes. Inspect
and stir, adding about half of the stock
or water.
6 Cook for 20 more minutes. Test for
tenderness. It should still have a bite, but
not be quite ready. It may need a while
more cooking. Add the remaining stock
or water.
7 Simmer for another 10–15 minutes,
then test again.
8 When it is as you like it, stir in the the
pepper, cucumber, coriander, mint and
garam masala, and add salt to taste. Let
it simmer for 5–10 minutes more, then
serve.

Balti Vindaloo

MEAT, CHUNKS OF POTATO AND COPIOUS AMOUNTS OF CHILLI POWDER MERGE TO CREATE A HOT BUT TASTY BALTI DISH.

serves 4

675 g (1½ lb) meat (lean leg of lamb, or pork, or stewing steak), weighed after discarding unwanted matter and diced into 3 cm (1¼ in) cubes
2–3 tablespoons ghee or corn oil
2–4 teaspoons chilli powder
3–6 garlic cloves, finely chopped
225 g (8 oz) onion, very finely chopped
2 tablespoons Balti masala paste (see page 39)
3–6 fresh red or green chillies, chopped
1 large potato, peeled and quartered
2 teaspoons fenugreek leaf
200 ml (7 fl oz) fragrant stock (see page 43) or water
1 tablespoon Balti garam masala (see page 41)
1 tablespoon fresh coriander leaves, very finely chopped
aromatic salt to taste (see page 43)
GARNISH
fresh coriander leaves

◆◆◆◆◆◆◆◆◆◆◆◆◆◆◆◆◆◆◆◆◆◆◆◆◆◆◆◆◆

1 Heat the ghee or oil in your Balti pan or wok on high heat. Stir-fry the chilli powder and garlic for 30 seconds.
2 Add the onion, and, reducing the heat, stir-fry for about 10 minutes, allowing it to become translucent and begin to brown.
3 Add the Balti masala paste, and stir-fry to the simmer. Add the meat, and stir-fry briskly to seal it, for about 5 minutes.
4 Place all the stir-fried ingredients in a large lidded casserole dish of 2.5–2.75 litre capacity (4–5 pints). Add the chillies, potato and fenugreek. Cover and place in the oven preheated to 190°C/375°F/ Gas 5.
5 Cook for about 20 minutes. Inspect and stir, adding about half of the stock or water.
6 Cook for 20 more minutes. Test for tenderness. It should still have a bite, but not be quite ready. It may need a while more cooking. Add the remaining stock or water.
7 Simmer for 10–15 minutes more then test again.
8 When it is as you like it, stir in the garam masala, fresh coriander leaves and salt to taste. Let it simmer for a final 5–10 minutes, then garnish and serve.

Balti Meat Tikka Masala

A BATCH OF COOKED MEAT TIKKA IS ADDED TO A RED GRAVY TO CREATE MANY PEOPLE'S FAVOURITE MEAT DISH.

serves 4

560 g (1¼ lb) cooked Balti Meat Tikka (see page 54)
THE GRAVY
2–3 tablespoons ghee or vegetable oil
3–6 garlic cloves, finely chopped
225 g (8 oz) onion, very finely chopped
2–3 tablespoons Balti masala paste (see page 39)
1 tablespoon red tandoori paste (see page 40)
4 canned plum tomatoes
1 tablespoon white spirit vinegar
1 tablespoon tomato ketchup
175 ml (6 floz) canned tomato soup
½ green pepper, chopped
4 green chillies, chopped
2 tablespoons coconut milk powder
1 tablespoon dried fenugreek leaves
1 tablespoon Balti garam masala (see page 41)
2 tablespoons fresh coriander leaves, very finely chopped
aromatic salt to taste (see page 43)

◆◆◆◆◆◆◆◆◆◆◆◆◆◆◆◆◆◆◆◆◆◆◆◆◆◆◆◆◆◆◆◆

1 Heat the oil in a large karahi or wok. Stir-fry the garlic for 30 seconds, add the onion and stir-fry for 8–10 minutes.
2 Add the pastes and stir-fry for a couple more minutes.
3 Add the tomatoes, vinegar, ketchup, soup, green pepper and chillies. Stir-fry until hot.
4 Add the coconut milk powder, fenugreek and the cooked meat tikka, and simmer for a further 10 minutes to make the tikka more tender, adding water as necessary to maintain a gravy consistency.
5 When it is as tender as you like it, stir in the garam masala, fresh coriander leaves and salt to taste. Give it a final 5 or 10 minutes simmering, then serve.

CHEF'S TIP
Meat will almost always be cooked 'on the bone' in the Balti area of Pakistan. If you wish to eat it like this, you can still use good quality leg meat, butcher diced, but get him to cut meat on the bone (into small boned pieces).

Venison Tikka Masala

◆ Balti Meat Pasanda

PASANDA MEANS 'BEATEN MEAT' AND IT WAS THE FAVOURITE DISH OF THE MOGHUL EMPERORS.

serves 4

675 g (1½ lb) lean lamb steaks
2–3 tablespoons ghee or corn oil
½ teaspoon turmeric
3–6 garlic cloves, finely chopped
225 g (8 oz) onion, very finely chopped
3–4 tablespoons Balti masala paste (see page 39)
150 ml (5 fl oz) single cream
⅓ block (65 g/2¼ oz) creamed coconut, chopped
2 teaspoons ground almonds
1 teaspoon white sugar
1 tablespoon Balti garam masala (see page 41)
1 tablespoon fresh coriander leaves, very finely chopped
aromatic salt to taste (see page 43)
GARNISH
desiccated coconut
coriander leaves

◆◆◆◆◆◆◆◆◆◆◆◆◆◆◆◆◆◆◆◆◆◆◆◆◆◆◆

1 Cut the lamb into chunks, then using a meat hammer, beat the chunks into thin pieces, about 5 x 2.5 cm (2 x 1 in), and less than 6 mm (¼ in) thick.
2 Heat the ghee or oil in your Balti pan or wok on high heat. Stir-fry the turmeric and garlic for 30 seconds.
3 Add the onion, and reducing the heat, stir-fry for about 10 minutes, allowing it to become translucent and begin to brown.
4 Add the masala paste, cream, coconut and the lamb. Raise the heat and bring to a brisk sizzle, stir-frying as needed for about 5 minutes.
5 Simmer and stir-fry on a lower heat for about 10 minutes, stirring as required, and adding just enough water to maintain a thickish texture.
6 To test that the lamb is cooked right through remove a piece and cut it in two. (Replace the halves in the pan.) If more cooking is needed keep testing.

When it is as you like it, add the ground almonds, sugar, garam masala, fresh coriander leaves and salt to taste.
7 Garnish and serve.

◆ Balti Dopiaza

LASHINGS OF ONIONS (PIAZA) ARE ADDED TO THE STANDARD BALTI BASE GRAVY TO CREATE A VERY SAVOURY DISH TEMPERED BY A HINT OF SWEETNESS AND BALTI HERBAL AROMATICS.

serves 4

675 g (1½ lb) meat (lean leg of lamb, or pork, or stewing steak), weighed after discarding unwanted matter and diced into 3 cm (1¼ in) cubes
2–3 tablespoons ghee or vegetable oil
1 teaspoon panch phoran (see page 43)
2–3 garlic cloves, finely chopped
225 g (8 oz) onion, thinly sliced
4–6 spring onion bulbs and leaves, chopped
3–4 tablespoons Balti masala paste (see page 39)
200 ml (7 fl oz) fragrant stock (see page 43) or water
1 tablespoon clear honey (optional)
1 tablespoon Balti garam masala (see page 41)
3 tablespoons fresh coriander leaves, very finely chopped
about 6 fresh basil leaves, chopped
aromatic salt to taste (see page 43)
GARNISH
fresh coriander leaves

◆◆◆◆◆◆◆◆◆◆◆◆◆◆◆◆◆◆◆◆◆◆◆◆◆◆◆◆◆◆

1 Heat the ghee or oil in your Balti pan or wok on high heat. Stir-fry the panch phoran for 20 seconds, then add the garlic and stir-fry for about 30 seconds more.
2 Add the sliced onion and reducing the heat, stir-fry for about 10 minutes, allowing it to become translucent and begin to brown.
3 Add the Balti masala paste, and stir-fry to the simmer. Add the meat and the spring onions and stir-fry briskly, to seal, for about 5 minutes.
4 Place all the stir-fried ingredients in a

large lidded casserole dish of 2.25–2.75 litre capacity (4–5 pints). Cover and place in an oven preheated to 190°C/375°F/Gas 5.
5 Cook for about 20 minutes. Inspect and stir, adding about half of the stock or water.
6 Cook for 20 more minutes. Test for tenderness. It should still have a bite, but not be quite ready. It may need a while more cooking. Add the remaining stock or water and the honey (if using).
7 Simmer for another 10–15 minutes, then test again.
8 When it is as you like it, stir in the garam masala, fresh coriander and basil leaves and salt to taste. Simmer for 5–10 minutes more, then garnish and serve.

MEAT COOKING TIME

The timings required to cook different meats for curry varies from meat to meat. Best beef seems to take less time than lamb, for example. And different cuts of beef will require different times. The tenderest, most expensive fillet will cook quicker than pie meat. The size of the cube will also affect timings. The smaller the cube the quicker the cooking. Whatever meat you use in Balti cooking it must be as tender as you can get it without it breaking up into a stringy mush. So the times I give must be regarded as average. Test by tasting and keep cooking until you are happy with the tenderness.

◆ Balti Jalfrezi

ʌLFREZI, ALSO SPELLED JAL FRIFI OR JALFRIZI,
ᴇANS DRY STIR-FRY, WHICH IS BALTI COOKING BY
ᴅFINITION. HERE WE ACHIEVE LIGHTNESS OF
ᴏUCH THROUGH BRIEF COOKING AND THE
ʀESHNESS OF THE SUPPORT INGREDIENTS, CHILLI,
ᴇSH GARLIC, GINGER, ONION, PEPPERS AND
ᴏRIANDER. NOTE TOO, THAT THE MEAT IS CUT
ᴇRY SMALL TO SPEED UP THE STIR-FRY TIME.

ᴇrves 4

75 g (1½ lb) meat (lean leg of lamb, or
    pork, or stewing steak), weighed after
    discarding unwanted matter
–3 tablespoons ghee or corn oil
–6 garlic cloves, finely chopped
5 cm (1 in) cube ginger, thinly sliced
10 g (4 oz) onion, thinly sliced
or 4 spring onions, bulbs and leaves,
    chopped
–3 tablespoons Balti masala paste (see
    page 39)
tablespoon green masala paste (see
    page 45)
2 a red pepper, cut into small diamond
    ʌapes
2 a green pepper, cut into small diamond
    shapes
–3 fresh green chillies, chopped
50 ml (7 fl oz) Balti chicken stock (see
    page 86) or water
tablespoon Balti garam masala (see
    page 41)
tablespoon fresh coriander leaves, very
    finely chopped
ʀomatic salt to taste (see page 43)
ᴘICES
½ teaspoons cummin seeds
2 teaspoon lovage seeds
2 teaspoon coriander seeds
ᴀRNISH
ᴇsh coriander leaves
ᴍon wedges and juice
ᴘrinkle of Balti garam masala

◆◆◆◆◆◆◆◆◆◆◆◆◆◆◆◆◆◆◆◆◆◆◆◆◆◆◆◆

1 Cut the meat into small pieces, about
2.5 x 2.5 x 1 cm (1 x 1 x ⅓ in).
2 Heat the ghee or oil in your Balti pan
or wok on high heat. Stir-fry the spices,
garlic and ginger for 30 seconds.
3 Add the onion and stir-fry for about
3 minutes.
4 Add the masala and green pastes, the
peppers, chillies and the meat. Raise the
heat and bring to a brisk sizzle, stir-
frying as needed for about 5 minutes.
5 Add a little stock or water. Simmer
and stir-fry, on a lower heat for about
10 minutes. (Note: it reduces quicker if
you add the stock bit by bit.)
6 To test that the meat is cooked right
through remove a piece and cut it in
two. (Replace the halves in the pan.) If
more cooking is needed keep testing.
When it is as you like it, add the garam
masala, fresh coriander leaves and salt to
taste.
7 Garnish and serve.

CHEF'S TIP

*To cut a pepper into diamonds:
cut the top off the pepper (where
the stalk used to be) and the
bottom. Stand the pepper on one
end and cut down throught the
flesh. Open it out and pare off
and discard the pith and seeds
You should now have a more or
less rectangular shape which you
can easily cut into equal-sized
diamonds, strips, squares or
rectangles.*

Poultry

Thousands of years ago, the flashy red jungle fowl *gallus gallus* spread around the world from its place of origin, India, and attached itself to man's campsite. It soon evolved into the fatter and larger domesticated chicken. The civilised inhabitants of the Indus valley bred chickens in 4500 BC and the ancient Egyptians operated egg hatcheries and incubators 2,000 years later. Today's loud and emotive argument about the battery hen is nothing new. 'Corn-fed' chicken can be confused with free range, but it does not necessarily follow that the hens are running about the farmyard scratching at grains of corn sprinkled by the farmer's wife. They are just as likely to be battery corn-fed, and yellow-coloured flesh can be induced by feeding turmeric or tartrazine. Free range corn-fed chicken can only be obtained from reputable sources.

Ducks and geese were also domesticated thousands of years ago by the Chinese. The most common domestic duck is the white Aylesbury with the yellow beak. The goose was farmed by the ancient Egyptians and the Romans. The grey domestic goose was probably descended from the wild greylag and the white from the snow goose.

The Aztecs domesticated the turkey centuries before the Spaniards 'discovered' the Americas. Just as they misnamed the islands they found as the West Indies, so they did the turkey, calling this enormous bird the 'Indian chicken'. Contrary to popular belief, the turkey did not originate in the country of that name; it arrived there, post-Columbus, and to this day its Turkish name is Hindi (or Indian)!

Game birds have always been used in traditional Balti cooking, simmered slowly on the bone, in a cast iron pot, over embers.

◆ Balti Chicken Bhoona Curry

A MEDIUM-STRENGTH, EASY-TO-PREPARE CURRY.

serves 4

675 g (1½ lb) chicken meat, weighed after discarding unwanted matter, including skin and bones and diced into 3 cm (1¼ in) cubes (see Chef's Tip, right)
2–3 tablespoons ghee or corn oil
½ teaspoon turmeric
3–6 garlic cloves, finely chopped
225 g (8 oz) onion, very finely chopped
3–4 tablespoons Balti masala paste (see page 39)
85 ml (3 fl oz) Balti chicken stock (see page 86) or water
2 tablespoons natural yoghurt
1 tablespoon Balti garam masala (see page 41)
1 tablespoon fresh coriander leaves, very finely chopped
aromatic salt to taste (see page 43)

◆◆◆◆◆◆◆◆◆◆◆◆◆◆◆◆◆◆◆◆◆◆◆◆◆◆◆

1 Heat the ghee or oil in your Balti pan or wok on high heat. Stir-fry the turmeric and the garlic for 30 seconds.
2 Add the onion and reducing the heat, stir-fry for about 10 minutes, until it becomes translucent and begins to brown.
3 Add the Balti masala paste and the chicken. Raise the heat and bring to a brisk sizzle, stir-frying as needed for about 5 minutes.
4 Add a little stock or water. Simmer and stir-fry, on a lower heat for about 10 minutes. (Note: it reduces quicker if you add the stock bit by bit.)
5 To test that the chicken is cooked right through remove a piece and cut it in two. (Replace the halves in the pan after testing.) If more cooking is needed keep testing. When it is as you like it, add the yoghurt, garam masala, fresh coriander leaves and salt to taste.
6 When simmering, it is ready to serve.

Previous pages: Balti Chicken Bhoona Curry

◆ Basic Balti Chicken Curry

THIS IS THE 'STANDARD' BENCHMARK MEDIUM-HEAT BALTI PREPARATION. IT COMPRISES TENDER BITE-SIZED CUBES OF CHICKEN IN A GOLDEN-BROWN SPICY GRAVY – NOT TOO HOT, NOT TOO MILD.

serves 4

675 g (1½ lb) chicken meat, weighed after discarding unwanted matter, including skin and bones and diced into 3 cm (1¼ in) cubes (see Chef's Tip, below)
2–3 tablespoons ghee or corn oil
3–6 garlic cloves, finely chopped
225 g (8 oz) onion, very finely chopped
3–4 tablespoons Balti masala paste (see page 39)
150 ml (7 fl oz) Balti chicken stock (see page 86) or water
1 tablespoon Balti garam masala (see page 41)
1 tablespoon fresh coriander leaves, very finely chopped
aromatic salt to taste (see page 43)

◆◆◆◆◆◆◆◆◆◆◆◆◆◆◆◆◆◆◆◆◆◆◆◆◆◆◆

1 Heat the ghee or oil in your Balti pan or wok on high heat. Stir-fry the garlic for 30 seconds.
2 Add the onion and reducing the heat stir-fry for about 10 minutes, allowing it to become translucent and begin to brown.
3 Add the Balti masala paste and the chicken. Raise the heat and bring to a brisk sizzle, stir-frying as needed for about 5 minutes.
4 Add a little stock or water. Simmer and stir-fry, on a lower heat for about 10 minutes. (Note: it reduces quicker if you add the stock bit by bit.)
5 To test that the chicken is cooked right through remove a piece and cut it in two. (Replace the halves in the pan after testing.) If more cooking is needed keep testing. When it is as you like it, add the garam masala, fresh coriander leaves and salt to taste and serve.

NOTE: this recipe can be used for any poultry or game. Adjust times accordingly.

CHEF'S TIP

It is cheaper to buy a whole chicken and butcher it yourself. Leg meat is just as tasty as breast, of course, and you can joint it as required, plus you can use the carcass to make stock (see page †). It is not essential to cut exact cube sizes in poultry, but obviously try to get them roughly the same. The best size of cube for Balti poultry (filleted and skinless) is roughly 3 cm (1¼ inch) . You may substitute any poultry or game for the recipes in this chapter.

POULTRY

Poultry is the generic term for domesticated chicken, turkey, goose and duck. It also covers a range of lighted game, which are either hand reared or are totally wild. In this chapter's Ingredients File, we examine all types of poultry, as well as joints, and cooking methods.

Left to right: quail, partridge, wood pigeon, guinea fowl

Chicken

This domesticated bird is the world's most popular main ingredient. As we see below, there are many culinary terms for chicken, which define its age and size. Here we see the largest chicken, a capon, alongside the smallest, a poussin, and for comparison

purposes, the smallest game bird, a quail. Chicken meat is rich in vitamin B and protein. Raw chicken meat meat averages 118 calories per 100 g (3½ oz) for white meat, and 126 calories for dark.

CHICKEN TYPES

Chicken is classified according to its age and weight at slaughter. All birds over one year old are referred to as 'fowl'.
Poussin – we start eating chicken at 4–6 weeks when it is called poussin and weighs 450–560 g (1–1¼ lb). These tiny birds are best cooked on the bone and will yield just enough meat for one.
Double poussin – aged between 6 and 10 weeks and at 675–900 g (1½–2 lb) serves 2, cooked on the bone.
  Spring or broiling (grilling) chicken – aged around 3–4 months and weighs 1.1–1.5 kg (2½–3½ lb). It yields between 3 and 4 servings.
  Roasting chicken – aged up to a year old and weighing 1.5–2.1 kg (3½–4½ lb); serves 4–6 people.
  Boiling chicken – over a year old and weighing 1.8–3.6 kg (4–8 lb); serves 5–7 people.
  Capon – a neutered cockerel over six months old weighing 1.8–4.5 kg (4–10 lb); serves 5–10 people.
  Poularde – a neutered hen over six months with almost the same characteristics as the capon. Both are generally bred to produce very tender white flesh.

Left to right: quail 200 g, poussin 400 g, spring chicken 1.1 kg, capon 2.5 kg

◆ Basic Balti Chicken Stock

AFTER BUTCHERING THERE IS STILL PLENTY OF GOODNESS LEFT IN POULTRY WHICH CAN BE MADE INTO A BALTI STOCK. THIS RECIPE USES A DRESSED ROASTING CHICKEN.

1 oven-ready roasting chicken
    (about 1.8 kg/4 lb)
6 garlic cloves, quartered
110 g (4 oz) onion, coarsely sliced
4 bay leaves
1 tablespoon Balti masala paste (page 39)
2 sticks celery, chopped
1 large carrot, chopped
1 tablespoon sugar
1 teaspoon salt

◆◆◆◆◆◆◆◆◆◆◆◆◆◆◆◆◆◆◆◆◆◆◆◆◆◆◆◆◆◆◆◆◆◆◆◆◆

1 Remove the skin from the carcass and discard. It will pull off relatively easily. Use a knife or kitchen scissors as needed.
2 Cut off the best of the meat, in pieces as large as you can get. Keep covered in the refrigerator, or freeze for future use.
3 Cut the carcass into joints small enough to go into the pot.
4 Choose a lidded pot large enough to contain the bones.
5 Put all the ingredients in the pot and bring to the boil.
6 Lower heat and maintain a rolling simmer for 30 minutes or so. Check and add water if needed. Continue to simmer for 30 more minutes.
7 Strain. Discard the solids. Cool the liquid. It should yield about 900 ml– 1 litre (1½ pints) of stock.
8 Pour about 200 ml (7 fl oz) into a yoghurt pot or equivalent. Repeat until all the stock is poured out then freeze for 24 hours.
9 Break the stock out of the moulds and put in a lidded container and straight back into the freezer. Use as required.

▶ THE INGREDIENTS FILE

cooking poultry

In the subcontinent of India, chicken is always eaten on the bone and without skin. The latter is only tasty when baked until it is crispy. Remember always to skin the joint before cooking. It is very easy: the skin more or less simply peels off. Discard it – it has no value even in stock. If there is fat present, remove as much of it as you can. Whole birds can only be slowly stewed or baked (see page 100), not stir-fried. Joints, e.g. legs, thighs, drumsticks, top and back quarters, can be grilled, baked, slow cooked or pan-fried. It is unnecessary to chop these joints into smaller pieces: the bone will probably splinter. When joints are cooked correctly, the meat will come of the bone easily prior to serving, or as it is being eaten, something relished by the population of the subcontinent. Cooking timings will vary depending on the size of the joint and the type of bird.

poultry cuts

Poultry and game can be purchased whole, but it is usual to buy them from the butcher, ready to cook, or 'dressed', i.e. with the feathers, neck and feet removed, and the giblets in a plastic bag inside the carcass.

Although jointed and filleted poultry meat is now readily available (and will be prepared to your requirements by a reputable poulterer) it is much cheaper if you buy a dressed carcass and joint it or fillet it to your own requirements. It is neither unpleasant nor difficult to do this. You will also have the advantage of having the remains of the carcass to make stock (see left). Following is a description of the different poultry cuts:

DRUMSTICK AND THIGH

The pestle-shaped lower leg of the fowl, above the ankle and below the knee joint is known as the drumstick. Its meat is redder than breast meat. The thigh is above the knee joint and up to the pelvic joint, on the bone.

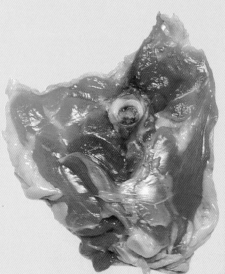

BACK QUARTER

The thigh and a connecting portion of the rear body.

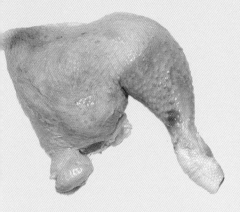

TOP QUARTER

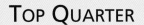

The wing and a connecting portion of the front body – should be cut away from the back at an angle so that it contains some white meat.

BREAST MEAT

Filleted breast meat often comes from capon or poularde and will weigh 175–300 g (6–10 oz), trimmed and fat-free. It is very lean providing an average 118 calories per 100 g (3½ oz),

and is rich in iron and high in protein. Poultry should always be skinned for use in Balti and curry cooking. It is easy to skin a fowl, but your poulterer will do it for you. It is also readily available filleted and skinned in supermarkets. It can then be beaten for pasanda curries, or diced for general currying.

DICED CHICKEN

Chicken breast meat, filleted, skinned and diced into 'bite-sized' cubes, is by far the most popular meat at the curry

and Balti house, and is the most expensive cut. It is white when cooked, extremely tender, and has good flavour, particularly if you can obtain it from a genuine free-range bird.

Other chicken meat, including the drumstick is darker than breast. Even so it is less fat-saturated than red meat, so is perceived to be 'healthier'.

The meat of other large birds can also be diced. For turkey, goose and duck the same applies as for chicken.

The best cube size for Balti poultry meat (filleted and skinless) is about 3 cm (1¼ in). Obviously it is not possible to cut exact cubes, nor will every one be exactly that size, but that should be the average.

BONED CHICKEN

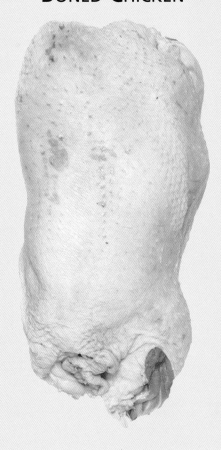

Whole birds can be boned, with practice and some care.

◆ Balti Chicken Garlic Curry

IT'S REMARKABLE HOW FEW INGREDIENTS IT TAKES TO MAKE SUCH A TASTY DISH.

serves 4

675 g (1½ lb) chicken, weighed after discarding unwanted matter, including skin and bones and diced into 3 cm (1¼ in) cubes (see Chef's Tip, page 84)
4 tablespoons butter, any type
12 garlic cloves, finely chopped
3–4 tablespoons Balti masala paste (see page 39)
150 ml (¼ pint) Balti chicken stock (see page 86) or water
1 tablespoon fresh coriander leaves, very finely chopped
aromatic salt to taste (see page 43)
GARNISH
fresh coriander leaves

◆◆◆◆◆◆◆◆◆◆◆◆◆◆◆◆◆◆◆◆◆◆◆◆◆◆◆

1 Heat the butter in your Balti pan or wok to quite a high heat, but watch it doesn't burn. Add the garlic and stir-fry for about 30 seconds. Add the masala paste and continue to stir-fry for a further 30 seconds, then add 3 or 4 tablespoons of stock or water and stir-fry for about 2 or 3 minutes more.
2 Add the chicken pieces and briskly stir-fry for about 2 minutes, then lower the heat a little, and over the next 5 minutes add the remaining stock or water, stirring as necessary.
3 To finish off, turn up the heat, add the coriander leaves and resume brisk stirring for about 5 minutes to reduce the remaining liquid to form a dryish gravy and coating.
4 Check that the chicken is cooked by cutting a piece in half. It should be white right through. If not continue stir-frying until it is. Salt to taste.
5 Garnish and serve as a starter with chutneys or as a main course with puris.

◆ Balti Chicken and Egg Curry

CHICKEN AND EGG IS A REMARKABLY GOOD COMBINATION IN THIS TASTY BALTI DISH.

serves 4

675 g (1½ lb) chicken meat, weighed after discarding unwanted matter, diced into 3 cm (1¼ in) cubes
2–3 tablespoons ghee or corn oil
½ teaspoon turmeric
3–6 garlic cloves, finely chopped
225 g (8 oz) onion, very finely chopped
3–4 tablespoons Balti masala paste (see page 39)
150 ml (5 fl oz) Balti chicken stock (see page 86) or water
1 tablespoon Balti garam masala (see page 41)
1 tablespoon fresh coriander leaves, very finely chopped
aromatic salt to taste (see page 43)
2–4 hardboiled eggs, grade 1 (see page 99)

◆◆◆◆◆◆◆◆◆◆◆◆◆◆◆◆◆◆◆◆◆◆◆◆◆◆◆

1 Heat the ghee or oil in your Balti pan or wok on high heat. Stir-fry the turmeric for 20 seconds then add the garlic for 30 seconds.
2 Add the onion and reducing the heat, stir-fry for about 10 minutes, allowing it to become brown.
3 Add the masala paste and the chicken. Raise the heat and bring to a brisk sizzle, stir-frying as needed for about 5 minutes.
4 Add a little stock or water. Simmer and stir-fry, on a lower heat for about 10 minutes. (Note: it reduces quicker if you add the stock bit by bit.)
5 To test that the chicken is cooked right through remove a piece and cut it in two. (Replace the halves in the pan after testing.) If more cooking is needed keep testing. When it is as you like it, add the garam masala, fresh coriander leaves and salt to taste.
6 Shell and quarter or halve the eggs and gently stir them into the chicken so that they don't break up. Serve.

◆ Balti Chilli Chicken Curry

SIMPLE TO MAKE, BUT VERY, VERY CHILLI HOT!

serves 4

675 g (1½ lb) chicken meat, weighed after discarding unwanted matter, including skin and bones and diced into 3 cm (1¼ in) cubes (see Chef's Tip page 84)
4 tablespoons butter, any type
4 teaspoons chilli powder
1 Scotch bonnet or habañero chilli, chopped (optional)
1 tablespoon Balti masala paste (see page 39)
150 ml (¼ pint) Balti chicken stock (see page 86) or water
1 tablespoon fresh coriander leaves, very finely chopped
aromatic salt to taste (see page 43)
GARNISH
fresh chilli

◆◆◆◆◆◆◆◆◆◆◆◆◆◆◆◆◆◆◆◆◆◆◆◆◆◆◆

1 Heat the butter in your Balti pan or wok to quite a high heat, but watch it doesn't burn. Add the chilli powder and stir-fry for about 30 seconds. Add the chillies (if using) and the masala paste and continue to stir-fry for a further 30 seconds, then add 3 or 4 tablespoons of stock or water and stir-fry for about 2 or 3 minutes more.
2 Add the chicken pieces and briskly stir-fry for about 2 minutes, then lower the heat a little, and over the next 5 minutes add the remaining stock or water, stirring as necessary.
3 To finish off, turn up the heat, add the coriander leaves and salt, and resume brisk stirring for about 5 minutes to reduce the remaining liquid to form a dryish gravy and coating.
4 Check that the chicken is cooked by cutting a piece in half. It should be white right through. If not continue stir-frying until it is. Salt to taste. Garnish and serve as a starter with chutneys or as a main course with puris.

Balti Chicken and Egg Curry

► THE INGREDIENTS FILE

duck

Magret de canard is a French term meaning the lean portion (of a fat duck) and refers to duck breasts, filleted with skin and fat still attached, which you or your poulterer must pare away. The resultant meat, though expensive, is the best for Balti cooking, and at 122 calories per 100 g (3½ oz) it is the healthiest too.

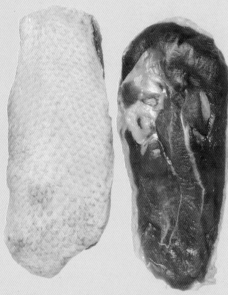

Magret de canard

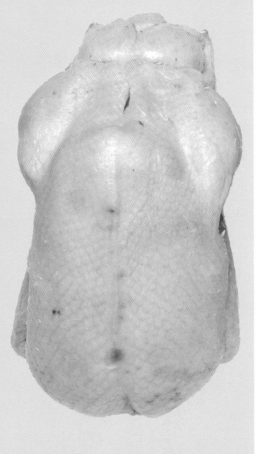

1.8 kg duck

goose

Goose yields less meat per equal weight of carcass than turkey, but it has a 'gamier' flavour.

A goose is table-ready at just three months, when it will weigh about 2.7 kg (6 lb). A slightly older bird at 3.5 kg (8 lb) will yield enough meat for 4–5 people.

Goose can be obtained up to 12 kg (26 lb) for special occasions but it can be tough. Raw goose meat, fat-free is rather high in calories at 260 calories

turkey

The best turkey in the UK is the Norfolk Black. A plump dressed hen weighs as little as 2.75 kg (6 lb) and serves 4–5 people. Older birds can weigh up to 13.5 kg (30 lb). Turkey is excellent for Balti cooking. Use leg meat or breast on or off the bone but always skinned and without fat when the raw meat is just 104 calories per 100 g (3½ oz). Turkey is slightly tougher than chicken, but is markedly cheaper.

◆ Balti Dhansak Chicken Curry

ONE OF THE ALL-TIME BALTI FAVOURITES – THE BALTI BASE IS THICKENED WITH CREAMY COOKED LENTILS (DHAL PURÉE).

serves 4

540 g (1 lb 3 oz) chicken meat, weighed after discarding unwanted matter, including skin and bones and diced into 3 cm (1¼ in) cubes (see Chef's Tip page 84)
2 tablespoons ghee or vegetable oil
4–6 garlic cloves, finely chopped
225 g (8 oz) onion, very finely chopped
2–3 tablespoons Balti masala paste (see page 39)
300 ml (11 fl oz) fragrant stock (see page 43)
100 g (3½ oz) masoor dhal, cooked
200 g (7 oz) canned ratatouille, mashed
2 tablespoons brinjal pickle
1 tablespoon white granulated sugar
2 teaspoons vinegar, any type
2 teaspoons Balti garam masala (see page 4?)
0–3 fresh green chillies, finely chopped
1 tablespoon fresh coriander leaves, very finely chopped
aromatic salt to taste (see page 43)
SPICES
1 teaspoon cummin seeds
½ teaspoon fenugreek seeds
GARNISH
fresh coriander leaves

◆◆◆◆◆◆◆◆◆◆◆◆◆◆◆◆◆◆◆◆◆◆◆◆◆◆◆

1 Heat the ghee or oil in your Balti pan or wok on high heat. Stir-fry the spices and garlic for 30 seconds.
2 Add the onion and chillies, reduce the heat and stir-fry for about 10 minutes, allowing the onion to become translucent and begin to brown.
3 Add the masala paste and the chicken. Raise the heat and bring to a brisk sizzle, stir-frying as needed for about 5 minutes.
4 Add a little stock or water, plus the masoor dhal, ratatouille, brinjal pickle, sugar and vinegar. Simmer and stir-fry, on a lower heat for about 10 minutes.

Note: it reduces quicker if you add the stock bit by bit.).

To test that the chicken is cooked right through remove a piece and cut it in two. (Replace the halves in the pan after testing.) If more cooking is needed keep testing. When it is as you like it, add the garam masala, fresh coriander leaves and salt to taste.

- Garnish and serve.

◆ Balti Chicken Kashmiri Curry

A COMBINATION FOR THOSE WHO LOVE THE CONTRAST OF FRUIT AND SAVOURY MEAT CURRY.

serves 4

675 g (1½ lb) chicken, weighed after discarding unwanted matter, including skin and bones and diced into 3 cm (1¼ in) cubes (see Chef's Tip, page 84)
2–3 tablespoons ghee or corn oil
4–6 garlic cloves, finely chopped
225 g (8 oz) onion, very finely chopped
3–4 tablespoons Balti masala paste (see page 39)
150 ml (7 fl oz) Balti chicken stock (see page 86) water
75 g (3 oz) lotus roots
150 g (5 oz) canned lychees, strained
2 tablespoons juice from the above
1 tablespoon dark muscovado sugar
1 tablespoon Balti garam masala (see page 41)
1 tablespoon fresh coriander leaves, very finely chopped
aromatic salt to taste (see page 43)
GARNISH
fresh coriander leaves

◆◆◆◆◆◆◆◆◆◆◆◆◆◆◆◆◆◆◆◆◆◆◆◆◆◆◆◆◆◆◆◆◆

1 Heat the ghee or oil in your Balti pan or wok on high heat. Stir-fry the garlic for 30 seconds.

2 Add the onion and reducing the heat, stir-fry for about 10 minutes, allowing it to become translucent and begin to brown.

3 Add the masala paste and the chicken. Raise the heat and bring to a brisk sizzle, stir-frying as needed for about 5 minutes.

4 Add a little stock or water and the lotus roots, lychees, juice and sugar. Simmer and stir-fry on a lower heat for about 10 minutes. (Note: it reduces quicker if you add the stock bit by bit.)

5 To test that the chicken is cooked right through remove a piece and cut it in two. (Replace the halves in the pan after testing.) If more cooking is needed keep testing. When it is as you like it, add the garam masala, fresh coriander leaves and salt to taste.

6 Garnish and serve.

◆ Balti Chicken Dopiaza Curry

LASHINGS OF ONIONS (PIAZA) ARE ADDED TO THE STANDARD BALTI BASE GRAVY TO CREATE A VERY SAVOURY DISH TEMPERED BY A HINT OF SWEETNESS AND BALTI HERBAL AROMATICS.

serves 4

675 g (1½ lb) chicken, weighed after discarding unwanted matter, including skin and bones and diced into 3 cm (1¼ in) cubes (see Chef's Tip, page 84)
1 teaspoon panch phoran (see page 43)
2–3 garlic cloves, finely chopped
225 g (8 oz) onion, thinly sliced
4–6 spring onions, bulbs and leaves, chopped
3–4 tablespoons Balti masala paste (see page 39)
125 ml (4 fl oz) fragrant stock (see page 43) or water
1 tablespoon clear honey (optional)
1 tablespoon Balti garam masala (see page 41)
3 tablespoons fresh coriander leaves, very finely chopped
about 6 fresh basil leaves, chopped
aromatic salt to taste (see page 43)
GARNISH
fresh coriander leaves

◆◆◆◆◆◆◆◆◆◆◆◆◆◆◆◆◆◆◆◆◆◆◆◆◆◆◆◆◆◆◆◆◆

1 Heat the ghee or oil in your Balti pan or wok on high heat. Stir-fry the panch phoran for 20 seconds, then add the garlic and stir-fry for about 30 seconds more.

2 Add both types of onion and, reducing the heat, stir-fry for about 10 minutes, allowing them to become translucent and begin to brown.

3 Add the masala paste and the chicken. Raise the heat and bring to a brisk sizzle, stir-frying as needed for about 5 minutes.

4 Add the stock or water and the honey (if using). Simmer and stir-fry, on a lower heat for about 10 minutes. (Note: it reduces quicker if you add the stock bit by bit.)

5 To test that the chicken is cooked right through remove a piece and cut it in two. (Replace the halves in the pan after testing.) If more cooking is needed keep testing. When it is as you like it, add the garam masala, fresh leaves and salt to taste.

6 Garnish and serve.

game birds

We examined the non-flighted game available in the previous chapter. There is a wide choice of game birds. Grouse, guinea fowl, partridge, pheasant, pigeon, quail, snipe, wild duck and woodcock are widely available. Most are seasonal (except pigeon and quail).

In France and the subcontinent wild birds as small as the warbler, lark and moorhen are eaten. The peacock, a Middle Eastern descendant of the pheasant, was prized in Britain at the time of the Crusaders. (It is protected in the Indian subcontinent, and may not be eaten, although I do have in my collection recipes from the Maharajas for peacock.) Swan was also highly sought-after in Europe in the Middle Ages, and was to be found on British royal tables until recently. Balti cooking derived from the nomadic, peripatetic and unpredictable lifestyle of the hunter-warrior, so game birds are perfect Balti subjects.

GROUSE

Of the several species of grouse, all ground-living, it is the Scottish or red grouse which is the most highly valued for flavour. The average carcass weighs 675 g (1½ lb) and yields a generous single portion of meat. Raw meat is 178 calories per 100 g (3½ oz).

GUINEA FOWL

This is related to the pheasant but is slightly larger as well as being similar in taste. A carcass weighs 1–1.5 kg (2¼–3½ lb). Raw fat-free guinea fowl meat is 156 calories per 100 g (3½ oz).

PARTRIDGE

Another relative of the pheasant, the grey-legged partridge is the most common game bird. The carcass weighs 350–400 g (12–14 oz) and will serve one. Raw fat-free partridge meat is 156 calories per 100 g (3½ oz).

PHEASANT

The most popular game bird, the young female provides the tenderest meat with the best flavour. Its carcass averages 1.1 kg (2½ lb) and should serve three. The cock bird is slightly larger at 1.3 kg (3 lb) but its meat is generally tougher, drier and yields less. Raw fat-free pheasant meat is 156 calories per 100 g (3½ oz).

PIGEON

The rock dove is the ancestor of the domestic pigeon. It has pale flesh which is not unlike chicken. Wild (wood) pigeon is larger with darker, stronger flavoured meat. Squab is young pigeon bred for the table. At just one month it weighs from 350 g (12 oz). An adult weighs 450–675 g (1–1½ lb). Small birds at these weights will serve one person; larger birds will serve two. Raw pigeon meat without fat is 166 calories per 100 g (3½ oz).

QUAIL

These tiny birds originated in the Middle East but are now found worldwide. Many are farm reared. At just 110–150 g (4–5 oz) per carcass they should be cooked whole, with skin on, and one will yield enough meat per

...rson for a starter or two for a main ...urse. They are available boned (a ...dly and difficult task to do oneself) ...d, as such, are delightful stuffed. ...aw quail meat, fat-free is 166 calories ...r 100 g (3½ oz).

SNIPE

...nother very tiny bird. Its weight and ...l other comments are as for the quail.

WILD DUCK

...allard, pintail, teal and widgeon are ...vourite wild duck species. There is ...uite a weight variation between ...ecies, and the largest (mallard) is ...nsiderably smaller than a ...mesticated duck. A mallard at 1.1 kg ...½ lb) will just serve three. A teal at ...0 g (12 oz) is enough for a single ...rtion.

WOODCOCK

...milar to the snipe and also a water ...rd. It is quite rare. At 150 g (5 oz) for ...arcass it yields sufficient meat for a ...arter for one.

◆ Balti Chicken Jalfrezi Curry

THIS IS A VERY QUICK AND SIMPLE DISH TO COOK. THE CHICKEN IS CUT VERY SMALL TO SPEED UP THE STIR-FRY TIME.

serves 4

675 g (1½ lb) chicken, weighed after discarding unwanted matter, including skin and bones and diced into 3 cm (1¼ in) cubes (see Chef's Tip, page 84)
2–3 tablespoons ghee or corn oil
3–6 garlic cloves, finely chopped
2.5 cm (1 in) cube ginger, thinly sliced
110 g (4 oz) onion, thinly sliced
3 or 4 spring onions, bulbs and leaves, chopped
2–3 tablespoons Balti masala paste (see page 39)
1 tablespoon green masala paste (see page 45)
½ a red pepper cut into small diamond shapes
½ a green pepper cut into small diamond shapes
1–3 fresh green chillies, chopped
150 ml (7 fl oz) Balti chicken stock (see page 86) or water
1 tablespoon Balti garam masala (see page 41)
1 tablespoon fresh coriander leaves, very finely chopped
aromatic salt to taste (see page 43)
SPICES
1½ teaspoons cummin seeds
½ teaspoon lovage seeds
½ teaspoon coriander seeds
GARNISH
squeezes of lemon juice
sprinkles of Balti garam masala
fresh coriander leaves

◆◆◆◆◆◆◆◆◆◆◆◆◆◆◆◆◆◆◆◆◆◆◆◆◆◆◆◆◆◆◆

1 Heat the ghee or oil in your Balti pan or wok on high heat. Stir-fry the spices, garlic and ginger for 30 seconds.
2 Add both types of onion and stir-fry for about 3 minutes.
3 Add the masala and green pastes, the peppers, chillies and the chicken. Raise the heat and bring to a brisk sizzle, stir-frying as needed for about 5 minutes.
4 Add a little stock or water. Simmer and stir-fry, on a lower heat for about 10 minutes. (Note: it reduces quicker if you add the stock bit by bit.)
5 To test that the chicken is cooked right through remove a piece and cut it in two. (Replace the halves in the pan after testing.) If more cooking is needed keep testing. When it is as you like it, add the garam masala, fresh coriander leaves and salt to taste.
6 Garnish and serve.

> ## CHEF'S TIP
> *To cut a pepper into diamonds: cut the top off the pepper (where the stalk used to be) and the bottom. Stand the pepper on one end and cut down through the flesh. Open it out and pare off and discard the pith and seeds. You should now have a more or less rectangular shape which you can easily cut into equal-sized diamonds, strips, squares or rectangles.*

◆ Balti Chicken Kofta Curry

KOFTAS ARE SMALL GROUND MEATBALLS, IN THIS CASE MADE WITH CHICKEN. SPICY AND DELICIOUS WHEN FLOATED IN THE TOMATO-FLAVOURED GRAVY, KOFTAS ARE EASY TO MAKE.

serves 4

FOR THE KOFTAS
560 g (1¼ lb) chicken breast, skinned
2 garlic cloves, finely chopped
2 tablespoons dehydrated onion flakes
1 tablespoon fresh coriander leaves, finely chopped
1 tablespoon masala powder (see page 39)
1 teaspoon garam masala
½ teaspoon salt
FOR THE BALTI KOFTA CURRY GRAVY
1 tablespoon ghee or vegetable oil
2–3 garlic cloves, finely chopped
300 g (10½ oz) Balti masala gravy (see page 42)
1 tablespoon tomato purée
175 g (6 oz) canned tomatoes, strained, juice reserved
1 teaspoon white granulated sugar
½ teaspoon dried fenugreek leaf
1 tablespoon fresh coriander leaves, very finely chopped
1 tablespoon fresh basil leaves, very finely chopped
aromatic salt to taste (see page 43)
GARNISH
fresh coriander leaves

◆◆◆◆◆◆◆◆◆◆◆◆◆◆◆◆◆◆◆◆◆◆◆◆◆◆◆◆◆

TO MAKE THE KOFTAS
1 Coarsely chop the chicken. Run everything once through a food processor, or twice through a hand mincer to achieve a finely textured paste.
2 Mix the paste thoroughly and divide it into four equal parts. Roll 6 small balls (koftas) from each part.
3 Preheat the oven to 375°F/190°C/ Gas 5.
4 Place the 24 koftas on an oven tray and bake them for 15 minutes.

TO MAKE THE BALTI KOFTA CURRY GRAVY
1 Heat the ghee or oil in the Balti pan or wok, and stir-fry the garlic for 30 seconds.
2 Add the Balti masala gravy, tomato purée, canned tomatoes, sugar and fenugreek leaf, and bring to the simmer.
3 Add the cooked koftas, with any juices they may have made, and stir-fry for about 3 minutes.
4 Add the fresh leaves and salt to taste. Simmer for a few more minutes and add the reserved tomato juice to keep things mobile.

◆ Balti Chicken Keema Curry

NORMALLY MADE WITH MINCED MEAT, THIS DISH CAN BE EQUALLY DELICIOUS USING MINCED POULTRY. MINCE IS ALMOST INDESTRUCTIBLE IN THE COOKING PROCESS, SO IT SIMPLY CANNOT BE OVERCOOKED. IT IS THEREFORE A GREAT DISH FOR THE BEGINNER.

serves 4

675 g (1½ lb) minced chicken, turkey or duck
2 tablespoons ghee or corn oil
4–6 garlic cloves, finely chopped
225 g (8 oz) onion, finely chopped
3–4 tablespoons Balti masala paste (see page 39)
1 tablespoon tomato purée
300 ml (11 fl oz) fragrant stock (see page 43)
1 tablespoon Balti garam masala (see page 41)
1 tablespoon fresh coriander leaves, chopped
aromatic salt to taste (see page 43)

◆◆◆◆◆◆◆◆◆◆◆◆◆◆◆◆◆◆◆◆◆◆◆◆◆◆◆◆◆

1 Put the mince into the Balti pan or wok with a teaspoon of oil, and stir-fry it for about 10 minutes. This 'seals' it and brings out the liquids which should be strained off and reserved. Transfer the meat to a large lidded casserole dish of 2.25–2.75 litre capacity (4–5 pints).

2 Heat the ghee or oil in your Balti pan or wok on high heat. Stir-fry the garlic for 30 seconds.
3 Add the onion and reducing the heat stir-fry for about 10 minutes, allowing it to become translucent and begin to brown.
4 Add the masala paste and the tomato purée. Raise the heat and bring to a brisk sizzle, stir-frying as needed for about 2 or 3 minutes.
5 Transfer all the stir-fried items to the casserole dish and place in the oven, preheated to 190°C/375°F/Gas 5.
6 Cook for about 20 minutes. Inspect and stir, adding about half of the stock or water.
7 Cook for 20 more minutes. Test for tenderness. It should still have a bite, but not be quite ready. It may need a while more cooking. Add the remaining stock or water.
8 Simmer for 10–15 minutes more then test again.
9 When it is as you like it, stir in the garam masala, fresh coriander leaves and salt to taste. Let it simmer for a final 5–10 minutes, then serve.

VARIATIONS
Balti Chicken Keema Mattar
Ingredients as for Balti Chicken Keema Curry with the addition of up to 250g (9 oz) frozen peas, thawed
Add the peas at stage 7.

Balti Chicken Keema Chana
Ingredients as for Balti Chicken Keema Curry with the addition of 400 g (14 oz) can chickpeas (strain off the liquid and reserve for other jobs). Add the chickpeas at stage 7.

Balti Duck Keema Curry

Balti Chicken Korma Curry

THIS BALTI KORMA IS TRADITIONALLY VERY MILD AND CREAMY, AND IT WORKS ESPECIALLY WELL WITH CHICKEN BREAST.

serves 4

675 g (1½ lb) chicken, weighed after discarding unwanted matter, including skin and bones and diced into 3 cm (1¼ in) cubes (see Chef's Tip, page 84)

2–3 tablespoons ghee or corn oil

3–6 garlic cloves, finely chopped

225 g (8 oz) onion, very finely chopped

3–4 tablespoons Balti masala paste (see page 39)

150 ml (7 fl oz) Balti chicken stock (see page 86) or water

100 ml (4 fl oz) double (thick) cream

100g (3½ oz) creamed coconut, chopped

1 teaspoon sugar

1 tablespoon Balti garam masala (see page 41)

10 whole almonds, peeled

1 tablespoon fresh coriander leaves, very finely chopped

aromatic salt to taste (see page 43)

SPICES

2 bay leaves

5 cm (2 in) cassia bark

4–6 green cardamoms

4–6 cloves

GARNISH

fresh coriander leaves

◆◆◆◆◆◆◆◆◆◆◆◆◆◆◆◆◆◆◆◆◆◆◆◆◆◆◆◆◆

1 Heat the ghee or oil in your Balti pan or wok on high heat. Stir-fry the spices and garlic for 30 seconds.

2 Add the onion and reducing the heat, stir-fry for about 10 minutes, allowing it to become translucent and begin to brown.

3 Add the masala paste and the chicken. Raise the heat and bring to a brisk sizzle, stir-frying as needed for about 5 minutes.

4 Add a little stock or water, plus the

Balti Chicken Korma Curry

cream and coconut. Simmer and stir-fry on a lower heat for about 10 minutes. (Note: it reduces quicker if you add the stock bit by bit.)

5 To test that the chicken is cooked right through remove a piece and cut it in two. (Replace the halves in the pan after testing.) If more cooking is needed keep testing.

6 When it is as you like it, stir in the sugar, garam masala, almonds, fresh coriander leaves and salt to taste. Give it a final 5 or 10 minutes simmering, then garnish and serve.

◆ Balti Chicken Madras Curry

MADRAS IS HOT BUT NOT SEARING AND THIS DISH CONTAINS INTERESTING FLAVOURINGS IN THE FORM OF TOMATO, LEMON AND ALMOND, ALONG WITH A CERTAIN AMOUNT OF CHILLI.

serves 4

675 g (1½ lb) chicken, weighed after discarding unwanted matter, including skin and bones and diced into 3 cm (1¼ in) cubes (see Chef's Tip, page 84)

2–3 tablespoons ghee or corn oil

3–6 garlic cloves, finely chopped

225 g (8 oz) onion, very finely chopped

3–4 tablespoons Balti masala paste (see page 39)

1 tablespoon tandoori paste (see page 40)

125 ml (4 fl oz) Balti chicken stock (see page 86) or water

6 oz (175 g) canned tomatoes, strained

2 tablespoons tomato ketchup

2 tablespoons ground almonds

1 tablespoon Balti garam masala (see page 41)

1 tablespoon fresh coriander leaves, very finely chopped

aromatic salt to taste (see page 43)

SPICES

2–4 teaspoons chilli powder

1 teaspoon cummin powder

GARNISH

fresh coriander leaves

◆◆◆◆◆◆◆◆◆◆◆◆◆◆◆◆◆◆◆◆◆◆◆◆◆◆◆◆◆◆◆

1 Heat the ghee or oil in your Balti pan or wok on high heat. Stir-fry the spices and garlic for 30 seconds.

2 Add the onion and reducing the heat, stir-fry for about 10 minutes, allowing it to become translucent and begin to brown.

3 Add the masala and tandoori pastes and the chicken. Raise the heat and bring to a brisk sizzle, stir-frying as needed for about 5 minutes.

4 Add a little stock or water, plus the tomatoes, ketchup and ground almonds. Simmer and stir-fry on a lower heat for about 10 minutes. (Note: it reduces quicker if you add the stock bit by bit.)

5 To test that the chicken is cooked right through, remove a piece and cut it in two. (Replace the halves in the pan after testing.) If more cooking is needed keep testing. When it is as you like it, add the garam masala, fresh coriander leaves and salt to taste.

6 Simmer for a while longer, garnish and serve.

◆ Balti Chicken Makhani Curry

IN THIS DISH, CHICKEN DRUMSTICKS ARE TANDOORI-MARINATED, THEN SERVED IN A BALTI GRAVY.

serves 4

8 large chicken drumsticks
FOR THE MARINADE
175 ml (6 fl oz) yoghurt
2 teaspoons paprika
1 teaspoon chilli
1 tablespoon tomato purée
2–3 tablespoons tandoori marinade
    (see page 54)
1/8 teaspoon red food colouring (optional)
FOR THE GRAVY
2–3 tablespoons ghee or corn oil
3–6 garlic cloves, finely chopped
5 cm (2 in) piece of fresh ginger, roughly
    chopped
225 g (8 oz) onion, very finely chopped
3–4 tablespoons Balti masala paste
    (see page 39)
6 canned plum tomatoes, chopped
1 tablespoon tomato ketchup
85 ml (3 fl oz) single cream
1 tablespoon Balti garam masala (see
    page 41)
1 tablespoon fresh coriander leaves,
    very finely chopped
aromatic salt to taste (see page 43)
SPICES
2 teaspoons paprika
1 teaspoon garam masala (see page 41)
1 teaspoon ground coriander
1/4 teaspoon yellow food colouring powder
    (optional)
1 teaspoon garlic powder

◆◆◆◆◆◆◆◆◆◆◆◆◆◆◆◆◆◆◆◆◆◆◆◆◆◆◆◆◆

1 Skin the chicken drumsticks, then lightly prick or gash the flesh.
2 Mix the marinade ingredients together in a non-metallic bowl. Add the chicken and mix well. Cover and place in the fridge for marination (see page 101).
3 To cook: preheat the oven to 190°C/375°F/Gas 5. Remove the chicken from the marinade, shaking off and

reserving any excess, but ensuring that there is still a liberal coating left on each piece. Place on an oven tray and bake for 20 minutes, then remove and keep warm. Strain liquid off oven tray and reserve.
4 Meanwhile, make the gravy: heat the ghee or oil in your Balti pan or wok on high heat. Stir-fry the garlic and ginger for 30 seconds.
5 Add the onion and, reducing the heat, stir-fry for about 10 minutes, allowing it to become translucent and begin to brown.
6 Add the masala paste, tomatoes, tomato ketchup, cream, garam masala, fresh coriander and salt to taste, and simmer for the few minutes it takes for it to start to darken in colour. Add the warm cooked chicken to the gravy plus any oven tray juices. Raise the heat and bring to a brisk sizzle, stir-frying as needed for about 5 minutes.
7 Simmer and stir-fry, on a lower heat for a further 5 minutes then serve.

COOKING POULTRY JOINTS
Legs, thighs and drumsticks, wings and backs can be baked or slow-cooked.
Timings will vary depending on the size of the joint and the type of bird. Remember always to skin the joint first and remove as much fat as you can, and cook the joint right through so that there is no pink or rare meat. It is unnecessary to chop joints into small pieces. The bone will probably splinter, and when cooked correctly will come off the bone easily prior to serving, or as it is being eaten.

◆ Balti Chicken Malaya Curry

TURN A BALTI INTO A MALAYAN BALTI BY ADDING MILD SPICES AND SWEET EXOTIC FRUIT SUCH AS PINEAPPLE.

serves 4

675 g (1½ lb) chicken, weighed after
    discarding unwanted matter, including
    skin and bones and diced into 3 cm
    (1¼ in) cubes (see Chef's Tip, page 84)
2–3 tablespoons ghee or corn oil
3–6 garlic cloves, finely chopped
225 g (8 oz) onion, very finely chopped
3–4 tablespoons Balti masala paste (see
    page 39)
150 ml (7 fl oz) Balti chicken stock (see page
    86) or water
6–8 chunks fresh or canned pineapple
1 tablespoon Balti garam masala (see
    page 41)
1 tablespoon fresh coriander leaves, very
    finely chopped
aromatic salt to taste (see page 43)

◆◆◆◆◆◆◆◆◆◆◆◆◆◆◆◆◆◆◆◆◆◆◆◆◆◆◆◆◆◆◆◆◆◆

1 Heat the ghee or oil in your Balti pan or wok on high heat. Stir-fry the garlic for 30 seconds.
2 Add the onion and reducing the heat, stir-fry for about 10 minutes, allowing it to become translucent and begin to brown.
3 Add the masala paste and the chicken. Raise the heat and bring to a brisk sizzle, stir-frying as needed for about 5 minutes.
4 Add a little stock or water and the pineapple chunks. Simmer and stir-fry, on a lower heat for about 10 minutes. (Note: it reduces quicker if you add the stock bit by bit.)
5 To test that the chicken is cooked right through, remove a piece and cut it in two. (Replace the halves in the pan after testing). If more cooking is needed keep testing. When it is as you like it, add the garam masala, fresh coriander leaves and salt to taste.
6 Serve.

▶ Balti Chicken Pasanda Curry

THIS RECIPE CAN BE USED FOR ANY POULTRY OR GAME. ADJUST TIMES ACCORDINGLY.

Serves 4

- 75 g (1½ lb) chicken, weighed after discarding unwanted matter, including skin and bones and diced into 3 cm (1¼ in) cubes (see Chef's Tip, page 84)
- teaspoon turmeric
- 2-3 tablespoons ghee or corn oil
- 4-6 garlic cloves, finely chopped
- 225 g (8 oz) onion, very finely chopped
- 3-4 tablespoons Balti masala paste (see page 39)
- 150 ml (5 fl oz) single cream
- block (65 g/2¼ oz) creamed coconut, chopped
- teaspoons ground almonds
- teaspoon white sugar
- tablespoon Balti garam masala (see page 41)
- tablespoon fresh coriander leaves, very finely chopped
- aromatic salt to taste (see page 43)

◆◆◆◆◆◆◆◆◆◆◆◆◆◆◆◆◆◆◆◆◆◆◆◆◆◆

Heat the ghee or oil in your Balti pan or wok on high heat. Stir-fry the turmeric and garlic for 30 seconds.

Add the onion and reducing the heat, stir-fry for about 10 minutes, until it becomes translucent and begins to brown.

Add the masala paste, cream, coconut, almonds, sugar and the chicken. Raise the heat and bring to a brisk sizzle, stir-frying as needed for about 5 minutes.

Simmer and stir-fry on a lower heat for about 10 minutes, stirring as required, and adding just enough water to keep a thickish texture.

To test that the chicken is cooked right through remove a piece and cut it in two. (Replace the halves in the pan after testing.) If more cooking is needed keep testing. When it is as you like it, add the garam masala, fresh coriander leaves and salt to taste.

▶ THE INGREDIENTS FILE

poultry giblets

Even the largest bird yields only a small amount of offal compared with meat (see page 70). The modern poulterer supplies the liver, kidneys and heart along with the neck in a plastic bag stored inside the bird's cavity. Always remember to remove these before roasting as melted plastic does nothing to enhance the flavour of the meat!

Use the neck for stock (see page 86). The liver, kidneys and heart are best kept frozen until you have a number of them. They will then make a great Balti stir-fry dish (using, for example, the recipe on page 56).

types of egg

The smallest egg shown is a quail's egg. then there's a bantam, poussin, and the four main classes of hen's eggs

An egg is protected by an inedible calcified shell which accounts for about 12 per cent of its total weight. It can be blue in the case of water birds, or it may be speckled. Chicken egg shells are white or brown. There is no difference between the eggs' contents, but brown seems to be preferred by the consumer. Within the egg's shell are a transparent fluid, the albumen, which contains some protein, and turns white and solid when cooked, and the yellow yolk, which nourishes the embryo. The yolk contains protein, fat, potassium and sodium. Some eggs contain two yolks. There are three grades and seven sizes of egg in EU countries. Grade A is fresh, Grade B is less fresh and Grade C has been refrigerated for some weeks and is almost exclusively used in food manufacturing. Size 1 is 70 g (almost 2½ oz) or over, size 4, at 55–60 g (around 2 oz), is the egg most commonly sold. Size 7 is 45 g (around 1½ oz) or under. Goose and turkey eggs are twice the size of chicken eggs and taste richer, as do duck eggs, which are about 10 per cent larger. Quails' eggs weigh about 15–20 g (around ½–¾ oz). Chicken eggs provide 76 calories per 100 g (3½ oz). Vegans will not eat eggs or any dish prepared with eggs at all.

handling poultry

Poultry has earned itself a bad reputation concerning salmonella which is endemic in, but causes no harm to certain animal hosts, especially poultry. It spreads particularly extensively when birds are kept in close confinement. Salmonella is not present in all poultry or game. Mostly, it is transmitted as a result of bad farming and bad feeding. Sadly, though, it is estimated that a fair proportion of battery-farmed poultry have the disease. Reputable retailers inspect their suppliers to satisfy themselves that all precautions have been taken. The salmonella bacteria cause food poisoning amongst humans, resulting in illness, or even death. Salmonella is easily killed at a minimum temperature of 77°C/170°F. Chicken should never therefore be served rare. In any case no Balti recipe would produce rare meat. However some further precautions are essential:

1 Buy only top-quality raw poultry or game and only from reputable poulterers or supermarkets. Avoid cheap sources. Selling meat in unrefrigerated conditions contravenes the Health Act, and is illegal.

2 Use it on the day of purchase or freeze it.
3 Keep it covered until required and in the fridge before and after preparation and cutting.
4 It is raw meat which can spread the bacteria. Always keep, prepare and cut the raw meat separately from other ingredients, especially cooked cold meats, salads, bread and other items eaten raw, and/or cold.
5 As soon as the meat is cut and prepared, wash the chopping board, work surface, dishes and knives in very hot disinfected water.
6 Store the raw meat in its own covered container at the lowest point in the fridge, where it can't drip on to other food (the lowest salad compartment is a good place).
7 If your poultry or game is frozen, it must be completely thawed in its own container.
8 As stated earlier, cook thoroughly at a minimum temperature of 77°C/170°F until it is ceases to be rare (or pink) at the centre of the meat, as all of my recipes indicate.
9 Once cooked, eat meat within 30 minutes, or cool and refrigerate or freeze it.

poultry baking

Although the recipes in this book do not require roasting, this information is given for reference purposes. A baking recipe for Kurzi chicken appears in this book's companion volume, the *Curry Bible*.

Whole birds require oven-baking or roasting, their timings relating to their carcass weight. Joints require less time than whole birds. The oven is preheated to 190°C /375°F /Gas 5.

Here are baking times for whole carcasses:

110–150 g (4–5 oz), i.e. quail, snipe and woodcock – 15 minutes
350–400 g (12–14 oz), i.e. partridge squab – 20-30 minutes
450 g (1 lb) – 40 minutes
For weights over 450 g (1 lb) – 40 minutes for the first 450 g (1 lb) plus 4 minutes per 110 g (¼ lb) thereafter OR 45 minutes for the first 500 g plus 3½ minutes per 100 g (3½ oz) thereafter

◆ Balti Chicken Tikka Masala Curry

THIS IS THE BALTI RESTAURANT VERSION OF THE UK'S MOST POPULAR CURRY DISH.

serves 4

675 g (1½ lb) chicken, weighed after discarding unwanted matter, including skin and bones and diced into 3 cm (1¼ in) cubes (see Chef's Tip, page 84)
2–3 tablespoons ghee or corn oil
3–6 garlic cloves, finely chopped
225 g (8 oz) onion, very finely chopped
1–2 tablespoons Balti masala paste (see page 39)
1–2 tandoori paste (see page 40)
150 ml (7 fl oz) cream of tomato soup
2 tablespoons coconut milk powder
1 tablespoon mango chutney, finely chopped
1 tablespoon Balti garam masala (see page 41)
1 tablespoon fresh coriander leaves, very finely chopped
aromatic salt to taste (see page 43)
FOR THE MARINADE
300 g (10 oz) Greek yoghurt
1 tablespoon dry fenugreek leaves, ground
1 tablespoon dry mint, ground
2 tablespoons tandoori paste (see page 40)
⅛ teaspoon orange/red dry food colouring (optional)
½ teaspoon salt

◆◆◆◆◆◆◆◆◆◆◆◆◆◆◆◆◆◆◆◆◆◆◆◆◆◆◆◆◆

1 Mix together the marinade ingredients in a non-metallic bowl. Immerse the chicken pieces, cover and place in the fridge to marinate (see left)
2 After marination, heat half the ghee in the Balti pan or wok. Spoon half the chicken and its marinade into the pan and briskly stir-fry for 5 minutes. Remove and repeat with the other half.
3 Clean the pan and heat the remaining ghee or oil on high heat. Stir-fry the garlic for 30 seconds.
2 Add the onion and, reducing the heat, stir-fry for about 10 minutes, allowing it to become translucent and

...gin to brown.

Add the masala and tandoori pastes ...d the chicken. Raise the heat and ...ing to a brisk sizzle, stir-frying as ...eeded for about 5 minutes.

Add the tomato soup and any ...maining marinade. Simmer and stir-fry ...a lower heat for about 10 minutes. ...ote: it reduces quicker if you add the ...ock and the soup bit by bit.)

To test that the chicken is cooked ...ght through remove a piece and cut it ...two. (Replace the halves in the pan ...ter testing.) If more cooking is needed ...ep testing. When it is as you like it, ...d the coconut milk powder, mango ...utney, garam masala, fresh coriander ...aves and salt to taste.

Simmer a while longer then serve.

◆ Balti Chicken ...eera Curry

...ERA IS CUMMIN. HERE WE USE BOTH GROUND ...D WHOLE CUMMIN, AND, WITH A LITTLE BALTI ...RAM MASALA AND BUTTER, HEY PRESTO, WE ...VE ONE OF THIS BOOK'S SIMPLEST YET TASTIEST ...LTIS.

...rves 4

...5 g (1½ lb) chicken breast, skinned and
  filleted
...) g (2 oz) butter, any type
...tablespoon cummin seeds
...tablespoon ground cummin
...tablespoon Balti garam masala (see
  page 41)
...0 ml (¼ pint) Balti chicken stock (see
  page 86) or water
...omatic salt to taste (see page 43)

...◆◆◆◆◆◆◆◆◆◆◆◆◆◆◆◆◆◆◆◆◆◆◆◆◆◆◆◆◆

Cut the chicken into chunks of about ...cm (1½ in) square.

Heat the butter in your Balti pan or ...ok to quite a high heat, but watch it ...esn't burn. Add the seeds and stir-fry ...r about 30 seconds. Add the ground ...mmin and garam masala and continue ...stir-fry for a further 30 seconds, then

add 3 or 4 tablespoons of stock or water and stir-fry for about 2 or 3 minutes more.

3 Add the chicken pieces and briskly stir-fry for about 2 minutes, then lower the heat a little, and over the next 5 minutes add the remaining stock or water, stirring as necessary.

4 To finish off, turn up the heat and resume brisk stirring for about 5 minutes to reduce the remaining liquid to form a dryish gravy and coating.

5 Check that the chicken is cooked by cutting a piece in half. It should be white right through. If not continue stir-frying until it is. Salt to taste and serve as a starter with chutneys or as a main course with puris.

◆ Balti Chicken Vindaloo Curry

CHICKEN, CHUNKS OF POTATO AND COPIOUS AMOUNTS OF CHILLI POWDER COMBINE TO CREATE A HOT BUT TASTY BALTI DISH.

serves 4

675 g (1½ lb) chicken, weighed after
  discarding unwanted matter, including
  skin and bones and diced into 3 cm
  (1¼ in) cubes (see Chef's Tip, page 84)
2–3 tablespoons ghee or corn oil
2–4 teaspoons chilli powder
3–6 garlic cloves, finely chopped
225 g (8 oz) onion, very finely chopped
3–4 tablespoons Balti masala paste (see
  page 39)
150 ml (7 fl oz) Balti chicken stock (see page
  86) or water
3–6 fresh red or green chillies, chopped
2 teaspoons fenugreek leaf
1 large potato, cooked, peeled and
  quartered
1 tablespoon Balti garam masala (see
  page 41)
1 tablespoon fresh coriander leaves, very
  finely chopped
aromatic salt to taste (see page 43)

◆◆◆◆◆◆◆◆◆◆◆◆◆◆◆◆◆◆◆◆◆◆◆◆◆◆◆◆◆◆

1 Heat the ghee or oil in your Balti pan or wok on high heat. Stir-fry the chilli powder and garlic for 30 seconds.
2 Add the onion and, reducing the heat, stir-fry for about 10 minutes, allowing it to become translucent and begin to brown.
3 Add the masala paste and the chicken. Raise the heat and bring to a brisk sizzle, stir-frying as needed for about 5 minutes.
4 Add the stock or water, chillies and fenugreek. Simmer and stir-fry on a lower heat for about 10 minutes. (Note: it reduces quicker if you add the stock bit by bit.)
5 To test that the chicken is cooked right through remove a piece and cut it in two. (Replace the halves in the pan after testing.) If more cooking is needed keep testing. When it is as you like it, add the potato, garam masala, fresh coriander leaves and salt to taste.

MARINATION
Score or cube your chicken and coat in marinade. It can be stored for up to 60 hours in the fridge but see tips on handling poultry, on page 100.

◆ Balti Murgh Masala Roast Chicken

THIS DISH REQUIRES A WHOLE SKINNED CHICKEN TO BE MARINATED THEN BAKED (OR ROASTED).

serves 4

1–1.8 kg (4 lb) roasting chicken, skinned (optionally boned), giblets removed (see page 99)
20–25 large spinach leaves, stalks trimmed off
MARINADE
3 tablespoons Balti masala paste (see page 39)
1 tablespoon Balti garam masala (see page 41)
1–3 teaspoons chilli powder (optional)
1 tablespoon fresh mint leaf, finely chopped
1 tablespoon fresh coriander leaves, finely chopped
3 garlic cloves, finely chopped
300 g (10 oz) Greek yoghurt
1 teaspoon salt
STUFFING
2 or 3 cupfuls plain rice, cooked

◆◆◆◆◆◆◆◆◆◆◆◆◆◆◆◆◆◆◆◆◆◆◆◆◆◆◆◆◆◆◆

1 Clean the chicken inside and out. Pat dry with kitchen paper. Make small incisions with your knife point in the deepest parts of the flesh.
2 Mix the marinade ingredients together.
3 Coat the chicken generously with the marinade then place in a non-metallic container. Cover it and refrigerate for 24 hours.
4 After that time: soften the spinach by steaming it for a minute (or microwaving for 30 seconds).
5 Preheat the oven to 375°F/190°C/ Gas 5. Stuff the chicken with the cold rice, then re-coat it with any excess marinade.
6 Carefully place the softened spinach leaves all over the chicken until it is totally covered. Keep on adding leaves until they are all used up.
7 Carefully cover with kitchen foil and place in the preheated oven on a rack above a tray.
8 Bake for about 1½ hours (see page 100). Check that it is cooked by removing the foil from a leg area and poking a small knife blade into the flesh. If the liquid runs out clear it is ready to be served with a delicious bread or rice and Balti vegetables. (If it needs more cooking replace the foil and return it to the oven.)

◆ Balti Chicken Methi Curry

METHI CURRIES CONTAIN FENUGREEK LEAF OR SEED, WHICH CREATES A VERY SAVOURY BALTI TASTE. FRESH FENUGREEK LEAF IS ALWAYS AVAILABLE FROM ASIAN GROCERS.

serves 4

675 g (1½ lb) chicken, weighed after discarding unwanted matter, including skin and bones and diced into 3 cm (1¼ in) cubes (see Chef's Tip, page 84)
2–3 tablespoons ghee or corn oil
3–6 garlic cloves, finely chopped
225 (8 z) onion, very finely chopped
3–4 tablespoons Balti masala paste (see page 39)
150 ml (7 fl oz) Balti chicken stock (see page 86) or water
1 tablespoon dried ground fenugreek leaf
OR 4 tablespoons fresh fenugreek leaf, de-stalked and chopped
1 tablespoon Balti garam masala (see page 41)
110 g (4 oz) rocket leaf, chopped
1 tablespoon fresh coriander leaves, very finely chopped
aromatic salt to taste (see page 43)
SPICES
1 teaspoon white cummin seeds
½ teaspoon black onion seeds

◆◆◆◆◆◆◆◆◆◆◆◆◆◆◆◆◆◆◆◆◆◆◆◆◆◆◆◆◆◆◆

1 Heat the ghee or oil in your Balti pan or wok on high heat. Stir-fry the spices and the garlic for 30 seconds.
2 Add the onion and, reducing the heat, stir-fry for about 10 minutes, allowing it to become translucent and begin to brown.
3 Add the masala paste and the chicken. Raise the heat and bring to a brisk sizzle, stir-frying as needed for about 5 minutes.
4 Add a little stock or water and the fenugreek leaf. Simmer and stir-fry on lower heat for about 10 minutes. (Note it reduces quicker if you add the stock bit by bit.)
5 To test that the chicken is cooked right through remove a piece and cut it in two. (Replace the halves in the pan after testing.) If more cooking is needed keep testing.
6 When it is as you like it, stir in the garam masala, rocket leaf, fresh coriander leaves and salt to taste. Give a final 5 or 10 minutes simmering, then serve.

Balti Turkey Methi Curry

Balti Chicken ?hal Curry

AL IS SERIOUSLY HOT, AND NOT TO BE EATEN BY
E UNINITIATED. SERIOUS CHILLI-HEADS WILL
JOY THE 'EXTRA-HOT' CHILLI POWDER AND MAY
P UP WITH SCOTCH BONNET OR HABAÑERO
ILLIES, THE HOTTEST AVAILABLE.

rves 4

'5 g (1½ lb) chicken, weighed after
 discarding unwanted matter, including
 skin and bones and diced into 3 cm
 (1¼ in) cubes (see Chef's Tip, page 84)
-3 tablespoons ghee or corn oil
or more teaspoons extra hot chilli powder
-6 garlic cloves, finely chopped
.5g (8 oz) onion, very finely chopped
tablespoons Balti masala paste (see
 page 39)
tablespoons tandoori paste (see page 40)
'5 g (6 oz) canned plum tomatoes,
 chopped
-8 fresh red and/or green chillies, whole or
 chopped
tablespoon vinegar, any type
0 ml (7 fl oz) Balti chicken stock (see page
 86) or water
tablespoon Balti garam masala (see
 page 41)
tablespoon fresh coriander leaves, very
 finely chopped
omatic salt to taste (see page 43)
ARNISH
esh coriander leaves

◆◆◆◆◆◆◆◆◆◆◆◆◆◆◆◆◆◆◆◆◆◆◆◆◆◆◆◆

Heat the ghee or oil in your Balti pan
wok on high heat. Stir-fry the chilli
owder and garlic for 30 seconds.
Add the onion and, reducing the
eat, stir-fry for about 10 minutes,
lowing it to become translucent and
egin to brown.
Add the masala and tandoori pastes
d the chicken. Raise the heat and
ring to a brisk sizzle, stir-frying as
eeded for about 5 minutes.
Add the tomatoes, fresh chillies,

alti Chicken Podina Curry

vinegar and a little stock or water.
Simmer and stir-fry on a lower heat for
about 10 minutes. (Note: it reduces
quicker if you add the stock bit by bit.)
5 To test that the chicken is cooked
right through remove a piece and cut it
in two. If more cooking is needed keep
testing. When it is as you like it, add the
garam masala, fresh coriander leaves
and salt to taste.
6 Garnish and serve.

◆ Balti Chicken Podina Curry

A DELICIOUS CREAMY CURRY WITH DELICATE
FLAVOURS OF CORIANDER AND MINT.

serves 4

675 g (1½ lb) chicken, weighed after
 discarding unwanted matter, including
 skin and bones and diced into 3 cm
 (1¼ in) cubes (see Chef's Tip, page 84)
FOR THE MARINADE
150 g (5 oz) natural yoghurt
1 teaspoon bottled minced coriander
6 tablespoons fresh spearmint, de-stalked
 and chopped
1 tablespoon green masala paste (see
 page 45)
SPICES
1 tablespoon coriander seeds
1 teaspoon green cardamom pods
1 teaspoon aniseed

2–3 tablespoons ghee or corn oil
1–2 garlic cloves, finely chopped
4–6 spring onions, bulbs and leaves, finely
 chopped
50 ml (2 fl oz) Balti chicken stock (see page
 86) or water
100 ml (3½ fl oz) single cream
1 tablespoon Balti garam masala (see
 page 41)
1 tablespoon fresh coriander leaves, very
 finely chopped
aromatic salt to taste (see page 43)
GARNISH
fresh mint leaves

◆◆◆◆◆◆◆◆◆◆◆◆◆◆◆◆◆◆◆◆◆◆◆◆◆◆◆◆

1 Roast and grind the spices (see page
41).
2 Mix the chicken with the marinade
ingredients. Cover and refrigerate to
marinate (see page 101).
3 Heat the ghee or oil in your Balti pan
or wok on high heat. Stir-fry the spices
and garlic for 30 seconds.
4 Add the onion and, reducing the
heat, stir-fry for about 2 minutes.
3 Add the chicken and all the marinade.
Raise the heat and bring to a brisk sizzle,
stir-frying as needed for about
5 minutes.
4 Add the stock or water. Simmer and
stir-fry on a lower heat for about
5 minutes.
5 Add the cream and keep simmering
for a further 5 minutes.
6 To test that the chicken is cooked
right through remove a piece and cut it
in two. (Replace the halves in the pan
after testing.) If more cooking is needed
keep testing. When it is as you like it,
add the garam masala, fresh coriander
leaves and salt to taste.
7 Simmer for a while longer, then
garnish and serve.

◆ Balti Chicken Rezala Curry

A RICH CREAMY CURRY (ORIGINALLY FROM BANGLADESH) BUT NOT MILD – WATCH THOSE CHILLIES, TEMPERED AS THEY MAY BE BY RAISINS.

serves 4

675 g (1½ lb) chicken, weighed after discarding unwanted matter, diced into 3 cm (1¼ in) cubes
3–4 tablespoons ghee or corn oil
10 garlic cloves, very finely chopped
225 g (8 oz) onion, very finely chopped
3–4 tablespoons Balti masala paste (see page 39)
3 or 4 fresh green chillies, sliced lengthways
410 g (1 lb) canned evaporated milk
20–30 strands saffron (optional)
1 tablespoon raisins (optional)
2 teaspoons white granulated sugar
2 tablespoons pistachio nuts, chopped
1 tablespoon ground almonds
1 tablespoon Balti garam masala (see page 41)
1 tablespoon fresh coriander leaves, very finely chopped
1 tablespoon rose water (optional)
aromatic salt to taste (see page 43)
SPICES
1 teaspoon turmeric
12 green cardamoms, crushed
3–4 5 cm (2 in) pieces cassia bark
2 teaspoons panch phoran (see page 43)

◆◆◆◆◆◆◆◆◆◆◆◆◆◆◆◆◆◆◆◆◆◆◆◆◆◆◆◆◆◆◆◆◆◆◆

1 Heat the ghee or oil in your Balti pan or wok on high heat. Stir-fry the spices and the garlic for 30 seconds.
2 Add the onion and, reducing the heat, stir-fry for about 10 minutes, allowing it to become translucent and begin to brown.
3 Add the masala paste, the chillies and the chicken. Raise the heat and bring to a brisk sizzle, stir-frying as needed for about 5 minutes.
4 Add a little evaporated milk, plus the saffron and raisins (if using), sugar, pistachio nuts and ground almonds. Simmer and stir-fry on a lower heat for about 10 minutes, adding the rest of the milk bit by bit.
5 To test that the chicken is cooked right through remove a piece and cut it in two. (Replace in the pan after testing.) If more cooking is needed keep testing. When it is as you like it, add the garam masala, fresh coriander, rosewater and salt to taste.

◆ Balti Chicken Rhogan Josh Curry

LITERALLY MEANING COOKED IN GHEE IN RED GRAVY, THE AUTHENTIC RHOGAN JOSH ORIGINATED AS A MEAT DISH IN KASHMIR AT THE TIME OF THE MOGHUL EMPERORS. IT USES AROMATIC WHOLE SPICES AND THE BALTI HOUSE VERSION INCORPORATES RED PEPPER FOR COLOUR.

serves 4

675 g (1½ lb) chicken, weighed after discarding unwanted matter, diced into 3 cm (1¼ in) cubes
2–3 tablespoons ghee or corn oil
3–6 garlic cloves, finely chopped
225 g (8 oz) onion, very finely chopped
3–4 tablespoons Balti masala paste (see page 39)
150 ml (7 fl oz) Balti chicken stock (see page 86) or water
1 tablespoon tomato purée
2 tablespoons ground almonds
1 red pepper, cut into diamonds
50 g (2 oz) fresh beetroot, peeled and shredded (optional)
1 tablespoon Balti garam masala (see page 41)
1 tablespoon fresh coriander leaves, very finely chopped
aromatic salt to taste (see page 43)
SPICES
6 cloves
2 bay leaves
1 5 cm (2 in) piece cassia bark
2 brown cardamoms
4 green cardamoms
½ teaspoon black cummin seeds
½ teaspoon paprika

◆◆◆◆◆◆◆◆◆◆◆◆◆◆◆◆◆◆◆◆◆◆◆◆◆◆◆◆◆◆◆◆◆◆◆

1 Heat the ghee or oil in your Balti pan or wok on high heat. Stir-fry spices and the garlic for 30 seconds.
2 Add the onion and, reducing the heat, stir-fry for about 10 minutes, allowing it to become translucent and begin to brown.
3 Add the masala paste and the chicken. Raise the heat and bring to a brisk sizzle, stir-frying as needed for about 5 minutes.
4 Add a little stock or water, and the tomato purée, ground almonds, red pepper and beetroot (if using). Simmer and stir-fry on a lower heat for about 10 minutes. (Note: it reduces quicker if you add the stock bit by bit.)
5 To test that the chicken is cooked right through remove a piece and cut it in two. (Replace the halves in the pan after testing.) If more cooking is needed keep testing. When it is as you like it, add the garam masala, fresh coriander leaves and salt to taste.

> **CHEF'S TIP**
> *To cut a pepper into diamonds: cut the top off the pepper (where the stalk used to be) and the bottom. Stand the pepper on one end and cut down through the flesh. Open it out and pare off and discard the pith and seeds. You should now have a more or less rectangular shape which you can easily cut into equal-sized diamonds, strips, squares or rectangles.*

Balti Partridge Rezala Curry

Fish & Shellfish

There is more water on our planet than land, and fishing was routine for hunter-gatherer tribes, long before man learned about agriculture. Fish were farmed by the ancient Egyptians, and preserved examples were discovered in the pyramids. Half the world's population catch fish, and even more eat it as their main protein intake, but not everyone likes fish. The British are rather unadventurous in their fish-eating. The Baltis are not particularly fond of fish either. In fact, Baltistan is over 900 miles from the sea, and at 16,000 feet, it seems unlikely that there would be any fish at all in the area. However, it is fed by countless streams, which pour down the mountains towering high above the Balti valleys, into the great river Indus. Add the numerous glacial lakes, and there is no shortage of fresh water fish and shellfish in the area.

The INGREDIENTS FILE in this chapter describes examples of the enormous range (it is estimated that there are over 20,000 edible fish species) of white round and flat fish and oily fish from the sea, freshwater, smoked and exotic fish and shellfish. Fish is tasty, nutritious and amazingly good for one's health, and these days many types are available fresh – even the tropical exotics – from our fishmongers and supermarkets. (And if a particular species is out of season, it is generally available frozen.) All of these ingredients work well curried Balti-style. The recipes which follow, and some in the Starters chapter, can be made with any variety from the FILE. Feel free to substitute the specified fish in any of the recipes in this chapter, for any other fish or shellfish.

◆ Balti Kampo

THE ART OF DRYING OR SMOKING FISH TO PRESERVE IT IS AN ANCIENT SKILL. FISH CAUGHT IN SUMMER ARE WINTER STAPLES WHEN THE LAKES AND RIVERS FREEZE OVER. SMOKED HADDOCK IS READILY AVAILABLE AND CREATES A FASCINATING BALTI DISH.

serves 4

657 g (1½ lb) smoked haddock (also called Finnan Haddies), weighed after filleting and skinning
2–3 tablespoons ghee or corn oil
3–6 garlic cloves, finely chopped
225 g (8 oz) onion, very finely chopped
3–4 tablespoons Balti masala paste (see page 39)
175 ml (6 fl oz) milk
3 fl oz (85 ml) single cream
1 tablespoon white granulated sugar
1 teaspoon Balti garam masala (see page 41)
1 tablespoon fresh coriander leaves, very finely chopped
aromatic salt to taste (see page 43)
SPICES
½ teaspoon lovage seeds
¼ teaspoon wild onion seeds

◆◆◆◆◆◆◆◆◆◆◆◆◆◆◆◆◆◆◆◆◆◆◆◆◆◆

1 Heat the ghee or oil in your Balti pan or wok on high heat. Stir-fry the spices and garlic for 30 seconds.
2 Add the onions and reducing the heat, stir-fry for about 10 minutes, allowing them to become translucent and begin to brown.
3 Add the masala paste and the fish. Raise the heat and bring to a brisk sizzle, stir-frying as needed for about 2 minutes.
4 Add the milk. Simmer and stir-fry on a lower heat for about 10 minutes. (Note: it reduces quicker if you add the milk bit by bit.)
5 When the fish is cooked right through, add the cream, sugar, garam masala, fresh coriander leaves and salt to taste.
6 Simmer for a while longer then serve.

Previous pages: Balti Kampo

◆ Basic Balti Fish Curry

THIS IS THE STANDARD BENCHMARK MEDIUM-HEAT BALTI PREPARATION. IT COMPRISES TENDER, BITE-SIZED CUBES OF FISH IN A GOLDEN-BROWN SPICY GRAVY – NOT TOO HOT, NOT TOO MILD.

serves 4

675 g (1½ lb) whole fish, filleted (or steaks) – any type
2–3 tablespoons ghee or corn oil
3–6 garlic cloves, finely chopped
225 g (8 oz) onion, very finely chopped
3–4 tablespoons Balti masala paste (see page 39)
175 ml (6 fl oz) milk
1 teaspoon Balti garam masala (see page 41)
1 tablespoon fresh coriander leaves, very finely chopped
aromatic salt to taste (see page 43)

◆◆◆◆◆◆◆◆◆◆◆◆◆◆◆◆◆◆◆◆◆◆◆◆◆◆

1 Heat the ghee or oil in your Balti pan or wok on high heat. Stir-fry the garlic for 30 seconds.
2 Add the onions and reducing the heat, stir-fry for about 10 minutes, allowing them to become translucent and begin to brown.
3 Add the masala paste and the fish. Raise the heat and bring to a brisk sizzle, stir-frying as needed for about 5 minutes.
4 Add the milk. Simmer and stir-fry on a lower heat for about 10 minutes. (Note: it reduces quicker if you add the milk bit by bit.)
5 To test that the fish is cooked right through. Remove a piece and cut it in two. (Replace the halves in the pan after

NOTE:
You can substitute shellfish (such as prawns, king prawns, lobster, crab, oyster, mussels, scallops) for fish in these recipes. For details see Ingredients file, pages 122–125.

testing.) If more cooking is needed keep testing. When it is as you like it, add the garam masala, fresh coriander leaves and salt to taste.

NOTE: you can use prawns and shellfish in place of white fish in this recipe. If using raw prawns, simply substitute peeled, raw prawns of any size for the 675 g (1½ lb) fish. For cooked prawns, reduce the cooking time of stage 3 to 2 minutes, and stage 4 to 3 minutes.

◆ Balti King Prawn Garlic Curry

IT'S REMARKABLE HOW FEW INGREDIENTS IT TAKES TO MAKE SUCH A TASTY DISH.

serves 4

24 large king prawns, peeled
4 tablespoons butter, any type
12 garlic cloves, finely chopped
3–4 tablespoons Balti masala paste (see page 39)
85 ml (3 fl oz) fragrant stock (see page 43) or water
1 tablespoon fresh coriander leaves, very finely chopped
aromatic salt to taste (see page 43)
GARNISH
fresh coriander leaves

◆◆◆◆◆◆◆◆◆◆◆◆◆◆◆◆◆◆◆◆◆◆◆◆◆◆

1 Heat the butter in your Balti pan or wok to quite a high heat, but watch it doesn't burn. Add the garlic and stir-fry for about 30 seconds.
2 Add the masala paste and continue to stir-fry for a further 30 seconds, then add 3 or 4 tablespoons of stock or water and stir-fry for about 2 or 3 minutes more.
3 Add the prawns and briskly stir-fry for about 2 minutes, then lower the heat a little and over the next 5 minutes add the remaining stock or water and the coriander leaves, stirring as necessary.
4 To finish off, turn up the heat and resume brisk stirring for about 2 minutes

o reduce the remaining liquid to form a dryish gravy and coating. Salt to taste, garnish and serve.

◆ Balti Jalfrezi Fish

JALFREZI MEANS DRY STIR-FRY. THE BRIEF COOKING TIME AND THE FRESHNESS OF THE INGREDIENTS — CHILLIES, FRESH GARLIC, GINGER, ONION, PEPPERS AND CORIANDER — COMBINE TO ACHIEVE A LIGHTNESS OF TOUCH.

serves 4

675 g (1½ lb) whole fish, filleted (or steaks)
   – any type – cut into bite-sized cubes
2–3 tablespoons ghee or corn oil
3–6 garlic cloves, finely chopped
2.5 cm (1 in) cube ginger, thinly sliced
110 g (4 oz) onion, thinly sliced
3 or 4 spring onions, bulbs and leaves,
   chopped
2–3 tablespoons Balti masala paste (see
   page 39)
1 tablespoon green masala paste (see
   page 45)
½ a red pepper, cut into small diamond
   shapes
½ a green pepper, cut into small diamond
   shapes
1–3 fresh green chillies, chopped
50 ml (2 fl oz) Balti fragrant stock (see page
   43) or water
1 tablespoon Balti garam masala (see
   page 41)
1 tablespoon fresh coriander leaves, very
   finely chopped
aromatic salt to taste (see page 43)
SPICES
1½ teaspoons cummin seeds
½ teaspoon lovage seeds
½ teaspoon coriander seeds
GARNISH
squeezes of lemon juice
sprinkles of Balti garam masala
fresh coriander leaves

◆◆◆◆◆◆◆◆◆◆◆◆◆◆◆◆◆◆◆◆◆◆◆◆◆

1 Heat the ghee or oil in your Balti pan or wok on high heat. Stir-fry the spices, garlic and ginger for 30 seconds.
2 Add both types of onion and stir-fry

for about 3 minutes.
3 Add the masala and green pastes, the peppers, chillies and the fish. Raise the heat and bring to a brisk sizzle, stir-frying as needed for about 5 minutes.
4 Add the stock or water. Simmer and stir-fry on a lower heat for about 10 minutes. (Note: it reduces quicker if you add the stock bit by bit.)
5 To test that the fish is cooked right through remove a piece and cut it in two. (Replace the halves in the pan after testing.) If more cooking is needed keep testing. When it is as you like it, add the garam masala, fresh coriander leaves and salt to taste.
6 Garnish and serve.

◆ Balti Ceylon Fish Curry

IN THIS DISH COCONUT, LEMON AND CHILLIES ARE ADDED TO THE STANDARD MEDIUM BALTI BASE SAUCE. THE RESULTING CURRY IS EVOCATIVE OF THE BALMY, PALMY, SUNNY LAND OF SRI LANKA. THE TART HOTNESS SHOULD BE TEMPERED BY THE COCONUT.

serves 4

675 g (1½ lb) whole fish, filleted (or steaks)
   – any type – cut into bite-sized cubes
2–3 tablespoons ghee or corn oil
2 teaspoons panch phoran (see page 43)
3–6 garlic cloves, finely chopped
225 g (8 oz) onion, very finely chopped
1–2 fresh green chillies, sliced
3–4 tablespoons Balti masala paste (see
   page 39)
175 ml (6 fl oz) milk
60 g (2 oz) creamed coconut block, chopped
juice of 1 lemon
1 teaspoon Balti garam masala (see page 41)
1 tablespoon fresh coriander leaves, very
   finely chopped
aromatic salt to taste (see page 43)

◆◆◆◆◆◆◆◆◆◆◆◆◆◆◆◆◆◆◆◆◆◆◆◆◆

1 Heat the ghee or oil in your Balti pan or wok on high heat. Stir-fry the panch phoran and garlic for 30 seconds.
2 Add the onions and chillies and, reducing the heat, stir-fry for about 10 minutes, allowing the onions to become translucent and begin to brown.
3 Add the masala paste and the fish. Raise the heat and bring to a brisk sizzle, stir-frying as needed for about 5 minutes.
4 Add the milk and creamed coconut. Simmer and stir-fry on a lower heat for about 10 minutes. (Note: it reduces quicker if you add the milk bit by bit.)
5 To test that the fish is cooked right through remove a piece and cut it in two. (Replace the halves in the pan after testing.) If more cooking is needed keep testing. When it is as you like it, add the lemon juice, garam masala, fresh coriander leaves and salt to taste.

FISH

Fish is quick and easy to cook. It is high in protein, low in cholesterol and a particularly good source of vitamins A, D and E. The oil in fish is polyunsaturated and is regarded as healthier than that in meat.

Fish come in all colours, shapes and sizes, the least beautiful perhaps being the monkfish, and the sleekest the shark. The largest edible fish is the tuna. An adult blue-fin tuna measures 3 m (10 feet) and weighs more than a beef carcass at 560 kg (half a ton). Even longer at 4.5 m (14½ feet) is the swordfish although it weighs less. At the other extreme is whitebait, the young of any round fish (usually the herring) which is a maximum of 32 mm (1¼ in).

The meat of most raw white fish is between 70 and 107 calories per 100 g (3½ oz). Most oily fish is between 196 and 323 calories per 100 g (3½ oz).

A wide range of fish are described here, together with tips for buying and handling them.

TYPES OF FISH

Fish is classified into two main types – freshwater and sea fish. Each of these types has three main categories: white fish, oily fish and shellfish.

white fish

White fish can be subdivided into two groups: round and flat. In both cases, the flesh of the fish is juicy and tasty, and it is not oily. Larger species produce quite big skinned and filleted steaks. Cod, hake, ling and monkfish, halibut and skate, catfish, pike and salmon are examples.

WHITE FISH, ROUND

A 600 g grey mullet and a 125 g cod steak

The larger round species are available as steaks, on or off the bone. Smaller round species are sold whole, trimmed, filleted and skinned as required.

Large species of round fish – over 1.5 m (almost 5 feet) – include: catfish (rockfish), conger eel, cod, hake, ling, monkfish (angler fish).

Medium species – up to 1.5 m (under 5 feet) – include: bass, chub, codling, coley, haddock, huss (dogfish), John Dory, grey mullet, perch, pollack, sea bream (black).

Small species – up to 50 cm (20 in) – include: codling, gurnard, red mullet, sea bream (red), whiting.

WHITE FISH, FLAT

he larger flat species are available as
eaks, on or off the bone. Smaller flat
pecies are sold whole, trimmed or
lleted as required.
Large species of flat fish – over 1.5 m
feet) – include: halibut and skate.
.edium species – up to 1.5 m (5 feet) –
clude: brill, flounder, plaice, lemon
le, Dover sole, turbot and witch sole.
mall species – up to 50 cm (20 in) –
clude: dab and megrim.

ght: whole Dover sole, 260 g

Above: skate wing, 350 g

Above: plaice fillets, 330 g

oily fish

ily fish has a high fatty acid/
olyunsaturated oil content, which can
elp to prevent blood clots. It is also
ood source of vitamins A and D, and
rtain minerals. Tuna is a large oily
ecies (see exotics). Smaller species are
ld trimmed or filleted as required.
Medium oily fish species – over 50 cm
0 in) – include: herring and mackerel
Very small species – up to 25 cm
0 in) include: anchovy, pilchard and
nelt.
Tiny species – under 12 cm (almost
in) include: sardine (young pilchard),
rats and whitebait.

Herring, 250 g

Whitebait, each 20 g

◆ Balti Fish Dhansak

ONE OF THE ALL-TIME BALTI FAVOURITES IN WHICH THE BALTI BASE IS THICKENED WITH CREAMY COOKED DHAL.

serves 4

540 g (1 lb 3 oz) whole fish, filleted (or
   steaks) – any type
4 tablespoons ghee or vegetable oil
4–6 garlic cloves, finely chopped
225 g (8 oz) onion, very finely chopped
2–3 fresh green chillies, finely chopped
2–3 tablespoons Balti masala paste (see
   page 39)
100 g (3½ oz) masoor dhal, cooked
200 g (7 oz) canned ratatouille, mashed
2 tablespoons brinjal pickle
1 tablespoon white granulated sugar
2 teaspoons vinegar, any type
2 teaspoons Balti garam masala (see page 41)
1 tablespoon fresh coriander leaves, very
   finely chopped
aromatic salt to taste (see page 43)
SPICES
1 teaspoon cummin seeds
½ teaspoon fenugreek seeds
GARNISH
fresh coriander leaves

◆◆◆◆◆◆◆◆◆◆◆◆◆◆◆◆◆◆◆◆◆◆◆◆◆◆◆◆◆◆

Heat the ghee or oil in your Balti pan or wok on high heat. Stir-fry the spices and garlic for 30 seconds.

Add the onions and chillies and, reducing the heat, stir-fry for about 10 minutes, allowing the onions to become translucent and begin to brown.

Add the masala paste and the fish. Raise the heat and bring to a brisk sizzle, stir-frying as needed for about 5 minutes.

Add the masoor dhal, ratatouille, brinjal pickle, sugar and vinegar. Simmer and stir-fry on a lower heat for about 10 minutes. (Note: you may need to add a little water to keep things mobile.)

To test that the fish is cooked right

Balti King Prawn Dansak

through remove a piece and cut it in two. (Replace the halves in the pan after testing.) If more cooking is needed keep testing. When it is as you like it, add the garam masala, fresh coriander leaves and salt to taste.

◆ Balti Fish Kofta Curry

FISH KOFTAS (OR RISSOLE BALLS) MAKE A LIGHT AND TASTY CURRY.

serves 4

THE KOFTAS
560 g (1¼ lb) filleted whole fish (or steaks)
   – any type
2 tablespoons gram flour
2 garlic cloves, finely chopped
2 tablespoons dehydrated onion flakes
1 tablespoon fresh coriander leaves, very
   finely chopped
1 tablespoon Balti masala paste (see
   page 39)
1 teaspoon garam masala (see page 41)
½ teaspoon salt
THE BALTI KOFTA CURRY GRAVY
1 tablespoon ghee or vegetable oil
2–3 garlic cloves, finely chopped
300 g (10½ oz) Balti masala gravy
   (see page 42)
1 tablespoon tomato purée
175 g (6 oz) canned tomatoes, strained,
   juice reserved
1 teaspoon white granulated sugar
½ teaspoon dried fenugreek leaf
1 tablespoon fresh coriander leaves, very
   finely chopped
1 tablespoon fresh basil leaves, very finely
chopped
aromatic salt to taste (see page 43)
GARNISH
fresh coriander leaves

◆◆◆◆◆◆◆◆◆◆◆◆◆◆◆◆◆◆◆◆◆◆◆◆◆◆◆◆◆◆

TO MAKE THE KOFTAS
1 Coarsely chop the fish. Run all the kofta ingredients through a food processor or twice through a hand mincer, to achieve a finely textured

paste.
2 Mix the paste thoroughly. Divide it into four equal parts. From each part roll 6 small balls (koftas).
3 Preheat the oven to 375°F/190°C/Gas5.
4 Put the 24 koftas on an oven tray and bake for 15 minutes.
TO MAKE THE BALTI KOFTA CURRY GRAVY
1 Heat the ghee or oil in the Balti pan or wok, and stir-fry the garlic for 30 seconds.
2 Add the Balti masala gravy, tomato purée, canned tomatoes, sugar and fenugreek leaf, and bring to the simmer.
3 Add the cooked koftas, with any juices they may have made, and stir-fry for about 3 minutes.
4 Add the remaining ingredients and salt to taste. Simmer for a few more minutes, adding the reserved tomato juice to keep things mobile.
5 Garnish and serve.

NOTE:
You can substitute shellfish (such as prawns, king prawns, lobster, crab, oyster, mussels, scallops) for fish in these recipes. For details see Ingredients file, pages 122–125.

freshwater fish

Any fish which inhabits inland lakes, streams or rivers fall into this category. Large freshwater fish species – over 1.5 m (5 feet) – include: catfish, pike and salmon.

Medium species – up to 1.5 m (5 feet) – include: carp, perch, salmon trout (sea trout), brown trout, rainbow trout and whitefish.

Small species – up to 50 cm (20 in) – include: grayling, roach and rudd. Very small species – up to 25 cm (10 in) – include: sprats

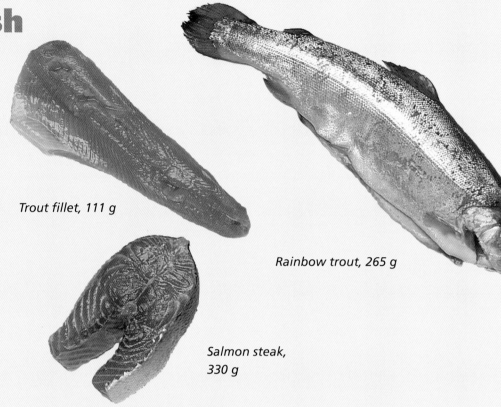

Trout fillet, 111 g

Rainbow trout, 265 g

Salmon steak, 330 g

exotic fish

Many exotic fish (that is those fish caught in tropical warm waters), also fall into the various categories above. There are thousands of exotic species, some of which are readily available fresh or frozen, including baracuda, croaker, drum, emperor bream, grouper, hilsa, marlin, rayfish, shark, snapper, swordfish and tuna.

Swordfish steak, 500 g

Tuna steak, 500 g

Tilapia

Pomfret

In the warm waters of the subcontinent are certain fish ideal for Balti curry cooking, particularly now that they are becoming more readily available fresh or frozen. These include rui or rhui, a kind of meaty, pink-fleshed carp; bekti, which is larger and white-fleshed with minimal bones; hilsa, a very bony type of herring; katla, a smaller carp; pomfret, a plump flattish, fleshy white fish; magur, a type of catfish; and boal, a kind of whiting.

◆ Balti Bhoona Prawn Curry

THIS IS A TASTY DRY CURRY.

serves 4

75 g (1½ lb) medium to large raw prawns, weighed after removing shells and heads
tablespoons ghee or vegetable oil
–6 garlic cloves, finely chopped
25 g (8 oz) onion, very finely chopped
–4 tablespoons Balti masala paste (see page 39)
5 ml (3 fl oz) milk
teaspoon Balti garam masala (see page 41)
tablespoon fresh coriander leaves, very finely chopped
romatic salt to taste (see page 43)

◆◆◆◆◆◆◆◆◆◆◆◆◆◆◆◆◆◆◆◆◆◆◆◆◆

Heat the ghee or oil in your Balti pan r wok on high heat. Stir-fry the garlic or 30 seconds.

Add the onions and, reducing the eat, stir-fry for about 10 minutes, llowing them to become translucent nd begin to brown.

Add the masala paste and the prawns. aise the heat and bring to a brisk sizzle, tir-frying as needed for about 5 inutes.

Add the milk. Simmer and stir-fry on a ower heat for about 10 minutes. (Note: reduces quicker if you add the milk bit y bit.)

Test that the prawns are cooked right hrough. Remove one and cut it in two. Replace the halves in the pan). If more ooking is needed keep testing. When it as you like it, add the garam masala, resh coriander leaves and salt to taste.

NOTE:
You can substitute shellfish (such as prawns, king prawns, lobster, crab, oyster, mussels, scallops) for fish in these recipes. For details see Ingredients file, pages 122–125.

◆ Balti Fish Dopiaza

LASHINGS OF ONIONS (PIAZA) ARE ADDED TO THE STANDARD BALTI BASE GRAVY TO CREATE A VERY SAVOURY DISH, TEMPERED WITH A HINT OF SWEETNESS.

serves 4

675 g (1½ lb) whole fish, filleted (or steaks) – any type – cut into bite-sized cubes
1 teaspoon panch phoran (see page 43)
2–3 garlic cloves, finely chopped
225 g (8 oz) onion, thinly sliced
4–6 spring onions, bulbs and leaves, chopped
3–4 tablespoons Balti masala paste (see page 39)
125 ml (4 fl oz) milk
1 tablespoon clear honey (optional)
1 tablespoon Balti garam masala (see page 41)
3 tablespoons fresh coriander leaves, very finely chopped
about 6 fresh basil leaves, chopped
aromatic salt to taste (see page 43)
GARNISH
fresh coriander leaves

◆◆◆◆◆◆◆◆◆◆◆◆◆◆◆◆◆◆◆◆◆◆◆◆◆◆

1 Heat the ghee or oil in your Balti pan or wok on high heat. Stir-fry the panch phoran for 20 seconds, then add the garlic and stir-fry for about 30 seconds more.
2 Add both types of onion and, reducing the heat, stir-fry for about 10 minutes, allowing them to become translucent and begin to brown.
3 Add the masala paste and the fish. Raise the heat and bring to a brisk sizzle, stir-frying as needed for about 5 minutes.
4 Add the milk and honey (if using). Simmer and stir-fry on a lower heat for about 10 minutes. (Note: it reduces quicker if you add the milk bit by bit.)
5 To test that the fish is cooked right through remove a piece and cut it in two. (Replace the halves in the pan after testing.) If more cooking is needed keep

testing. When it is as you like it, add the garam masala, fresh leaves and salt to taste.

◆ Balti Kashmiri Fish

THE AROMATIC SPICES, YOGHURT, AND NUTS COMBINE TO PRODUCE A SUPERB LIGHTLY AND AUTHENTICALLY FLAVOURED DISH. SERVE FRESH WITH NAAN BREAD AND CHUTNEY.

serves 4

675 g (1½ lb) filleted whole fish (or steaks) – any type
7 fl oz (200 ml) milk
½ teaspoon turmeric
2 tablespoons ghee or sesame oil
5 cm (2 in) cube ginger, finely chopped
110 g (4 oz) Greek yoghurt
aromatic salt to taste (see page 43)
SPICES
1 teaspoon cumin seeds
½ teaspoon coriander seeds
½ teaspoon fennel seeds
½ teaspoon lovage seeds
GARNISH
20–30 cashew nuts, fried and crumbled
1 tablespoon fresh herbs – coriander, parsley or basil

◆◆◆◆◆◆◆◆◆◆◆◆◆◆◆◆◆◆◆◆◆◆◆◆◆◆

1 Roast, cool and grind the spices.
2 Add the milk to the turmeric and soak the fish in it for 1½–2 hours.
3 Heat the ghee or oil in the Balti pan or wok and stir-fry the ground spices for 20 seconds. Add the ginger and continue for 20 more seconds.
4 Add the yoghurt and once simmering, add the fish with its marinade.
5 Gently stir-fry for about 10–15 minutes or until the fish is cooked right through.
6 Salt to taste. Garnish with the crumbled nuts and fresh herbs.

◆ Balti Bengali Fish Curry

A DRY FISH CURRY, TO WHICH POTATO, TOMATO, SUGAR AND CHILLI ARE ADDED.

serves 4

675 g (1½ lb) whole, filleted fish (or steaks) – any type
2–3 tablespoons ghee or corn oil
2 teaspoons chilli powder
3–6 garlic cloves, finely chopped
225 g (8 oz) onion, very finely chopped
3 or 4 red chillies, chopped
2–3 tablespoons Balti masala paste (see page 39)
2 large potatoes, cooked and halved
2 fresh plum tomatoes
2 teaspoons jaggery or brown sugar
175 ml (6 fl oz) milk
1 teaspoon Balti garam masala (see page 41)
1 tablespoon fresh coriander leaves, very finely chopped
aromatic salt to taste (see page 43)

◆◆◆◆◆◆◆◆◆◆◆◆◆◆◆◆◆◆◆◆◆◆◆◆◆◆◆◆◆◆◆◆◆◆◆

1 Heat the ghee or oil in your Balti pan or wok on high heat. Stir-fry the chilli powder and garlic for 30 seconds.
2 Add the onions and chillies and, reducing the heat, stir-fry for about 10 minutes, allowing the onions to become translucent and begin to brown.
3 Add the masala paste and the fish. Raise the heat and bring to a brisk sizzle, stir-frying as needed for about 5 minutes.
4 Add the tomatoes, jaggery or brown sugar and the milk. Simmer and stir-fry on a lower heat for about 10 minutes. (Note: it reduces quicker if you add the milk bit by bit.)
5 Add the potatoes. To test that the fish is cooked right through remove a piece and cut it in two. (Replace the halves in the pan after testing.) If more cooking is needed keep testing. When it is as you like it, add the garam masala, fresh coriander leaves and salt to taste.

Note: this recipe can also be made using prawns. If using raw prawns, simply substitute peeled, raw prawns of any size for the 675 g (1½ lb) fish. For cooked prawns, reduce the cooking time of stage 3 to 2 minutes, and stage 4 to 3 minutes.

◆ Balti Fish Korma

KORMAS ARE USUALLY MADE WITH MEAT OR CHICKEN, BUT THIS BALTI FISH VERSION IS EQUALLY DELICIOUS. TRY IT BOTH WITH AND WITHOUT THE COCONUT FOR DIFFERENT FLAVOURS.

serves 4

675 g (1½ lb) filleted whole fish (or steaks) – any type
2–3 tablespoons ghee or corn oil
3–6 garlic cloves, finely chopped
225 g (8 oz) onion, very finely chopped
3–4 tablespoons Balti masala paste (see page 39)
175 ml (6 fl oz) milk
50 ml (2 fl oz) double cream
3–4 tablespoons chopped creamed coconut
1 teaspoon sugar
20 fried almonds, whole
20–25 saffron strands (optional)
1 teaspoon Balti garam masala (see page 41)
1 tablespoon fresh coriander leaves, very finely chopped
aromatic salt to taste (see page 43)
SPICES
2 bay leaves
5 cm (2 in) cassia bark
4–6 green cardamom
4–6 cloves
GARNISH
fresh coriander leaves

◆◆◆◆◆◆◆◆◆◆◆◆◆◆◆◆◆◆◆◆◆◆◆◆◆◆◆◆◆◆◆◆◆◆◆

1 Heat the ghee or oil in your Balti pan or wok on high heat. Stir-fry the spices and garlic for 30 seconds.
2 Add the onions and reducing the heat, stir-fry for about 10 minutes, allowing them to become translucent and begin to brown.
3 Stir in the masala paste then add the fish. Raise the heat and bring to a brisk sizzle, stir-frying as needed for about

2 minutes.
4 Add the milk. Simmer and stir-fry, on a lower heat for about 10 minutes. (Note: it reduces quicker if you add the milk bit by bit.)
5 Add the cream, coconut, sugar, almonds and saffron (if using). When simmering, test that the fish is cooked right through by removing a piece and cutting it in two. (Then replace the halves in the pan.) If more cooking is needed keep testing. When it is as you like it, add the garam masala, fresh coriander leaves and salt to taste. Simmer just a while longer, then serve.

> **NOTE:**
> *You can substitute shellfish (such as prawns, king prawns, lobster, crab, oyster, mussels, scallops) for fish in these recipes. For details see Ingredients file, pages 122–125.*

Balti Bengali Fish Curry

▶ THE INGREDIENTS FILE

smoked fish

Smoking is an ancient method of preservation. The meat or fish in question is first coated in salt to draw out any moisture. It is then hung to dry. Finally it is placed above a smoking fire. This seals the fish and imparts flavour. Any white fish can be smoked and supplied filleted. Common examples include: kippers (herring), finnan haddies (haddock) and salmon.

general information

When buying fresh fish always check the following:

1 The eyes should be clear and bright, not sunken.
2 The fins should not be flabby.
3 The gills should be firm and difficult to open.
4 The scales should all be in place; the skin should look shiny and moist.
5 There should not be a bad smell.
6 White fish fillets should be neat and trim and a white translucent colour. Avoid any with a blue tint.
7 Frozen fish should be hard with no sign of partial thawing. Packaging should not be damaged.

Your fishmonger will clean, skin and fillet fish. He will also descale and trim the whole fish, removing the head, fins and tail.

Fresh fish and shellfish can be frozen at home providing they have not been frozen before. Interleave the fish or fillets with stretch film. To thaw frozen fish, place in a covered container in the bottom of the refrigerator (allowing 12 hours minimum). Do not thaw in water as there will be loss of texture, flavour and valuable nutrients.

To prevent fish from breaking up in Balti cooking, always cook it in largish pieces. Cut into bite-size pieces after cooking, just before serving.

◆ Balti Fish Keema

THE SUBJECT HERE IS MINCED FISH. IT IS QUICK TO COOK AND DELICIOUS TO EAT.

serves 4

675 g (1½ lb) whole fish, filleted (or steaks) – any type
2 tablespoons ghee or corn oil
4–6 garlic cloves, finely chopped
225 g (8 oz) onion, finely chopped
3–4 tablespoons Balti masala paste (see page 39)
1 tablespoon tomato purée
1 tablespoon Balti garam masala (see page 41)
1 tablespoon fresh coriander leaves, chopped
aromatic salt to taste (see page 43)

◆◆◆◆◆◆◆◆◆◆◆◆◆◆◆◆◆◆◆◆◆◆◆◆◆◆◆◆◆

1 Remove all skin and unwanted matter from the fish, then slowly run it through a mincer. (A food processor is too violent.)
2 Heat the ghee or oil in your Balti pan or wok on high heat. Stir-fry the garlic for 30 seconds.
3 Add the onion and, reducing the heat, stir-fry for about 5 minutes, allowing it to become translucent.
4 Add the masala paste and tomato purée. Raise the heat and bring to a brisk sizzle, stir-frying as needed for about 2 or 3 minutes.
5 Add the minced fish, and stir-fry for about 5 minutes, adding just enough water to keep things mobile.
6 The fish should be virtually cooked by now. When it is, stir in the garam masala, fresh coriander leaves and salt to taste. Give it a final 2-minute simmer, then garnish and serve.

Balti Fish Madras

BALTI MADRAS GIVES HEAT LOVERS A TASTY, BUT NOT TOO HOT CURRY, AND USING FISH IT MAKES A GREAT CHANGE.

serves 4

675 g (1½ lb) filleted whole fish (or steaks) – any type
2–3 tablespoons ghee or corn oil
3–6 garlic cloves, finely chopped
225 g (8 oz) onion, very finely chopped
150 ml (5 fl oz) milk
2–4 tablespoons Balti masala paste (see page 39)
1 tablespoon tandoori paste (see page 40)
6 oz (175 g) canned tomatoes, strained
2 tablespoons tomato ketchup
2 tablespoons ground almonds
1 teaspoon Balti garam masala (see page 41)
1 tablespoon fresh coriander leaves, very finely chopped
aromatic salt to taste (see page 43)
SPICES
2–4 teaspoons chilli powder
1 teaspoon cummin powder
GARNISH
fresh coriander leaves

Heat the ghee or oil in your Balti pan or wok on high heat. Stir-fry the spices and garlic for 30 seconds.

Add the onions and, reducing the heat, stir-fry for about 10 minutes, allowing them to become translucent and begin to brown. If it dries up, add a few splashes of milk to keep things mobile.

Add the pastes and the fish. Raise the heat and bring to a brisk sizzle, stir-frying as needed for about 5 minutes.

Add the remaining milk. Simmer and stir-fry on a lower heat for about minutes. (Note: it reduces quicker if you add the milk bit by bit).

Add the tomatoes, the ketchup and ground almonds, and continue to stir-fry for a further 5 minutes.

To test that the fish is cooked right through, remove a piece and cut it in two (then replace the halves in the pan). If more cooking is needed keep testing. When it is as you like it, add the garam masala, fresh coriander leaves and salt to taste. Simmer a while longer and serve.

Balti Fish Tikka Masala Curry

THIS IS THE BALTI RESTAURANT VERSION OF THE UK'S MOST POPULAR CURRY DISH.

serves 4

675 g (1½ lb) filleted whole fish (or steaks) – any type
2–3 tablespoons ghee or corn oil
3–6 garlic cloves, finely chopped
225 g (8 oz) onion, very finely chopped
2–3 tablespoons Balti masala paste (see page 39)
1–2 tablespoons tandoori paste (see page 40)
150 ml (7 fl oz) cream of tomato soup
300 ml (14 fl oz) fragrant stock (see page 43)
2 tablespoons coconut milk powder
1 tablespoon mango chutney, finely chopped
1 tablespoon Balti garam masala (see page 41)
1 tablespoon fresh coriander leaves, very finely chopped
aromatic salt to taste (see page 43)
MARINADE
10 oz (300 ml) Greek yoghurt
1 tablespoon dry fenugreek leaves, ground
1 tablespoon dry mint, ground
2 tablespoons tandoori paste (see page 00)
⅛ teaspoon orange/red dry food colouring (optional)
½ teaspoon salt

1 Mix together the marinade ingredients in a non-metallic bowl. Immerse the fish pieces, cover and refrigerate for 1–2 hours.
2 After marination, heat half the ghee in the Balti pan or wok. Spoon half the fish and its marinade into the Balti pan or wok and briskly stir-fry for 5 minutes. Remove and repeat with the other half.
3 Clean the Balti pan or wok and heat the remaining ghee or oil in your Balti pan or wok on high heat. Stir-fry the garlic for 30 seconds.
4 Add the onion and, reducing the heat, stir-fry for about 10 minutes, allowing it to become translucent and begin to brown.
5 Add the masala and tandoori pastes and the fish. Raise the heat and bring to a brisk sizzle, stir-frying as needed for about 5 minutes.
6 Add a little of the soup and any remaining marinade. Simmer and stir-fry on a lower heat for about 10 minutes. (Note: it reduces quicker if you add the stock bit by bit.)
7 To test that the fish is cooked right through remove a piece and cut it in two (then replace the halves in the pan). If more cooking is needed keep testing. When it is as you like it, add the coconut milk powder, mango chutney, garam masala, fresh coriander leaves and salt to taste.
8 Simmer a while longer then serve.

> **NOTE:**
> You can substitute shellfish (such as prawns, king prawns, lobster, crab, oyster, mussels, scallops) for fish in these recipes. For details see Ingredients file, pages 122–125.

TYPES OF SHELLFISH

Shellfish are divided into three categories (one of which in fact has no shell!):
Crustaceans – these have a tough crusty covering (or shell) – include crabs, crayfish, crawfish, lobster, prawns/shrimps, and scampi.
Molluscs – invertebrates protected by a strong shell – include: limpets, whelks and winkles, abalone, clams, mussels, oysters and scallops.
Cephalopeds – invertebrates with no shell – include: cuttlefish, octopus, squid and sea urchins.

crustaceans

All members of the crustacean group have an external shell which varies in toughness from species to species. The tiniest prawn's is edible while the largest lobster's is almost indestructible. Despite this, all crustaceans shed their shells regularly. The shells of live crustaceans are naturally camouflaged in sea colours, such as blue-greys, greens and browns, which are a component part of their molecular protein-pigment structure. Also present, but obscured are carotenoids which have red and yellow pigments. Once cooking begins, heat changes the protein-pigment structure, causing the carotenoid colours to dominate quickly turning the shell into the familiar pink or scarlet. The cooked flesh turns white, with pink tinges. Crustaceans give the best flavour cooked live (see below), but this is not for the squeamish, for whom uncooked or ready-cooked produce, fresh or frozen, is more acceptable. Crustaceans contain no carbohydrates, minimal fat and are rich in protein and certain minerals.

Raw prawn averages 90 calories per 100 g (3½ oz), scampi 110, lobster 120, and crab 127.

LOBSTERS

The luxury item of the shellfish department is, of course, lobster. There are three species of miniature lobster, and two distinctly different species of large lobster. One has huge pincer-like claws, and is exclusively found in the waters of the northern Atlantic. Called the *homard* in French, there are two main types: the larger American lobster weighing up to and over 4 kg (9 lb), and the virtually identical, but smaller European lobster. The other species is known as the spiny lobster, which can grow to 50 cm (20 in) in length. These are native to, but are scarce in European waters. They are commonly fished in Asia and in Australia. Called *langouste* in French, the spiny lobster should correctly be called saltwater crayfish. However, they are also known as crawfish in Britain and crayfish in Australia. Spiny lobsters do not grow in American waters, and when imported there (mostly from Australia) they are called rock lobsters. What the Americans call crawfish is the freshwater crayfish, or simply the crayfish of Europe. It is a

From left to right: Spiny lobster or crayfish; crayfish tails; European lobster

CRAB

miniature lobster, complete with
pincers, and it is found in freshwater
lakes and streams. It grows to a length
of about 15 cm (6 in). In France they
are known as *écrevisse*, and in
Australia, yabbies.

Another miniature lobster species is
the Australian sand lobster or bay bug
a small clawless crustacean with
lobster-like flesh in the tail.

The Norway lobster has long thin
claws and a thin body yielding juicy
flesh. It is also called the Dublin Bay
Prawn, and the *langoustine* in France.
Larger individuals, up to 25 cm (10 in)
in length, specially caught in the bay of
Naples, are called scampi.

COOKING LOBSTER

To Prepare a Lobster

Though unappealing, it is easy to cook
a live lobster.

Place it into boiling water for a
minimum of 3 minutes (for uncooked
flesh) and for 20 minutes (for cooked
flesh).

Twist off the legs and pincers.
Extract the flesh using pliers and a
pick. Discard cartilage.

If you are using the shell, halve it by
simply cutting down the centre line.
Keep the tail on.

Wash the shell halves when the flesh
has been removed.

Discard the hard and soft material in
the head area. Cut the flesh away from
the shell, and separate it. Spoon out the
creamy white liver and red eggs (coral)
if present.

Cut up and mix all the meat, liver
and coral.

An 800 g (1¾ lb) lobster yields about
225 g (8 oz) of meat.

The most common Atlantic and
Mediterranean crab is the common or
edible crab. It grows up to 20 cm (8 in),
though the average crab is smaller.
White meat is found in the claws and
legs, and dark meat in the body shell.
Other crabs of around the same size,
include: the Jonah, found in American
waters; the blue crab, in America and
Europe; and the mud crab in Asia and
Australia.

COOKING CRAB

1 If alive, immerse the crab in warm
water for 30 minutes, to prevent it from
shedding its claws.

2 Bring the same water to the boil and
simmer for 10 minutes per 450 g (1 lb).
Drain and allow to cool.

3 Place it on its back and pull off the
claws and legs. Extract the flesh using
pliers and a pick.

4 Remove and discard the tail, then
twist the body out of the shell with a
knife.

5 Discard the finger-like grey gills and
the stomach behind the eyes, any
spongy inner parts, and intestines.
Keep both the white and brown or
yellow-brown meat.

6 Wash the body shell. Using pliers
crack off the top shell and discard.
Wash again.

A 450g (1 lb) crab yields about
175–200 g (6–8 oz) of meat.

PRAWNS AND SHRIMPS

It is often assumed that shrimps are tiny versions of prawns. In America they are indeed called shrimps until they reach about 6 cm (2½in) in length, after which the term king prawn is used. According to the professionals, prawns and shrimps are one and the same thing – they measure them by how many you get to the pound (450 g). It is easier to apply this rule when visualising portion sizes, especially with larger prawns. But their sizes do vary enormously from 6 mm (⅓ in) to 23 cm (9 in) in length, from tip to extended tail. There are some fifteen species of cold water prawns (Atlantic or Norwegian) and 40 deep water and tropical warm-watered species available at our fishmongers. They are sold live sometimes, or raw or cooked, to use trade terms, with shell-on or shell-off (including the tail) and head-on or head-off. The term peeled, correctly

means shell-off and head-off. Larger prawns, peeled, but with the tail left on are quite attractive.

The tiniest prawns are sometimes called 'brown shrimps', because although their shells are translucent when raw, their colour when cooked is browner than the pink of most crustaceans (see lobster). Their shells are so soft and fiddly to peel, it is easier to consume them, with their shells on. Indeed the crunchiness improves their taste and texture. A little taste trial on each occasion, as to how much shell to leave on a particular prawn may be needed.

Tiny prawns can yield as many as 500 per 450 g (1 lb). At about 4 cm (1½ in) unpeeled prawns yield an average 200–300 to the pound and are known as common prawns. Expect about 90–120 to the pound for medium-sized – 4 cm (1½ in) prawns.

King prawns range from 21–25, 16–20 and 8–12 to the pound.

The largest prawns are warm water species called jumbo or tiger prawns (because of the tiger-like stripe). Though expensive, and not that easy to track down, the jumbo at under 5 to the pound, yields a massive 110 g (4 oz) when peeled and cooked, its flesh being almost as good as lobster.

Cooking times for raw prawns depend on their size. The shells will go pink first, but the flesh will take longer, and is not ready until it is white right through. Cooked prawns merely need heating right through.

Cheap Prawns

There is no such thing as cheap prawns, yet prices can vary enormously, particularly for frozen sachets. Cheap products can include a large percentage of water and chlorine (up to half the weight of the packet!).

Sizes range from the Giant King Prawn (110 g) down to tiny ones (2 g)

Molluscs

ome molluscs have a single round shell nclosing the creature's soft body, hich extends some way out of the hell's small aperture for feeding. Other olluscs have a hinged double shell hich the creature can open to feed self, and close completely for rotection. The former include limpets, helks and winkles. The latter include palone clams, mussels, oysters and allops.

All molluscs can be curried, with articularly good results coming from ams, mussels and scallops.

he clam lives in sand and mud flats round coastal waters. Its first corded use was in China in the Tang ynasty of the eighth century, when e clams were fished from the Yangtze ver. Today they are farmed in the SA and are readily available frozen. lthough they are available shelled, ey are actually better in their ells. They come in three sizes in eir shells: small – averaging per 450 g (1 lb); medium – per 450 g; and large – 10 per 50 g.

Mussels are best bought live. heck that their shells are tightly osed. Place in cold water in the idge overnight, and discard any pen-shelled or floating mussels – ey are dead. After currying in mple watery gravy, the reverse is the se. Discard any which have remained osed.

The scallop is a British native and is so found in seas and oceans orldwide. Its shell is ribbed, flatish nd relatively large, often tinged with oral pink, and pretty enough to be sed to serve the scallops on. Although enerally scallops are sold frozen ithout shells, most fishmongers will pply shells if required.

callops come in three sizes: small – 0–40 per kg (2.2 lb); medium –

20–30 per kg; and large – 10–20 per kg. Four small, three medium or two large is ample per person for a starter. Scallops contain white meat (the round muscle) which is attached to the creamy white and coral pink roe, known as the foot. All this is edible.

Opening Molluscs

You need a special oyster knife (available from cookshops) which has a thick, wide, stubby blunt blade. A wide screwdriver can substitute, but a kitchen knife blade is too thin and is liable to break.

Clocwise from top left: oysters, New Zealand blue mussels, European mussels, cockles, scallops

1 Hold the clam in a tea-towel with its shell hinge facing you.
2 Insert the blade near the hinge and wiggle and twist until the hinge separates. Separate the two halves of the shell.
3 Run the blade all around the shell half containing the flesh, to cut the mollusc away from the shell.
4 Discard any molluscs which are dried up, off-colour or are bubbled.
5 Remove and discard the gut and gill.

Balti Nagopa

THIS RECIPE – A TYPE OF PAKORA – THE FISH IS
[CO]ATED IN A SPICY BATTER AND DEEP-FRIED.

[se]rves 4

[s]mall white fish fillets (any type), about
  85 g (3 oz) each
[6] tablespoons ghee or vegetable oil
[lem]on wedges
[TH]E BATTER
[15]0 g (5 oz) gram flour
[25]g (1 oz) coconut milk powder
[g]arlic cloves, finely chopped
[t]ablespoon vinegar
[t]ablespoons Greek yoghurt
[t]ablespoon Balti garam masala (see
  page 41)
[t]ablespoons Balti masala paste (see
  page 39)
[t]easpoons salt
[t]easpoons sugar
[t]easpoon white cummin seed
[t]easpoon lovage seeds
[f]resh green chillies, finely chopped

◆◆◆◆◆◆◆◆◆◆◆◆◆◆◆◆◆◆◆◆◆◆◆◆◆

Wash the fish fillets and pat them dry.
Mix the batter ingredients, adding
[en]ough water to achieve a thickish,
[po]urable paste.
Immerse the fish fillets in the batter in
[a l]arge bowl. Cover and refrigerate for
[1–]2 hours.
Use a large flat frying pan. Heat the
[gh]ee. Unless your pan is huge you will
[pro]bably only be able to fit 2 or 4 fillets
[in]at a time.
Fry them for 5–8 minutes then turn
[th]em and fry the other side for the same
[tim]e.
Serve whilst still crisp with lemon
[we]dges, dhal and plain rice.

[Ba]lti Nagopa

◆ Balti Malaya Fish Curry

IN THIS RECIPE THE BALTI AROMATICS COMBINE
BEAUTIFULLY WITH FISH AND THE SWEET, EXOTIC
FLAVOUR OF PINEAPPLE.

serves 4

675 g (1½ lb) filleted whole fish (or steaks)
  – any type
2–3 tablespoons ghee or corn oil
3–6 garlic cloves, finely chopped
225 g (8 oz) onion, very finely chopped
3–4 tablespoons Balti masala paste
  (see page 39)
175 ml (6 fl oz) milk
6–8 chunks fresh or canned pineapple
3–4 tablespoons coconut milk powder
sprinkling of desiccated coconut
1 teaspoon Balti garam masala (see page 41)
1 tablespoon fresh coriander leaves, very
  finely chopped
aromatic salt to taste (see page 43)
SPICES
½ teaspoon lovage seeds
½ teaspoon yellow mustard seeds
½ teaspoon chilli powder
½ teaspoon asafoetida (optional)
GARNISH
fresh coriander leaves

◆◆◆◆◆◆◆◆◆◆◆◆◆◆◆◆◆◆◆◆◆◆◆◆◆◆◆◆

1 Heat the ghee or oil in your Balti pan
or wok on high heat. Stir-fry the spices
and garlic for 30 seconds.
2 Add the onions and reducing the
heat, stir-fry for about 10 minutes,
allowing them to become translucent
and begin to brown.
3 Add the masala paste and the fish.
Raise the heat and bring to a brisk sizzle,
stir-frying as needed for about 5
minutes.
4 Add the milk and the pineapple
chunks. Simmer and stir-fry, on a lower
heat for about 10 minutes. (Note: it
reduces quicker if you add the milk bit
by bit).
5 Test that the fish is cooked right
through by removing a piece and cutting
it in two. (Then replace the halves in the
pan.) If more cooking is needed keep
testing. When it is as you like it, add the
coconut milk powder, garam masala,
fresh coriander leaves and salt to taste.
6 Simmer until it is cooked to your
liking. Garnish and serve.

NOTE:

*You can substitute shellfish (such as
prawns, king prawns, lobster, crab,
oyster, mussels, scallops) for fish in
these recipes. For details see
Ingredients file, pages 122–125.*

◆ Balti Phal Fish Curry

WE CAME ACROSS PHAL – THE HOTTEST BALTI DISH A COOK CAN MAKE – EARLIER. HERE'S A FISH VERSION, AND PLEASE REMEMBER, IT'S ONLY FOR SERIOUS HOT-HEADS, AND CERTAINLY NOT FOR THE NOVICE.

serves 4

675 g (1½ lb) filleted whole fish (or steaks)
    – any type
2–3 tablespoons ghee or corn oil
4 or more teaspoons extra hot chilli powder
3–6 garlic cloves, finely chopped
225 g (8 oz) onion, very finely chopped
3–4 tablespoons Balti masala paste (see page 39)
2 tablespoons tandoori paste (see page 40)
6 oz (175 g) tomato, chopped
4–8 fresh red and/or green chillies, whole or chopped
175 ml (6 fl oz) milk
1 teaspoon Balti garam masala (see page 41)
1 tablespoon fresh coriander leaves, very finely chopped
1 tablespoon vinegar, any type
aromatic salt to taste (see page 43)
GARNISH
fresh coriander leaves

◆◆◆◆◆◆◆◆◆◆◆◆◆◆◆◆◆◆◆◆◆◆◆◆◆◆◆◆◆

1 Heat the ghee or oil in your Balti pan or wok on high heat. Stir-fry the chilli powder and garlic for 30 seconds.
2 Add a few splashes of water, then the onions and, reducing the heat, stir-fry for about 10 minutes, allowing them to become translucent and begin to brown.
3 Stir in the pastes then add tomato, fresh chilli and the fish. Raise the heat and bring to a brisk sizzle, stir-frying as needed for about 3 minutes.
4 Add the milk. Simmer and stir-fry on a lower heat for about 12 minutes. (Note: it reduces quicker if you add the milk bit by bit).
5 To test that the fish is cooked right through, remove a piece and cut it in two (then replace the halves in the pan). If more cooking is needed keep testing.

When it is as you like it, add the garam masala, fresh coriander leaves and vinegar and salt to taste. Simmer until it is cooked to your liking.
6 Garnish and serve.

◆ Balti Patia

THIS DISH IS SWEET, HOT AND SAVOURY ALL AT THE SAME TIME. IT WAS CREATED CENTURIES AGO BY INDIA'S PARSEE COMMUNITY; HERE IT IS GIVEN THE BALTI TREATMENT.

serves 4

675 g (1½ lb) filleted whole fish (or steaks)
    – any type
2–3 tablespoons ghee or corn oil
3–6 garlic cloves, finely chopped
225 g (8 oz) onion, very finely chopped
2 tablespoons Balti masala paste (see page 39)
200 g (7 oz) Balti masala gravy (see page 42)
1 tablespoon tomato purée
2 or 3 tomatoes, finely chopped
½ red pepper, very finely chopped
2 teaspoons brown sugar
1 tablespoon lime juice, freshly squeezed
1 teaspoon Balti garam masala (see page 41)
1 tablespoon fresh coriander leaves, very finely chopped
aromatic salt to taste (see page 43)
SPICES
2 teaspoons paprika
1 teaspoon chilli powder
½ teaspoon panch phoran (see page 43)

◆◆◆◆◆◆◆◆◆◆◆◆◆◆◆◆◆◆◆◆◆◆◆◆◆◆◆◆◆◆◆

1 Heat the ghee or oil in your Balti pan or wok on high heat. Stir-fry the spices and garlic for 30 seconds.
2 Add the onions and, reducing the heat, stir-fry for about 10 minutes, allowing them to become translucent and begin to brown. Add a few splashes of water if needed to keep things mobile.
3 Add the masala paste and the fish. Raise the heat and bring to a brisk sizzle, stir-frying as needed for about 2 minutes.
4 Add the gravy. Simmer and stir-fry, on

a lower heat for about 8 minutes.
5 Add the tomato purée, tomatoes, re[d] pepper, sugar and lime juice, and continue stir-frying at a gentle simmer for a further 8 minutes.
6 Test that the fish is cooked right through by removing a piece and cuttin[g] it in two. (Then replace the halves in th[e] pan.) If more cooking is needed keep testing. When it is as you like it, add th[e] garam masala, fresh coriander leaves and salt to taste.

NOTE:
You can substitute shellfish (such as prawns, king prawns, lobster, crab, oyster, mussels, scallops) for fish in these recipes. For details see Ingredients file, pages 122–125.

Balti Patia Seafood

CEPHALOPODS

Cephalopods are molluscs with tentacles on their heads. This family includes cuttlefish, octopus, squid and sea urchins.

Squid makes an interesting occasional subject for currying. To prepare it:

1 Carefully pull the head with its tentacles away from the body (being careful not to puncture the ink sac which can optionally be used in cooking).

2 Pull out and discard the flat transparent cartilage and the innards.

3 Cut off and keep the tentacles, and discard the head.

4 Rinse the squid to remove the purple-tinged membrane.
The conical-shaped body can be kept whole. It deep-fries rather spectacularly, or it can be cut into rings or squares.

FROG'S LEGS

Beloved by the French and Cajuns, frogs bred and farmed for the table are quite large. Only the legs are marketed, available in pairs of various weights, and classified as seafood. Their flesh is white, and more like chicken than fish. Indeed, if you do decide to use them, cook them on the bone using chicken recipe timings.

DE-VEINING PRAWNS

Prawns of all sizes have a so-called vein which runs down the back (the outside of the curved prawn). It is in fact the intestine, and sometimes this can be dark coloured and dirty. Even if it is clean you should remove this vein. It's rather like stringing beans.

1 Use a small, sharp paring knife and make an incision right down the back of the prawn.

2 Pull the vein away and discard it, washing the prawn after it is done.

De-veining is impractical in the case of tiny prawns which are too fiddly, so pragmatism must prevail here (or a lot of hard work).

◆ Balti Satpara Nyashi

serves 4

675 g (1½ lb) filleted whole fish (or steaks) – any type
2–3 tablespoons ghee or corn oil
225 g (8 oz) onion, very finely chopped
2 teaspoons Balti masala mix (see page 39)
5 cm (2 in) ginger, thinly sliced
175 ml (6 fl oz) milk
25–30 saffron strands
1 tablespoon fresh coriander leaves, chopped
2–3 tablespoons pistachio nuts, chopped
2 teaspoons white granulated sugar
aromatic salt (see page 43) to taste
THE MARINADE
6 garlic cloves, chopped
2 oz (50 g) onion, chopped
3 tablespoons coconut milk powder
1 tablespoon gram flour
1 tablespoon vegetable oil
0–4 red chillies, chopped
2 teaspoons paprika
1 tablespoon tomato purée
SPICES
1 teaspoon sesame seeds
½ teaspoon green cardamom seeds
½ teaspoon black cummin seeds
½ teaspoon fenugreek seeds
½ teaspoon aniseed
GARNISH
1 tablespoon coriander seeds, roasted and lightly crushed
any green herbs

◆◆◆◆◆◆◆◆◆◆◆◆◆◆◆◆◆◆◆◆◆◆◆◆◆◆◆◆◆◆◆

1 Grind together the marinade ingredients in a blender, food processor or in the old-fashioned mortar and pestle with enough water to achieve a thick but pourable paste.

2 Immerse the fish in the marinade in a non-metallic bowl, cover and refrigerate r 2 or 3 hours.

Heat the oil in the Balti pan or wok.
ir-fry the spices for 30 seconds. Add
e onion, masala mix and the ginger
d stir-fry at the sizzle for 3 or 4
inutes.

Add the milk and when simmering
d the fish and all the marinade.

Simmer for 10–15 minutes, adding a
tle extra milk or water if it starts
icking.

Add the saffron, coriander leaves,
ts, sugar and salt to taste and simmer
r a final 5 minutes or until the fish is
oked.

Garnish with the coriander seeds and
rbs. Serve with plain rice.

> **NOTE:**
> *You can substitute shellfish (such as prawns, king prawns, lobster, crab, oyster, mussels, scallops) for fish in these recipes. For details see Ingredients file, pages 122–125.*

◆ Balti Tapa

THIS RECIPE USES PILCHARDS OR THEIR YOUNG – SARDINES (OILY FISH GRILL WELL). THE WHOLE FISH IS COATED WITH THE PASTE. GRILL OR BAKE AND SERVE WITH YOGHURT RAITA, ONION SALAD, NAAN BREAD.

serves 4

4 whole pilchards, about 25 cm (10 in) long
OR 16 10 cm (4 in) sardines
THE PASTE
6 tablespoons Balti masala paste (see
    page 39)
2 garlic cloves, finely chopped
2.5 cm (1 in) ginger, finely chopped
110 g (4 oz) onion, finely chopped
2 tablespoons melted ghee or butter
2 teaspoons dried mint
2 teaspoons aromatic salt
1 tablespoon ground almonds
4 tablespoons Greek yoghurt
GARNISH
garam masala
aromatic salt
chilli powder (optional)

◆◆◆◆◆◆◆◆◆◆◆◆◆◆◆◆◆◆◆◆◆◆◆◆◆◆◆◆◆◆◆

1 Grind together the paste ingredients in a blender, food processor or the old-fashioned mortar and pestle, with enough water to achieve a thick but pourable paste.
2 Preheat the grill to medium hot and line the grill tray with kitchen foil (to catch drips and make cleaning up easier). Put the grill rack into the tray. Place the fish on the rack, close together.
3 Coat the top side of the fishes with half of the marinade.
4 Place the tray at the midway position and grill for 5–8 minutes (depending on fish and size and actual heat level). The fish should by then be cooking but not burned.
5 Remove the tray. Turn the fish keeping them close together and coat the remaining marinade over them.
6 Repeat the grilling on the other side (stage 4).
7 Sprinkle with the garnish ingredients to taste and serve piping hot.

◆ Balti Chilli Squid

SQUID, LOVE OR HATE IT, COOKS AS EASILY AND AS QUICKLY AS PRAWNS OR CHICKEN. THIS STIR-FRY IS REMARKABLE FOR ITS MINIMAL INGREDIENTS.

serves 4

300g (11 oz) squid rings
2 tablespoons ghee or vegetable oil
4 to 6 garlic cloves, finely chopped
1 to 3 teaspoons chilli powder
2 teaspoons Balti garam masala (see page
    41)
2 to 3 tablespoons fresh lime juice
2 tablespoons fresh coriander, finely chopped
aromatic salt to taste (see page 43)
some dried chilli and lime wedges to garnish

◆◆◆◆◆◆◆◆◆◆◆◆◆◆◆◆◆◆◆◆◆◆◆◆◆◆◆◆◆◆◆

1 Heat the ghee or oil in the karahi. Stir-fry the garlic for 20 seconds, then add the chilli and garam masala and continue to stir-fry for a further 20 seconds.
2 Stir in the lime juice, and when the sizzling slows (a few seconds) add the squid. Lower the heat to prevent too rapid cooking, and briskly stir-fry until it is cooked to your liking.
3 Add the coriander, stir-fry for a further minute. Salt to taste, garnish and serve.

Vegetables

Vegetables have always been part of man's diet. For centuries, those living in harsh climates and mountainous areas preserved vegetables for use in times of crop failure or in hard winters. The rugged Baltistan territory is one such area. There, root vegetables which grow prolifically in the short hot summer can be stored at cool temperatures and they last for months. Legumes become dried beans, peas and lentils when dried, and store indefinitely. Onions ginger and garlic can be dried and reconstituted. But as well as vegetables being scarce for parts of the year, meat and poultry are scarce at the best of times. To stretch this limited supply, vegetables almost always accompany Balti meat dishes, providing interesting combinations. Meat with sweetcorn and potato, chicken with celery, and fish with lobia beans are just three examples.

Legumes are extremely popular in the mountainous regions of the subcontinent. They provide great nourishment, and are very tasty indeed when spiced the Balti way. They require rather more time to cook than most vegetables, but they freeze well, and work well combined with vegetables and/or meat or fish. In fact, it is exactly this seemingly infinite capacity to 'mix and match' that has made the UK Balti house popular.

◆ Balti Achari Bhajee

ACHAR MEANS 'PICKLE', AND ACHARI BHAJEE MEANS 'VEGETABLES CURRIED IN A PICKLE BASE'. THE MOST POPULAR PICKLES ARE LIME, MANGO, OR MIXED PICKLE. OTHER OPTIONS ARE BRINJAL, CHILLI, VEGETABLE OR PRAWN BALLICHOW PICKLES. THE PICKLE GIVES THE CURRY A VERY POWERFUL TASTE. THE MAIN INGREDIENT NEED NOT BE LIMITED TO CHICKEN.

serves 2

300 g (11 oz) vegetables of your choice, weighed after stage 1
2 tablespoons ghee or vegetable oil
1/3 teaspoon turmeric
1/2 teaspoon white cummin seeds
1/2 teaspoon mustard seeds
3 garlic cloves, finely chopped
2.5 cm (1 in) piece fresh ginger, finely chopped (optional)
1 tablespoon Balti masala mix (see page 39)
1/2 large Spanish onion, peeled and chopped
2 or more green chillies, sliced
1 tablespoon green pepper, seeded and coarsely chopped
1 tablespoon red pepper, seeded and coarsely chopped
1 tablespoon freshly chopped coriander leaves
2 or 3 fresh cherry tomatoes, halved
2 tablespoons brinjal pickle, chopped
1 tablespoon lime pickle, chopped
2 teaspoons garam masala (see page 41)
salt to taste
lemon juice

◆◆◆◆◆◆◆◆◆◆◆◆◆◆◆◆◆◆◆◆◆◆◆◆◆◆◆◆◆

1 Prepare the vegetables by divesting them of unwanted matter, washing them as required, then cutting them into the shapes of your choice. Cook them using one of the three methods described on this page.
2 Heat the ghee or oil and fry the turmeric and seeds for about 30 seconds. Add the garlic and ginger and stir-fry for about 30 seconds more, then add the

Previous pages: Balti Achari Bhajee

masala mix, with just enough water to make a paste, and stir for a further minute.
3 Add the onion, chillies and peppers and continue to stir-fry for about 5 more minutes.
4 Add the coriander, tomatoes, chopped pickles and garam masala, and stir-fry for about a minute on medium heat. Add the cooked vegetables, and a little water if needed.
6 When everything is hot, salt to taste, and serve with a squeeze of lemon juice over the top.

◆ Three Cooking Methods for Vegetables

HERE ARE THREE METHODS FOR COOKING VEGETABLES FOR BALTI – BY BOILING, STEAMING OR MICROWAVING.

serves 2

300 g (11 oz) vegetables of your choice, weighed after stage 1

◆◆◆◆◆◆◆◆◆◆◆◆◆◆◆◆◆◆◆◆◆◆◆◆◆◆◆◆◆

METHOD 1: BOILING
1 Prepare the vegetables by divesting them of unwanted matter, washing them as required, then cutting them into the shapes of your choice.
2 Bring ample water to the boil in a saucepan.
3 Place vegetables in water then simmer for 3–4 minutes, or longer for some vegetables such as potatoes.
4 Strain and add hot to the Balti curry of your choice.
5 Stir-fry for a few moments until everything is well mixed and serve as a side dish or added to other Baltis.
6 If adding the vegetables cold, allow enough time to get them hot.

METHOD 2: STEAMING
You can use Chinese bamboo tiered steamers held above a saucepan

containing boiling water. Or use a double boiler, or cheapest of all, simply place a strainer above the pan.
1 Prepare the vegetables by divesting them of unwanted matter, washing them as required, then cutting them int the shapes of your choice.
2 Bring ample water to the boil in a saucepan.
3 Put the vegetables into the steamer tray, upper half of the double boiler or the strainer. Place over the boiling wate
4 Follow the above boiling recipe from stages 4–6.

METHOD 3: MICROWAVING
The microwave is a brilliant tool for cooking vegetables whilst retaining the colour. Simply put the chosen vegetable(s) into a non-metallic bowl with minimal water and microwave on maximum power for the least amount o time to achieve the texture you require. In rapid time, the vegetable is piping hot, yet minimal flavour is lost due to minimal water being involved in the cooking process. Most domestic microwaves are powered at 600–700 watts. Occasionally they come at lower wattages, in which case increase the timings accordingly. Catering microwaves can be powered as high as 2,000 watts, and timings will need to be reduced accordingly.

1 Prepare the vegetables by divesting them of unwanted matter, washing them as required, then cutting them int the shapes of your choice.
2 Place 50 ml (2 floz) water and the vegetables into a suitably sized wide lidded non-metallic bowl.
3 Run the microwave for 1½ minutes. Test and continue until the vegetable is as you want it. A little more water may be needed if it dries out.
4 Follow the boiling recipe above from stages 4–6.

VEGETABLES

Fruit and vegetables are getting good press these days, although the debate about organic cultivation versus chemicals is loud and clear. I recently conducted an experiment for a well-known food magazine, in which I cooked a number of dishes using organic vegetables and then the same dishes with non-organic vegetables. They were then blind-tasted by a panel of foodies. Most of the panel members preferred the organic dishes which is all very well, but the cost of the ingredients was up to four times that of their non-organic equivalents. Organic vegetables do have the edge in terms of flavour, but you must make your own choice based also on what suits your pocket. Of course, if you are a gardener, there is nothing more satisfying than growing your own produce. But it is hard work, and you need time, not to mention a suitable garden and equipment.

The latest thinking is that each person must consume five items of fruit or vegetable a day. As this section of the Ingredients File shows, there is plenty of choice; our greengrocers and supermarket are brimming over with items, that even a few years ago, were unobtainable. Fresh ginger, for example, only became widely available during the mid-eighties. The nineties have seen the arrival of many different species: Sainsbury's, for example, offer six chilli species, and many exotic vegetables.

The better shops ensure that their produce is fresh and the turnover is fast. Sometimes items held in chill cabinets become a little too cold, and this decreases and even eliminates storage life at home. The general rule is to select a good-looking specimen which smells attractive. Colour should be bright and even, not blotchy, or with dark patches. Leaves, especially herbs and lettuce, should be crisp, not limp. Roots and tubers, such as onions and potatoes should be firm, not soft and their skins should have a sheen. Produce with any decay or dryness, or conversely showing signs of weeping, should be avoided.

There is no better way to enjoy vegetables than with Balti spices.

Here we examine a wide selection of vegetables, followed by storage tips.

ASPARAGUS

The word asparagus originated from the Greek word meaning to 'stalk' or 'shoot'. It is a member of the lily family, with about 300 species native to places from Siberia to Africa. Asparagus has been in Britain since the 16th century, when it grew wild on the shores. Within 100 years it was cultivated in a village outside London called Battersea (now SW11) which became famous as much for its bundles of asparagus, as its for its cockney slang: 'sparrow grass'. British asparagus have an excellent full flavour because the climate allows the stems to grow slowly. The tips and tops of the stalks are the delicacy; discard the stalk at the point where it becomes tough. Asparagus are a good source of fibre, potassium and iron, and vitamins B and C. Raw asparagus are 18 calories per 100 g (3½ oz).

AUBERGINE

The aubergine originated in south-east Asia and belongs to the nightshade family (as do tomatoes and potatoes). It is a long, pear- or egg-shaped vegetable, hence its alternative name, eggplant, and it is generally deep purple in colour. Grill or bake whole until it burns slightly, for a gorgeous smoky taste, then scoop out and purée the flesh. Alternatively slice into bite-sized pieces (retaining the skin) and cook. Either way discard the pith and seeds in the centre. Aubergine is a good source of fibre and iron, and vitamins C and A. It is 14 calories per 100 g (3½ oz).

BELL PEPPER

This highly flavoured vegetable goes under a number of names, for example: paprika, pepper, red pepper, green pepper, sweet pepper, pimento and capsicum – names which all refer to some other vegetable and thus create ambiguity. In fact it is unrelated to pepper, and is just one member of the massive capsicum family, to which chillies also belong (see page 137). The fleshy, hollow fruit capsule is bell or heart-shaped, and measures up to around 11 cm (4½ in) in length. Unlike the chilli, the bell pepper contains no capsaicin, the 'heat-giving' agent. But it has a distinctive flavour, and is now bred in white, yellow, orange and purple, as well as red and green. The bell pepper is attractive to use in Balti dishes, giving good colour contrasts. The red, orange and yellow colours stand up better to prolonged cooking than do green, which go rather grey if cooked for some time (though this does not affect their taste). To counter this, you can blanch, steam or microwave the pre-cut bell pepper, softening it and heating it sufficiently to enable it to be added at a relatively late stage of cooking. Alternatively omit the softening stage and add it after the fry-up stage of the spices, garlic, onion and masala paste. Roasting the bell pepper, then removing its skin, gives it a whole new taste dimension. Discard the stalk, pith and seeds. Bell pepper is one of the richest sources of Vitamin C (red more than green), and it is a good source of fibre and potassium and Vitamin A. Raw, it provides 14 calories per 100 g (3½ oz).

BITTER GOURD – KARELA

The bitter gourd is a knobbly, long cylindrical and pointed green gourd, growing native and greatly enjoyed in the subcontinent, and now available in the West. It is very bitter and is an acquired taste yielding 21 calories per 100 g (3½ oz).

BROCCOLI OR CALABRESE

A type of brassica with short fleshy green buds, clustered in a single head, which was developed in Italy in the 1500s, (*brocco* meaning arm or branch in Italian). It resembles cauliflower, for which it can be substituted. Cut into small florets having discarded the leaves and stalks, then boil, steam or microwave until tender. Broccoli is an excellent source of vitamins B, E and in particular C, fibre, folate, potassium and iron, and provides 25 calories per 100 g (3½ oz)

CABBAGE

abbage is a member of the brassica mily and one of the most ancient egetables. It originated in Asia minor d the eastern Mediterranean, and ew wild as far north as Britain. riginally the cabbage comprised osely packed, dark green edible aves, growing from a stubby stalk on low plant. Cultivation created crisp

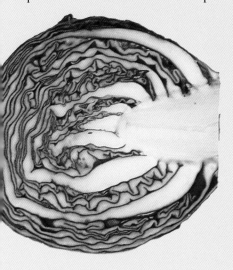

ghtly-packed leaves, whose colours nge through hues of green, white and d. The Brussels sprout could be the riginal miniature vegetable. It was riginated in Brussels in the 1200s, om wild cabbage. Cabbage is good for ore, folate, potassium, iron and tamins C, B and E. It provides 18 lories per 100 g (3½ oz).

CARROT

his long cylindrical tapering root is a ember of the parsley family, and riginated in Persia, Afghanistan and akistan. The Asian variety is a deep, most beetroot-coloured red, whilst e more familiar European varieties e bright orange in colour. The colour omes from large amounts of arotenoid, present to some extent in any vegetables, and in shellfish.

Carrots can be eaten raw, so need minimal cooking. For large carrots, discard tops and tails, wash then pare them, then cut into strips, rounds or cubes. Baby carrots are best whole. Carrots are a good source of fibre, folate, potassium, iron, and vitamins B, E and in particular A. They yield 21 calories per 100 g (3½ oz)

CAULIFLOWER

Originating in the Middle East, these brassicas are made up of short stems with numbers of florets, which are normally white, but can be green, yellow or red. Cauliflower is an excellent source of vitamin C, and is also good for fibre, potassium, iron, and vitamin K. It provides 14 calories per 100 g (3½ oz).

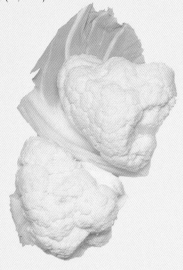

CELERY

Celery is an herbaceous plant of the carrot/parsley family with long white or green fleshy, slightly stringy stems. It was grown in ancient Greece. Celery can be eaten raw, so minimal cooking is needed. It is good for vitamin C and potassium, and provides 7 calories per 100 g (3½ oz).

CHILLI

The hot member of the capsicum family (described more fully on page 136). Wash, de-stalk and chop the chilli into narrow rings or slices, or keep it whole. You may discard the seeds if the chilli is pithy, but that's a bit like throwing the baby out with the bath water since it is the seeds which provide the heat and, contrary to some schools of thought, they do not cause indigestion in those who are used to them. Chilli needs no pre-boiling, steaming or microwaving. Simply add to the recipe of your choice after the spices, garlic and onion are fried, or as directed.

Chillies are one of the richest sources of vitamin C (red more than green) and are a good source of fibre, potassium and vitamin A. Fresh chilli, like onion and garlic, actively helps to reduce blood pressure and cholesterol. Chillies yield 21 calories per 100 g (3½ oz).

◆ Balti Aloo

serves 2 (see below)

2 large potatoes (or 4 medium/10–12 small
new)

1 Scrub the potatoes clean. Dice large
ones into roughly equal bite-sized cubes.
Small ones can be halved or left whole.
New potatoes should be scrubbed only.
2 Boil, steam or microwave to tender
(see page 134).
3 You will need around 10–15 minutes
depending on the potato type.
Alternatively deep-fry the chunks to
tender.
4 Either add to other Balti dishes
towards the end of cooking or cook as a
dish in their own right following the
recipe on page 141 for Balti Bombay
Potato.

VARIATION
Balti Aloo Mithai
Red and white sweet potatoes and yam
are cooked exactly as potatoes. Use the
recipe above.

Vegetable Portions

A meat or fish main course dish for four
people is usually around 675 g
(1½ lb),assuming it is accompanied by,
for example, vegetable side dishes.
Often, it is more interesting to serve a
number of vegetables dishes together as
a main course in themselves. All the
vegetable recipes here are therefore
portioned at around 325 g (just under
11 oz) which will provide a very
generous single portion served with rice
or bread, or an adequate portion for
two if served with another similar sized
dish and rice or bread. For four, it can be
used as one of several accompaniment
dishes. Remember also that with certain
vegetables, it is more convenient to
portion visually than by weight.
Potatoes, for example are best portioned
by the number of potatoes each diner
will eat.

◆ Balti Bhajee

BHAJIA OR *BHAJA* MEANS TO FRY, HENCE ONION
BHAJI. *BHAJEE* OR *BHAJI*, MEAN LITERALLY IN
BENGALI, 'A DRYISH VEGETABLE CURRY'. ANY
VEGETABLES CAN BE COOKED THIS WAY. HERE IT IS
BALTI STYLE, WITH MY OWN CHOICE OF
VEGETABLES, THOUGH YOU CAN USE ANY
COMBINATION OF YOUR OWN CHOICE.

serves 2 (see left)

300 g (11 oz) vegetables of your choice,
weighed after stage 1
OR
2 large carrots, cooked and chopped into
roundels
60 g (2 oz) sweetcorn
60 g (2 oz) mangetout
60 g (2 oz) frozen peas, thawed
6 cauliflower florettes
2 tablespoons sunflower oil
110 g (4 oz) onion, thinly sliced
3 cloves garlic, finely chopped
1–2 fresh green cayenne chillies, chopped
1 tablespoon green pepper, chopped
2 cherry tomatoes, chopped
1–2 teaspoons sugar
1 teaspoon Balti garam masala (see page 41)
1 tablespoon freshly squeezed lemon juice
aromatic salt to taste (see page 43)
MASALA
½ teaspoon turmeric
1 teaspoon coriander
4 cloves, crushed
1 piece cassia bark
2 green cardamom pods, crushed

1 Heat the oil in a karahi or wok, then
stir-fry the masala ingredients for about
a minute. Add the onion, garlic, chillies,
pepper and tomatoes and continue to
stir-fry for about 3 minutes.
2 Add the cooked vegetables. Stir in
enough water to keep things mobile.
Simmer for 2 more minutes.
3 Add the sugar and garam masala and
stir and simmer for a final minute.
4 Stir in the lemon juice, salt to taste
and serve.

▶ THE INGREDIENTS FILE

COURGETTE

Also called zucchini,
courgette is a kind
of mini marrow
and a member of
the squash family.
It is a good source
of vitamin C and
provides 15
calories per 100 g
(3½ oz).

DRUMSTICK

A member of the gourd family, native
to south India, the drumstick is long
and thin, growing up to half a metre
(20 in). Its ribbed tough outer casing
contains soft juicy tasty flesh.
To cook, chop it into

pieces, then boil or curry. To eat it the
drumstick is halved, and the flesh
sucked off. Only then is the inedible
skin discarded. The drumstick provide
20 calories per 100 g (3½ oz).

GOURDS AND SQUASHES

Curcurbitacae, from which the word
gourd derives, is the botanical name of
this family of ancient vegetables whos
soft, high water-content flesh is encase
in a harder rind-like inedible casing,

which in some species is smooth, in others knobbly or ribbed. The family is thought to have originated in the Bengal area of India, though it is so ancient, that wild species developed in the Americas before continental drift caused the tectonic plates to separate. Anything called squash is native American as is the pumpkin and chayote (*christophene*). The snake squash, custar squash and spaghetti

squash, are but a few examples. In the Old World, the gourd family includes the cucumber, the marrow (which originated in Persia, and grows to quite huge dimensions, averaging 30 cm/ 12 in), and a whole range of exotic gourds from India. These include the

ribbed gourd (*looki*), bottle gourd (*doodi*), round gourd (*papdi*), drumsticks (*sajjar*), bitter gourd (*kerela*) and snake gourd (see separate entries for the last three). These vegetables require minimal cooking and supply relatively few nutrients. Depending on the species they yield between 7 and 25 calories per 100 g (3½ oz).

GREEN BEAN

The green bean originated in the Americas and was taken east post-Columbus. Before that in the Old World, beans were varieties with large seeds, such as the broad bean, and

virtually inedible scaly casings (see Pulses, page 162–163). The term green bean is used to distinguish between those and species such as the runner bean, snap bean, French or Kenyan bean, and the Indian long bean. All are fleshy pods with soft seeds. Usually they are green but sometimes purple or yellow. The largest are long beans growing up to a metre in length (40 in). Runner beans grow up to 25 cm (10 in) in length. The smallest, the snap bean, is about 10 cm (4 in). All are suitable for currying. Top, tail and string (if necessary), then use whole, sliced or diced. Green beans are good for fibre, folate, and vitamin C. They yield 28 calories per 100 g (3½ oz).

KAKROL

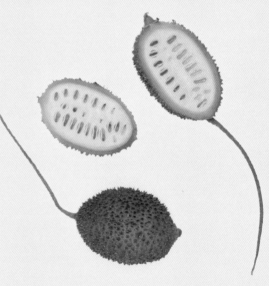

Also known as *Kantola*, these vegetables have no English translation. They are especially popular in Bangladesh and can be used like courgettes. The outer case and seeds are edible. Try them sliced and stir-fried. They yield 15 calories per 100 g (3½ oz).

LEEK

A member of the onion family, native to the Mediterannean, and introduced to Britain by the Romans, the leek is now an important symbol to the Welsh. To prepare, cut off the roots and the tops of the leaves. Discard any damaged outer leaves, ensure there is no gritty soil between the remaining leaves, then slice either lengthways or into roundels (these, incidentally are great for garnishing). Leeks are an excellent source of vitamin C and are also good for vitamins A, B and E, potassium, fibre, iron and magnesium. The leek provides 30 calories per 100 g (3¹/₂ oz).

LOTUS ROOT

A rather extraordinary perforated aquatic root, indigenous to, and very popular in Baltistan and Kashmir, the lotus root is available canned and occasionally fresh at specialist Asian greengrocers in the UK. Peel the fresh root, and cut it into roundels. Keep immersed until you cook it. Boil, steam or microwave until tender, or blanch and stir-fry. The lotus root provides 70 calories per 100 g (3¹/₂ oz).

MAIZE

Maize is a member of the grass family, and more popularly known as sweetcorn. It is native to the Americas, where it has been used dried to make flour, and fresh as a vegetable since pre-

Columbus times. It is a cereal crop, providing many well-known dried breakfast products as well as popcorn. As a vegetable, the familiar cob yields hundreds of golden, soft, tasty grains. They are very high in starch and sugar and excellent for protein. Boiling converts the starch to sugar, but try slowly frying them, and allowing them to caramelise. Miniature cobs (baby corn) are popular in oriental cookery. On the cob, corn provides 123 calories per 100 g (3¹/₂ oz); unsweetened canned it is 76 calories per 100 g (3¹/₂ oz).

MANGETOUT

The fleshy pods and tiny seeds are a member of the pea family (hence its alternative names, snow pea or sugar pea). Mangetout are in fact pulses, but are eaten before they mature, and like green beans, the whole thing – pod and seeds – is eaten after topping and tailing. It contain small amounts of lectin, the toxin present in all pulses, so

should ideally be cooked before eating. Being flat and relatively small, it makes a perfect Balti stir-fry subject. Mangetout are an excellent source of vitamin C and are also good for fibre, magnesium, iron, and vitamin B. Raw mangetout yield 56 calories per 100 g (3¹/₂ oz).

MANGO

The mango (am) originated in the East Indies. It has been cultivated in India for over 6000 years, and is the most revered fruit there, earning the title 'Queen of Fruit', as well as substantial revenue as an export crop. Mango is also used as a vegetable, particularly for pickling. Mangoes grow seasonally on a pretty tree, whose dark leaves spread out like a huge parasol. In Britain and the West, we are fortunate enough to be supplied with fresh mangoes virtually all year round, with imports from many countries. In India, this is not the case, and the mango season is a much anticipated, but rather short highlight of the year. Mangoes are an excellent source of vitamins A and C and are also good for sugar, fibre, potassium, and vitamin B. They provide 15 calories per 100 g (3¹/₂ oz).

◆ Balti Bhoona Vegetable

serves 2 (see page 138)

300 g (11 oz) vegetables of your choice, weighed after stage 1
2 tablespoons vegetable ghee or oil
5 cm (2 in) cube ginger, thinly sliced into matchsticks
1 tablespoon Balti masala mix (see page 39)
200 g (7 oz) onion, thinly sliced
2 tablespoons fresh coriander leaves, chopped
aromatic salt to taste (see page 43)

Clean and prepare the vegetables as appropriate.

Heat the ghee or oil in your Balti pan or wok. Stir-fry the ginger for 20 seconds. Add the masala mix and stir-fry for a further minute. Add the onion. Stir-fry for around 5 minutes.

Meanwhile steam, boil or microwave the vegetables to readiness (see page 134) then drain.

Add the drained hot vegetables and the coriander to the pan and mix in well. Simmer for a couple of minutes more, then salt to taste and serve.

CHEF'S TIP

If you wish to skin tomatoes (I don't normally bother) pierce them once, immerse in water which has just boiled but is off the heat, for 1 minute. Remove them with a slotted spoon and when cool enough, peel off the skins. Canned plum tomatoes are an excellent highly flavoured alternative to fresh.

◆ Balti Bindi Bhajee

OKRA (BINDI) ALSO KNOWN AS 'LADIES' FINGERS' ARE APPALLING IF COOKED BADLY, WHEN THEY OOZE AN UNPLEASANTLY STICKY, THOUGH TASTELESS, SAP. THIS CAN EASILY BE PREVENTED BY COOKING THEM IN THE BRIEFEST POSSIBLE TIME, WITHOUT CUTTING THEM, AND IMMEDIATELY PRIOR TO SERVING THEM.

serves 4 as an accompaniment

250g (9 oz) okra
3 tablespoons vegetable oil
1 teaspoon black mustard seeds
½ teaspoon panch phoran (see page 43)
4 tablespoons chopped onion
2 tomatoes, finely chopped
1 teaspoon Balti garam masala (see page 39)
1 teaspoon sugar
1 lemon, freshly squeezed
1 tablespoon chopped coriander leaves
aromatic salt to taste (see page 43)
SPICES
⅓ teaspoon turmeric
1 teaspoon cummin
1 teaspoon coriander
½ teaspoon chilli powder
½ teaspoon green cardamom seeds, ground

1 Carefully wash the okra.
2 Heat the oil in a Balti pan or wok, stir-fry the seeds, spices and panch phoran for 30 seconds, then add the onion and stir-fry for 5 minutes.
3 Add the tomatoes, garam masala and sugar and stir-fry for 5 minutes.
4 Add the whole okra to the pan and stir-fry for 5 minutes. Stir gently. If the okra is bruised or cut it will go very sappy. Add water by the spoonful to keep things mobile.
5 Add the lemon juice and the chopped coriander leaves.
6 Stir-fry for 5 minutes more. If the okra were tender to start with they are now cooked perfectly. Add salt to taste and serve at once. Do not refrigerate or freeze this dish – it will go sappy and mushy.

◆ Balti Bombay Potato

THE TOMATO AND THE POTATO WERE IGNORED BY THE MOGHULS, INDIANS AND BRITISH ALIKE, UNTIL AMERICAN MISSIONARIES BROUGHT THEM TO INDIA IN THE 19TH CENTURY. CONSEQUENTLY THERE ARE NO TRADITIONAL POTATO DISHES, ALTHOUGH FORTUNATELY THE POTATO IS NOW FULLY ACCEPTED IN INDIA. THIS DOES EXPLAIN THOUGH WHY THIS ONE, NOW A CURRY-HOUSE CLASSIC, WAS LIKE SO MANY OTHER CURRIES A BRITISH RESTAURANT INVENTION.

serves 2 (see page 138)

2 large potatoes (or 4 medium/10–12 small new) cooked as per recipe on page 138
2 tablespoons sunflower oil
85 g (3 oz) onion, thinly sliced
1 tablespoon yellow bell pepper, finely chopped
2 tomatoes, roughly chopped
1 tablespoon fresh coriander leaves, chopped
aromatic salt to taste (see page 43)
MASALA
2 teaspoons coriander
1 teaspoon Balti garam masala (see page 41)
½ teaspoon turmeric
½ teaspoon chilli powder

1 Heat the oil, and stir-fry the masala ingredients for 30 seconds. Add the onion and the pepper, and continue to stir-fry for a further 3 minutes.
2 Add about 8 tablespoons water and the tomatoes and leaves and stir-fry for 2 minutes.
3 Add the cooked potato and simmer until hot. Salt to taste and serve.

◆ Balti Broccoli

BROCCOLI IS A SUPERB SUBJECT FOR BALTI.

serves 2 (see page 138)

300 g (11 oz) broccoli florets
2 tablespoons sunflower oil
½ teaspoon sesame seeds
1 teaspoon mustard seeds
½ teaspoon turmeric
1 tablespoon green masala paste (see
    page 45)
2 teaspoons fresh ginger, finely chopped
3 tablespoons onion, finely chopped
3 tablespoons fresh spinach leaves
1 tablespoon fresh coriander leaves
2 teaspoons Balti garam masala (see page 41)

◆◆◆◆◆◆◆◆◆◆◆◆◆◆◆◆◆◆◆◆◆◆◆◆◆◆◆◆◆◆◆◆◆

1 Boil, steam or microwave the broccoli
florets until they are tender.
2 Heat the oil in your Balti pan or wok
until quite hot. Stir-fry the seeds, and
turmeric for 30 seconds, then add the
paste and the ginger and stir-fry for a
further 30 seconds. Add the onion and
stir-fry for 2 or 3 minutes. Add the
broccoli and just enough water to keep
things mobile.
3 When hot and sizzling (after about
3 or 4 minutes) add the fresh leaves,
garam masala and salt to taste.

◆ Balti Begum Burta

BURTA, MEANING MASH, WORKS AS WELL WITH
AUBERGINE AS IT DOES WITH POTATO.

serves 2 (see page 138)

350 g (12 oz) whole raw aubergine
2 tablespoons fresh coriander leaves
1 tablespoon Balti garam masala (see
    page 41)

◆◆◆◆◆◆◆◆◆◆◆◆◆◆◆◆◆◆◆◆◆◆◆◆◆◆◆◆◆◆◆◆◆

1 Grill or bake the aubergine until it
burns slightly, for a smoky taste.
2 Cut the aubergine in half lengthways,

discard the pith and seeds in the centre,
then scoop out and mash the flesh.
Discard the peel.
3 Simply add the mashed aubergine to
the heated Balti pan, and just enough
water to keep things mobile.
4 When hot and sizzling (after about 3
or 4 minutes) add the fresh leaves, Balti
garam masala and salt to taste.

◆ Balti Jalfrezi

JALFREZI, THE CLASSIC DRY STIR-FRY, IS IDEAL FOR
BALTI VEGETABLES.

serves 2 (see page 138)

300 g (11 oz) vegetables of your choice,
    weighed after stage 1
2 tablespoons ghee or vegetable oil
2–3 garlic cloves, finely chopped
1 tablespoon green masala paste (see
    page 45)
110 g (4 oz) onion, thinly sliced
1 tablespoon red pepper, cut into small
    diamond shapes
1 tablespoon green pepper, cut into small
    diamond shapes
2–4 tablespoons fresh coriander, finely
    chopped
aromatic salt to taste (see page 43)
squeeze of lemon juice
sprinkles of Balti garam masala (see page 41)
SPICES
1½ teaspoons cummin seeds
½ teaspoon lovage seeds
½ teaspoon coriander seeds

◆◆◆◆◆◆◆◆◆◆◆◆◆◆◆◆◆◆◆◆◆◆◆◆◆◆◆◆◆◆◆◆◆

1 Prepare the vegetables, then cut into
the shapes of your choice. Cook the
vegetables using one of the three
methods on page 134.
2 Heat the oil in the karahi. Stir-fry the
spices for 30 seconds then add and stir-
fry the garlic for a further 30 seconds.
Add the masala paste and stir-fry for a
further minute. Add the onion and stir-
fry for 3 more minutes.
3 Add the vegetables and all the
remaining ingredients, salt to taste, and
briskly stir-fry until it is cooked.

◆ Balti Brinjal Begum

BRINJAL IS AUBERGINE, WHICH IS VERY POPULAR I
THE SUBCONTINENT. AUBERGINE CAN TASTE BITTE
(A TASTE ENJOYED BY PAKISTANIS) BUT YOU CAN
DRAW OUT THE BITTERNESS BY SOAKING THE
AUBERGINE IN PLENTY OF COLD WATER TO WHICH
SUGAR AND SALT HAVE BEEN ADDED (ABOUT 1
TABLESPOON EACH TO 500 ML /17½ FL OZ
WATER). IMMERSE THE SLICED OR HALVED
AUBERGINES IN THIS SOLUTION FOR AN HOUR OR
TWO THEN RINSE, STEAM OR BOIL TO TENDERNESS
FOR USE IN THIS RECIPE. PEELING IS OPTIONAL, BU
THE SKIN IS PART OF THE ATTRACTION OF THE DISH

serves 2 (see page 138)

300 g (11 oz) aubergine
4 tablespoons sesame oil
½ teaspoon mustard seeds
½ teaspoon sesame seeds
½ teaspoon wild onion seeds
2 teaspoons fresh garlic, finely chopped
4 tablespoons onion, finely chopped
2 tablespoons fresh coriander leaves
1 tablespoon Balti garam masala (see
    page 41)
salt to taste

◆◆◆◆◆◆◆◆◆◆◆◆◆◆◆◆◆◆◆◆◆◆◆◆◆◆◆◆◆◆◆◆◆

1 Pre-soak the aubergine as described
above. Cut in half lengthways, discard
the pith and seeds in the centre, cut into
bite-sized pieces, then steam or boil.
Alternatively you can dry the aubergine
after soaking (or omit the soaking
altogether), then deep-fry (at
190°C/375°F) for about 5 minutes.
2 Heat the oil in your Balti pan or wok
until quite hot. Stir-fry the seeds and th
garlic for a further 30 seconds.
3 Add the onion and stir-fry for 2 or
3 minutes. Add the aubergine and just
enough water to keep things mobile.
4 When hot and sizzling (after about
3 or 4 minutes) add the fresh leaves,
Balti garam masala and salt to taste.
Serve hot.

Balti Brinjal Begum

◆ Balti Celery

serves 2 (see page 138)

175 g (6 oz) celery
2 tablespoons mustard blend or light oil
1 teaspoon panch phoran (see page 43)
$^1/_3$ teaspoon green cardamom seeds
1 or 2 star anise
2 teaspoons fresh garlic, finely chopped
2 tablespoons onion, finely chopped
15–20 saffron stamens
4 or 5 tablespoons double cream
2 tablespoons fresh coriander leaves, finely
    chopped
3 or 4 fresh mint leaves, chopped
1 teaspoon Balti garam masala (see page 41)
salt to taste

◆◆◆◆◆◆◆◆◆◆◆◆◆◆◆◆◆◆◆◆◆◆◆◆◆◆◆◆◆◆◆◆◆◆

1 Cut the pithy base off the bunch of
celery, trim off the leaves and tops of the
stalks if needed, and discard. Wash the
stalks and cut into bite-size pieces.
2 Heat the oil in your Balti pan or wok
until quite hot. Stir-fry the seeds and the
garlic and stir-fry for 30 seconds. Add
the onion and stir-fry for 2 or 3 minutes.
3 Add the celery and saffron and stir
with just enough water to make things
mobile. Stir as needed and add a little
water until the celery is soft. Then stir in
the cream, fresh leaves, garam masala,
and salt to taste. Serve hot.

◆ Balti Chilli

THE CHILLI IS THE HOT MEMBER OF THE CAPSICUM
FAMILY. THE BEST CHILLI FOR BALTI CURRIES IS THE
CAYENNE WHICH IS THE LONG, THIN, CYLINDRICAL
TAPERING POD, MEASURING 5–10 CM (2–4 IN).
CHILLI NEEDS NO PRE-PREPARATORY BOILING,
STEAMING OR MICROWAVING. SIMPLY CUT OFF THE
STALK, THEN ADD TO THE RECIPE OF YOUR CHOICE
AFTER FRYING THE SPICES, GARLIC AND ONION, OR
AS INDIVIDUAL RECIPES DIRECT. FOR THOSE WHO
TRULY ADORE HEAT, CHILLIES CAN BE USED TO
MAKE A DISH IN THEIR OWN RIGHT. BIG CHILLIES
(15–20 CM/6–8 IN LONG) ARE MILDER, AND CAN
BE STUFFED WITH CURRIED FILLINGS (SEE PAGE 49).

serves 2 (see page 138)

200 g (7 oz) cayenne chillies
3 tablespoons vegetable oil
2 teaspoons black mustard seeds
$^1/_2$ teaspoon black cummin seeds
4 tablespoons pink onion, chopped
2 tomatoes, finely chopped
1 lemon, freshly squeezed
1 tablespoon coriander leaves, chopped
salt to taste
MASALA
$^1/_2$ teaspoon turmeric
1 tablespoon Balti garam masala (see
    page 41)
1 or more teaspoons chilli powder

◆◆◆◆◆◆◆◆◆◆◆◆◆◆◆◆◆◆◆◆◆◆◆◆◆◆◆◆◆◆◆◆◆◆

1 Wash and de-stalk the chillies.
2 Heat the oil in the Balti pan or wok,
stir-fry the seeds for 30 seconds, then
add the masala ingredients and onion
and stir-fry for 5 minutes.
3 Add the tomatoes and chillies and
stir-fry for 5 minutes. Add water by the
spoonful to keep things mobile.
4 Add the lemon juice and the chopped
coriander leaves and stir-fry for 5
minutes more.

◆ Balti Courgettes

COURGETTES ARE A TYPE OF SQUASH OR MARROW.
THEY ARE AN IDEAL SUBJECT FOR BALTI STIR-FRIES.

serves 2 (see page 138)

300 g (11 oz) courgettes, weighed after
    stage 1
2 tablespoons sesame oil
1 teaspoon sesame seeds
$^1/_3$ teaspoon black cummin seeds
$^1/_3$ teaspoon lovage seeds
2 teaspoons fresh garlic, finely chopped
110 g (4 oz) onion, finely chopped
2 tablespoons fresh coriander leaves
1 tablespoon Balti garam masala (see
    page 41)
salt to taste

◆◆◆◆◆◆◆◆◆◆◆◆◆◆◆◆◆◆◆◆◆◆◆◆◆◆◆◆◆◆◆◆◆◆

1 Wash then slice the courgettes
diagonally or square-on, discarding tip
and tail as necessary.
2 Heat the oil in your Balti pan or wok
until quite hot. Stir-fry the seeds and the
garlic for 30 seconds. Add the onion and
stir-fry for 2 or 3 minutes.
3 Add the courgettes and stir with just
enough water to keep things mobile.
Continue doing this as necessary until
the courgettes are tender.
4 After about 5 minutes add the fresh
leaves, garam masala and salt to taste.
Serve hot.

Balti Celery

◆ Balti Egg

Hardboiled eggs make Balti egg curry, and halved, quartered or sliced, they make attractive garnishes.

To hardboil a size 4 egg, immerse it in boiling water. Remove after exactly 15 minutes and cool at once in running cold water. Longer cooking results in a blue ring around the yolk. A quail egg takes 4 minutes to boil. To prevent cracking during boiling, rather than adding salt or vinegar to the water, simply bring the egg to room temperature overnight, prick the blunt end (where the air sac is located) with a pin, then place it in ample boiling water and start timing. You will immediately notice a stream of bubbles coming out of the pinhole. The release of this air prevents expansion, and the egg will not crack.

serves 2

4 hardboiled eggs, shelled and halved
2 tablespoons sunflower oil
225 g (8 oz) onion, thinly sliced
4 cloves garlic, finely chopped
1 tablespoon chopped green pepper
2 cherry tomatoes, chopped
1–2 teaspoons sugar
1 teaspoons Balti garam masala (see page 41)
1 tablespoon freshly squeezed lemon juice
aromatic salt to taste (see page 43)
SPICES
½ teaspoon turmeric
1 teaspoon coriander
4 cloves, crushed
1 piece cassia bark
2 green cardamom pods, crushed

◆◆◆◆◆◆◆◆◆◆◆◆◆◆◆◆◆◆◆◆◆◆◆◆◆◆◆◆

1 Heat the oil in a karahi or wok, then stir-fry the spices for about a minute.
2 Add the onion, garlic, pepper and tomato and continue to stir-fry for about 3 minutes.
3 Add the sugar and garam masala and stir in enough water to keep things mobile. Simmer for 2 more minutes.
4 Add the eggs and carefully stir until they are heated right through
5 Stir in the lemon juice. Salt to taste.

◆ Balti Green Beans

Runner bean, snap bean, French or Kenyan bean: all are fleshy pods, usually green but sometimes purple or yellow, and they are now available all year round. The largest are runners growing up to 25 cm (10 in) in length. The smallest, the snap bean, is about 10 cm (4 in).

serves 2 (as an accompaniment)

300 g (11 oz) green beans of your choice, weighed after topping and tailing – and, in the case of runners, pulling off the stringy part – then cut into strips or crosswise
3 tablespoons sunflower oil
1 teaspoon mustard seeds
½ teaspoon black cummin seeds
1 teaspoon fresh garlic, finely chopped
2 teaspoons fresh ginger, finely chopped
2 tablespoons fresh coriander leaves, finely chopped
2 teaspoons Balti garam masala (see page 41)
salt to taste

◆◆◆◆◆◆◆◆◆◆◆◆◆◆◆◆◆◆◆◆◆◆◆◆◆◆◆◆

1 Boil, steam or microwave to tender as described on page 134.
2 Heat the ghee or oil in your Balti pan or wok until quite hot. Stir-fry the seeds for 30 seconds, add the garlic and ginger together and stir-fry for a further 30 seconds.
3 Add the green beans and stir with just enough water to make things mobile. When hot and sizzling add the fresh leaves, garam masala and salt to taste. Serve hot.

◆ Balti Ghobi

Ghobi means cabbage or cauliflower, which is also called phulghobi. Cut the florets so that they are quite small. This makes their cooking brief so that you get crunchy, tasty results.

serves 2 (see page 138)

300 g (11 oz) washed cauliflower florets, weighed after removing leaves and stalks
2 tablespoons sunflower oil
½ teaspoon sesame seeds
1 teaspoon mustard seeds
½ teaspoon turmeric
2 teaspoons fresh ginger, finely chopped
3 tablespoons onion, finely chopped
3 tablespoons fresh spinach leaves, shredded
1 tablespoon fresh coriander leaves
20 or so saffron stamens
1–2 teaspoons Balti garam masala (see page 41)
salt to taste

◆◆◆◆◆◆◆◆◆◆◆◆◆◆◆◆◆◆◆◆◆◆◆◆◆◆◆◆

1 Boil, steam or microwave the florets until they are as tender as you like them (see page 134).
2 Heat the oil in your Balti pan or wok until quite hot. Stir-fry the seeds, and turmeric for 30 seconds, then add the ginger and stir-fry for a further 30 seconds. Add the onion and stir-fry for 2 or 3 minutes.
3 Add the florets, saffron and just enough water to make things mobile.
4 When hot and sizzling (after about 3 or 4 minutes) add the fresh leaves, garam masala and salt to taste. Serve hot.

VARIATION
Balti Ghobi Aloo
Simply add some cooked potatoes at stage 3.

Balti Ghobi Aloo

◆ Balti Kofta Vegetable

Vegetables make very attractive koftas.

serves 2 or more (see page 138)

For the Vegetable Koftas
Makes 16
60 g (2 oz) peas, cooked or frozen and
    thawed, partly mashed
225 g (8 oz) mashed potato
2 garlic cloves, finely chopped
2 tablespoons dehydrated onion flakes
1 tablespoon fresh coriander leaves, finely
    chopped
2 green chillies, finely chopped
1 egg, beaten
1 teaspoon aromatic salt (see page 43)
2 tablespoons Balti garam masala (see
    page 41)
½ teaspoon lovage seeds
1 teaspoon chilli powder
40 g (1½ oz) gram flour
oil for deep-frying
For the Balti Kofta Curry Gravy
1 tablespoon ghee or vegetable oil
2–3 garlic cloves, finely chopped
2 tablespoons Balti masala paste (see
    page 39)
1 tablespoon tomato purée
225 g (8 oz) Balti masala gravy (see page 42)
175 g (6 oz) canned tomatoes, strained,
    juice reserved
1 teaspoon white granulated sugar
½ teaspoon dried fenugreek leaf
aromatic salt to taste (see page 43)

◆◆◆◆◆◆◆◆◆◆◆◆◆◆◆◆◆◆◆◆◆◆◆◆◆◆◆◆

To make the Koftas
1 Mix the kofta ingredients together to create a mouldable mixture.
2 Divide the mixture into 16 equal-sized portions, and mould them into balls.
3 Mix the gram flour with just enough water to make a thick batter.
4 Heat the deep-frying oil to 190°C/375°F, then dip each kofta into the batter and fry for about 5 minutes. Serve hot with chutney.
To make the Balti Kofta Curry Gravy
1 Heat the oil in the Balti pan or wok

and stir-fry the garlic for 30 seconds. Add the masala paste and tomato purée and stir-fry for a further minute.
2 Add the Balti masala gravy, tomatoes sugar and fenugreek and bring it to the simmer for a few minutes.
3 Salt to taste. Add the koftas, and simmer until they are hot.

◆ Balti Vegetable Keema

A type of mince, made from dehydrated soya bean pulp and high in fibre, is available at specialist shops. It is almost indistinguishable from meat and is a perfect substitute in recipes such as this one.

serves 2 (see page 138)

300 g (11 oz) dehydrated soya mince
    granules
2 tablespoons ghee or corn oil
4 garlic cloves, finely chopped
225 g (8 oz) onion, finely chopped
3 tablespons Balti masala paste (see page 39)
1 tablespoon tomato purée
400 ml (14 fl oz) fragrant stock (see page 43)
1 tablespoon Balti garam masala (see
    page 41)
1 tablespoon fresh coriander leaves,
    chopped
aromatic salt to taste (see page 43)

◆◆◆◆◆◆◆◆◆◆◆◆◆◆◆◆◆◆◆◆◆◆◆◆◆◆◆◆

1 Soak the soya granules for a couple of hours to rehydrate them, then drain.
2 Heat the ghee or oil in your Balti pan or wok on high heat. Stir-fry the garlic for 30 seconds.
3 Add the onion and, reducing the heat, stir-fry for about 10 minutes, allowing it to become translucent and begin to brown.
4 Add the masala paste and the tomato purée. Raise the heat and bring to a brisk sizzle, stir-frying as needed for about 2 or 3 minutes.
5 Add the soya to the pan and stir-fry until sizzling again.
6 Little by little add the stock (and if

needed some water to ensure it is not sticking), to achieve a nice creamy curry texture.
7 Add the garam masala, and coriander leaves and salt to taste.
8 It is ready to serve after a few minutes, but can be kept simmering.

◆ Balti Korma

Vegetable Korma is creamy and delicious.

serves 2 (see page 138)

300 g (11 oz) vegetables of your choice,
    weighed after stage 1
1 tablespoon ghee or vegetable oil
2–3 garlic cloves, finely chopped
1 tablespoon Balti masala paste (see
    page 39)
225 g (8 oz) Balti masala gravy (see page 42)
100 ml (4 fl oz) double cream
1 teaspoon sugar
20 fried almonds, whole
aromatic salt to taste
20–25 saffron strands lightly roasted
Spices
2 bay leaves
5 cm (2 in) cassia bark
4–6 green cardamoms
4–6 cloves
Garnish
fresh coriander leaves

◆◆◆◆◆◆◆◆◆◆◆◆◆◆◆◆◆◆◆◆◆◆◆◆◆◆◆◆

1 Prepare the vegetables: remove any unwanted matter, wash as required, then cut into the shapes of your choice. Cook using one of the three methods described on page 134.
2 Heat the oil in the karahi. Stir-fry the spices for 30 seconds then add the garlic and stir-fry for a further 30 seconds. Add the masala paste and stir-fry for a further minute.
3 Add the gravy and bring it to the simmer, adding the remaining ingredients, including the vegetables, and salt to taste. Simmer until it is cooked to your liking.

MUSHROOM

Technically the mushroom is not a vegetable, but an edible fungus of which there are literally hundreds of species to choose from. The most familiar species are mass-cultivated and include field, cup, button and flat mushrooms. Other less familiar cultivated varieties include beefsteak fungus, parasol, cep, blewit, pleurotte and oyster. All have distinctive flavours, and are handled in the same way, which is to wipe them clean (peeling only if necessary), then cut as required, adding without further cooking to the curry of your choice. Mushrooms are a good source of vitamin B, potassium and fibre and provide 14 calories per 100 g (3½ oz).

generally eaten fresh. Unless the pod is very juvenile, it is inedible (see Mangetout page 140). Fresh peas are available in season and are a welcome alternative to the frozen equivalent, although it should be said that the frozen pea is one of the best frozen products. Peas are an excellent source of protein, sugar, starch and numerous minerals. They also contain small amounts of lectin, the toxin present in all pulses, so should ideally be cooked before eating. Peas provide 52 calories per 100 g (3½ oz).

PLANTAIN

Bananas and the cooking species, plantains, originated in south-east Asia. When the green skin is peeled (and discarded), its flesh, which is much firmer than the banana's, can be sliced or diced and cooked. The plantain is an excellent source of vitamins B6 and C, is good for fibre, carbohydrate and potassium, and provides 120 calories per 100 g (3½ oz).

OKRA

The green, tapering, seed capsule, with a pointed tip and longitudinal grooves is native to Africa and Asia. Okra sizes range from about 6 cm (2½ in) to as much as to 25 cm (10 in). Select soft not scaly specimens, no more than about 11 cm (4½ in) long. Okra, also known as bindi or ladies' fingers, can be eaten raw. Once cut they ooze sap so cut just before a light stir-fry and eat at once. Okra is a good source of vitamin C, potassium and fibre and provides 17 calories per 100 g (3½ oz).

PEA

The small green spheres which grow in a pod are called garden peas, and though they can be dried, when they become a pulse, they are

◆ Balti Mangetout

TO PREPARE MANGETOUT SIMPLY TOP AND TAIL THEM AND IF THEY HAVE A 'STRING' PULL IT OFF. THEY NEED BRIEF COOKING TO REMOVE THE TOXIN LECTIN WHICH IS PRESENT IN SMALL QUANTITIES.

serves 2 (see page 138)

300 g (11 oz) mangetouts, topped and tailed
2 tablespoons mustard oil
1/2 teaspoon panch phoran (see page 43)
2 teaspoons fresh garlic, finely chopped
1 teaspoon white granulated sugar
1 tablespoon chopped coriander leaves
aromatic salt to taste

1 Heat the oil in the Balti pan or wok. Stir-fry the panch phoran and garlic for 30 seconds.
2 Add the mangetout and after a short sizzle lower the heat. Add splashes of water and stir regularly.
3 After about 5 minutes, add the sugar, the fresh coriander and salt to taste. Serve at once.

◆ Balti Karela

THIS KNOBBLY, POINTED CYLINDRICAL GREEN GOURD IS VERY BITTER AND AN ACQUIRED TASTE. TO DRAW OUT ITS BITTERNESS YOU SHOULD SOAK THE KARELA IN PLENTY OF COLD WATER TO WHICH SUGAR AND SALT HAVE BEEN ADDED (ABOUT 1 TABLESPOON OF EACH TO 500 ML/17 1/2 FL OZ WATER). IMMERSE THE SLICED OR HALVED KARELA IN THIS SOLUTION FOR AN HOUR OR TWO THEN RINSE AND USE AS DESCRIBED BELOW.

serves 2 (see page 138)

175 g (6 oz) karela, weighed after washing, discarding the top and tail and dicing into bite-size pieces (and soaking if desired)

1 Boil, steam or microwave to tender using one of the methods described on page 134.

◆ Balti Madras Vegetable

MADRAS IS THE AFFICIONADO'S HOT DISH – HOT BUT NOT SEARING – CONTAINING INTERESTING FLAVOURINGS IN THE FORM OF TOMATO AND ALMOND ALONG WITH CHILLI.

serves 2 (see page 138)

300 g (11 oz) vegetables of your choice, weighed after stage 1
1 tablespoon ghee or vegetable oil
2–3 garlic cloves, finely chopped
1 tablespoon Balti masala paste (see page 39)
1 tablespoon tandoori paste (see page 40)
175 g (6oz) canned tomatoes, strained
2 tablespoons tomato ketchup
2 tablespoons ground almonds
2 tablespoons dehydrated fried onion flakes
aromatic salt to taste
SPICES
2–4 teaspoons chilli powder
1 teaspoon cummin powder
GARNISH
fresh coriander leaves

1 Heat the oil in the Balti pan, stir-fry the spices for 30 seconds then add and stir-fry the garlic for a further 30 seconds. Add and stir-fry the pastes for a further minute.
2 Add the vegetables and briskly stir-fry for about 3 minutes.
3 Add the remaining ingredients and salt to taste. Simmer until it is cooked to your liking.
4 Garnish and serve.

◆ Balti Lotus Roots

A RATHER EXTRAORDINARY PERFORATED ROOT, INDIGENOUS TO AND VERY POPULAR IN BALTISTAN AND KASHMIR, AND AVAILABLE AT SPECIALIST ASIAN GREENGROCERS IN THE UK.

serves 2 (see page 138)

175 g (6 oz) fresh lotus root (weighed after peeling), washed and cut as required, or canned lotus root
1 tablespoon ghee or vegetable oil
2–3 garlic cloves, finely chopped
2 tablespoons Balti masala paste (see page 39)
1 tablespoon tomato puree
225 g (8 oz) Balti masala gravy (see page 42)
175 g (6 oz) canned tomatoes, strained, juice reserved
1 teaspoon white granulated sugar
1/2 teaspoon dried fenugreek leaf
aromatic salt to taste (see page 43)
GARNISH
fresh coriander leaves

1 Boil, steam or microwave the lotus roots to tender using one of the methods described on page 134.
2 Heat the ghee or oil in the Balti pan or wok and stir-fry the garlic for 30 seconds. Add the masala paste and tomato purée and stir-fry for a further minute.
3 Add the Balti masala gravy and bring it to the simmer.
4 Add the tomatoes, sugar and fenugreek and continue simmering for a few more minutes.
5 Salt to taste. Add the lotus roots, and simmer until they are hot.
6 Garnish and serve.

Balti Lotus Roots

◆ Balti Mooli and Carrot

Mooli is the large white radish which is delightful raw. It is also extremely good in Balti cooking, especially when combined with carrot.

serves 2 (see page 138)

300 g (11 oz) carrot or mooli, or a
    combination of both, weighed after
    stage 1
3 tablespoons sunflower oil
¼ teaspoon white cummin seeds
¼ teaspoon mustard seeds
¼ teaspoon fenugreek seeds
¼ teaspoon fennel seeds
¼ teaspoon wild onion seeds
2 teaspoons fresh garlic, finely chopped
1 teaspoon fresh ginger, finely chopped
2 tablespoons fresh parsely, chopped
2 tablespoons fresh coriander leaves,
    chopped
2 teaspoons Balti garam masala (see page
    41)
salt to taste

◆◆◆◆◆◆◆◆◆◆◆◆◆◆◆◆◆◆◆◆◆◆◆◆◆◆◆◆

1 Wash and scrape the mooli and carrots then either chop into small 5–8 mm (¼–⅜ in) cubes, or you can shred them.
2 Heat the oil in your Balti pan or wok until quite hot. Stir-fry the seeds for 30 seconds then add the garlic and ginger together and stir-fry for a further 30 seconds.
3 Add the mooli and carrot and stir with just enough water to make things mobile. When hot and sizzling repeat this, adding water for 3 or 4 minutes, or until the mooli and carrots are at the tenderness of your liking.
4 Add the fresh leaves and garam masala and salt to taste. Serve hot.

◆ Balti Mushroom

Mushrooms absorb liquids and flavours very readily. For that reason I prefer to keep them dry, peel on, if possible before cooking. Of course, if they are very dirty then wash and dry them. Mushrooms can be added to any dish, or they can be cooked on their own, as in this recipe which results in tasty mushrooms with a gorgeous bite and flavour.

serves 2 (see page 138)

400 g (13 oz) mushroom, any type, whole
    or chopped
3 tablespoons vegetable or sunflower oil
½ teaspoon white cummin seeds
¼ teaspoon black cummin seeds
¼ teaspoon fennel seeds
2 teaspoons fresh garlic, finely chopped
2 teaspoons fresh ginger, finely chopped
2 or 3 tablespoons onion, finely chopped
1 tablespoon fresh coriander, chopped
1 teaspoon Balti garam masala (see page 41)
salt to taste

◆◆◆◆◆◆◆◆◆◆◆◆◆◆◆◆◆◆◆◆◆◆◆◆◆◆◆◆

1 Heat the oil in your Balti pan or wok until quite hot. Stir-fry the seeds for 30 seconds, then add the garlic and ginger together and stir-fry for a further 30 seconds.
2 Add the onion and stir-fry for 2 or 3 minutes.
3 Add the mushrooms and just enough water to make things mobile.
4 When hot and sizzling (after about 3 or 4 minutes) add the fresh leaves, garam masala and salt to taste. Serve hot.

◆ Balti Gourd or Squash

This recipe can be used for any gourd or squash, including marrow and pumpkin.

serves 2 (see page 138)

300 g (11 oz) marrow or other gourd,
    weighed after stage 1
4 tablespoons sunflower oil
1 teaspoon sesame seeds
½ teaspoon fennel seeds
½ teaspoon lovage seeds
2 teaspoons fresh garlic, finely chopped
1 teaspoon fresh ginger, finely chopped
2 tablespoons fresh coriander leaves
2 tablespoons fresh basil leaves
2 teaspoons Balti garam masala (see page
    41)
aromatic salt to taste (see page 43)

◆◆◆◆◆◆◆◆◆◆◆◆◆◆◆◆◆◆◆◆◆◆◆◆◆◆◆◆

1 Cook the marrow to tender first (by boiling in plenty of water for 15 or so minutes). Cool enough to halve, de-seed and cut into bite-size cubes (or you can use a melon scoop to make balls).
2 Heat the oil in your Balti pan or wok until quite hot. Stir-fry the seeds for 30 seconds, add the garlic and ginger together and stir-fry for a further 30 seconds.
3 Add the marrow and stir with just enough water to make things mobile. When it is hot and sizzling (after about 2 or 3 minutes) add the fresh leaves, garam masala and salt to taste. Serve hot.

Balti Gourd with Okra

Balti Tibetan Stir-fry

BALTISTAN SHARES ITS BORDER WITH CHINA (ITS PEOPLE ACTUALLY LOOK MORE LIKE TIBETANS THAN INDO-PAKISTANIS). THIS RECIPE REFLECTS THIS INFLUENCE USING BABY SWEETCORN, BEAN SPROUTS, SPRING ONIONS, PEPPERS (ALL OF WHICH ARE AVAILABLE FRESH), AND WATER CHESTNUTS AND STRAW MUSHROOMS (THESE WILL PROBABLY BE CANNED). ALTERNATIVELY YOU COULD USE FRESH CHINESE STIR-FRY MIXED VEGETABLES AVAILABLE IN PACKETS IN THE VEGETABLE DEPARTMENT.

serves 2 (see page 138)

300 g (11 oz) vegetables of your choice, weighed after stage 1
3 or 4 baby sweetcorn sliced
125 g (4 oz) beansprouts
3 or 4 pieces sliced bamboo shoots (optional)
3 or 4 halved water chesnuts (optional)
200 g (7 oz) canned straw mushrooms, drained
OR 250 g (8 oz) fresh oyster mushrooms
3 tablespoons sesame oil
1 teaspoon sesame seeds
½ teaspoon fennel seeds
2 or 3 star aniseed
4 cloves
1 small piece mace
5 cm (2 in) piece cassia bark
2 or 3 bay leaves
2 teaspoons fresh garlic, finely chopped
2 teaspoons fresh ginger, finely chopped
6 or 7 spring onion bulbs and leaves
1 tablespoon red pepper, chopped
2 tablespoons fresh coriander leaves
2 teaspoons Balti garam masala (see page 41)
salt to taste

◆◆◆◆◆◆◆◆◆◆◆◆◆◆◆◆◆◆◆◆◆◆◆◆◆◆◆◆◆◆◆

Wash, chop and mix the sweetcorn, bamboo shoots, chestnuts and mushrooms (keep the bean sprouts whole).
Heat the ghee or oil in your Balti pan or wok until quite hot. Stir-fry the seeds and spices for 30 seconds, then add the garlic and ginger together and stir-fry for a further 30 seconds.
3 Add the spring onions and stir-fry for 2 or 3 minutes.
4 Add the mixed vegetables and stir with just enough water to make things mobile. Stir-fry until hot and sizzling (after about 3 or 4 minutes) then add the red pepper, fresh leaves, garam masala and salt to taste. Serve hot.

Balti Sweetcorn

HIGH-QUALITY IMPORTS MAKE FRESH SWEETCORN AVAILABLE FOR MOST OF THE YEAR. BUY FRESH COBS, BOIL THEM, CUT OFF THE CORNS AND USE IN THIS RECIPE OR FREEZE FOR SUBSEQUENT USE. FAILING THAT, USE FROZEN OR CANNED SWEETCORN.

serves 2 (see page 138)

375 g (12 oz) sweetcorn grains (removed from the cobs)
3 tablespoons ghee or corn oil
½ teaspoon fennel seeds
½ teaspoon sesame seeds
⅓ teaspoon green cardamom seeds
2 teaspoons fresh garlic, finely chopped
2 tablespoons fresh parsely, finely chopped
1 tablespoon fresh coriander leaves, finely chopped
1 teaspoon Balti garam masala (see page 41)
salt to taste

◆◆◆◆◆◆◆◆◆◆◆◆◆◆◆◆◆◆◆◆◆◆◆◆◆◆◆◆◆◆◆

1 Heat the ghee or oil in your Balti pan or wok until quite hot. Stir-fry the seeds, for 30 seconds, then add the garlic and stir-fry for a further 30 seconds.
2 Add the sweetcorn and stir with just enough water to make things mobile. Stir-fry for about 3 or 4 minutes.
3 Add the fresh leaves, garam masala and salt to taste. Serve hot.

Balti Pea

PEAS CAN BE ADDED TO ALL THE RECIPES IN THIS BOOK. IF YOU INTEND TO ADD THEM, DO SO TOWARDS THE END OF COOKING TO RETAIN THEIR GORGEOUS GREEN COLOUR. FROZEN PEAS WILL DO, OF COURSE, BUT THERE IS NOTHING QUITE LIKE SHELLING FRESH PEAS. WITH FROZEN PEAS, SIMPLY THAW THEM, AND ADD THEM TO THE RECIPE AT STAGE 3.

serves 2 (see page 138)

300 g (11 oz) fresh peas, shelled and washed, or frozen peas, thawed
3 tablespoons sunflower oil
1 teaspoon white cummin seeds
½ teaspoon mustard seeds
2 teaspoons fresh garlic, finely chopped
3 or 4 fresh mint leaves, chopped
2 teaspoons Balti garam masala (see page 41)
salt to taste

◆◆◆◆◆◆◆◆◆◆◆◆◆◆◆◆◆◆◆◆◆◆◆◆◆◆◆◆◆◆◆

1 Boil, steam or micorwave the peas to tender (see page 134).
2 Heat the oil in your Balti pan or wok until quite hot. Stir-fry the seeds for 30 seconds, then add the garlic and stir-fry for a further 30 seconds.
3 Add the peas and stir with just enough water to make things mobile. Stir-fry until hot and sizzling (3–5 minutes should be plenty of time).
4 Add the fresh leaves, garam masala and salt to taste. Serve hot.

Balti Tibetan Stir-fry

◆ Balti Cha-Spi-Dhal-Chi

MIXED VEGETABLES WITH SPINACH, DHAL AND CHICKPEAS – THE ARCHETYPAL MIX'N'MATCH COMBINATION BELOVED BY BALTI-MANIACS. MAKING UP THIS COMBINATION WOULD BE LABORIOUS WERE IT NOT FOR THE FREEZER. USE FROZEN MIXED VEGETABLES, FRESH OR FROZEN SPINACH, DHAL AND CHICKPEAS (CHANA) WHICH YOU'VE PRE-COOKED IN BULK AND FROZEN IN BATCHES (SEE PAGES 162-163), OR FOR EVEN QUICKER RESULTS USED TINNED LENTILS.

serves 4

1 tablespoon ghee or vegetable oil
1 portion (6 oz/175 g) Tarka Dhal (see page 162)
1 portion (6 oz/175 g) Kabli Chana Dhal (see page 164)
6 oz (175 g) mixed vegetables, frozen
1 portion (6 oz/175 g) Balti Sag (see page 161)
aromatic salt to taste
some fresh coriander leaves, whole

◆◆◆◆◆◆◆◆◆◆◆◆◆◆◆◆◆◆◆◆◆◆◆◆◆◆◆◆◆

1 Heat the ghee or oil in the karahi.
2 Add the dhal and chickpeas and bring to the simmer. Add the mixed vegetables, and bring back to the simmer again. If frozen this will take a while longer.
3 Add the spinach and any extra tastes of your choice (see page 134). Add a little water if it needs it. Salt to taste. Serve at once, garnished with the fresh coriander leaves.

◆ Balti Tropical Vegetables

EQUAL AMOUNTS OF ANY SIX BALTI VEGETABLES OF YOUR CHOICE. HERE IS AN EXAMPLE, USING A LEAF, A BEAN, A LEGUME, A ROOT, A FRUIT VEGETABLE AND A SQUASH: CAULIFLOWER, GREEN BEANS, RED KIDNEY BEANS, PARSNIP, TOMATO AND MARROW. THIS PARTICULAR COMBINATION GIVES A GOOD VARIETY OF COLOUR AND TEXTURE.

serves 4

EITHER
2 tablespoons ghee or vegetable oil
3–6 garlic cloves, finely chopped
225 g (8 oz) onion, very finely chopped
1–2 tablespoons Balti masala paste (see page 39)
6 to 8 tablespoons cooked red kidney beans (see page 163)
150 g (5½ oz) cooked green beans
10–12 smallish cooked cauliflower florets
1 diced cooked parsnip
6 halved cherry tomatoes
300 g (11 oz) cooked gourd squash or marrow
10–12 baby spinach leaves, chopped
2 teaspoons Balti garam masala (see page 41)
2 tablespoons chopped fresh coriander leaves
aromatic salt to taste (see page 43)

◆◆◆◆◆◆◆◆◆◆◆◆◆◆◆◆◆◆◆◆◆◆◆◆◆◆◆◆◆◆◆

1 Heat the ghee or oil in the balti pan or wok. Stir-fry the garlic for 30 seconds. Add the onions and the paste and continue stir-frying for at least 5 minutes.
2 Add the beans, florets, parsnip, tomatoes, and gourd, and just enough water to keep things mobile, and gently stir to the simmer for a couple of minutes.
3 Add the spinach, garam masala and fresh coriander. Add a little more water if it needs it. Simmer for a couple more minutes, salt to taste and serve.

▶ THE INGREDIENTS FILE

POTATO

It is hard to believe that the potato, was not 'discovered' until the 16th century in the Americas. It was said to be introduced to England by Francis Drake, following his voyage to Virginia in 1584. It eventually found its way to India and her cooking. The potato is a tuber, round or oval, varying in size. It belongs to the nightshade family (as do the aubergine and tomato). No other vegetable is as versatile as the potato, which can be boiled, baked, roasted, fried, cut into shapes or mashed. There are numerous varieties of potato. Most large red potatoes are best for roasting most large whites are best for frying and boiling, ergo currying. New potatoes are best scrubbed unpeeled, and boiled whole, and are superb in curries.

Store potatoes in the dark. Old potatoes can develop the toxin solanine in the form of sprouts or green patches and should be discarded. Potatoes are high in starch, sugar, fibre and protein and the newer they are, the more vitamin C they have. Boiled or baked potatoes provide 80 calories per 100 g (3½ oz).

Radish

Radish originated in China as an herbaceous plant with a thick tap root. The varieties which are favoured in European salads are small round or oval specimens with a bright red skin and brilliant white flesh. The version favoured in the Orient, and now available in the West, is the white radish known in Chinese as *loh baak*, in Japanese as *daikon*, and in Hindi as *mooli*. The white radish grows long and thin, to between 10 and 40 cm (4–16 in). Its overall colour is white. It has a high water content and few nutrients. Its attributes are its crispy texture and appealing light peppery taste. It can be eaten raw, or briefly stir-fried in curries. Radishes provide 15 calories per 100 g (3½ oz).

Red and White Sweet Potato, Yam, Parsnip and Turnip

There is debate about whether the sweet potato originated in eastern Asia or South America. It is evidently so ancient, that wild species may have developed before continental drift caused the tectonic plates to separate. Sweet potato appears in Chinese recipes dating from before 1492, yet it is on record as having been 'discovered' in 1500 in Brazil by the Portuguese who brought it to Africa to feed slaves. It had become popular in Britain by the mid-1500s. (Shakespeare makes potato references which predate the true potato's arrival in Britain in 1584.)

Although the sweet potato does yield an edible potato-like flesh, it is not related to the ordinary potato. The sweet potato is the thick root of a tropical plant. There are a number of varieties, with smooth skin, whose colours vary from light yellow to reddish-violet, giving rise to their general names, red or white sweet potato. The flesh of red sweet potato is orange, and it is very sweet. The flesh of the white sweet potato is yellow,

drier and less sweet and makes an excellent and colourful potato substitute. Cook as potatoes. Sweet potatoes are high in starch, sugar, fibre and protein. Boiled or baked sweet potatoes provide 85 calories per 100 g (3½ oz).

The sweet potato is sometimes erroneously called a yam. In fact, the yam has a crinkled-brown, tough, sometimes hairy skin, and though sizes start quite small, some varieties are much larger than the sweet potato. The yam and the sweet potato are unrelated. The yam is not a root; it is a tuber, indisputably native to China. It had reached Africa by AD900, probably via the Spice Route, and did not reach the West Indies until the 1500s, being taken there, in reverse so to speak, by the Portuguese. The skin should be peeled and discarded. The white flesh which is not so sweet as the sweet potato's, is cooked as for potato. Yams are high in starch, but low in sugar, fibre and protein. Boiled or baked yams provide 120 calories per 100 g (3½ oz).

Parsnip is a native European cream-coloured root vegetable with a pleasant sweet flesh. Peel and then cook as potatoes. The parsnip is high in starch, and provides some sugar, fibre and protein. It provides 56 calories per 100 g (3½ oz).

Turnip is high in water content, and low in sugar, hence less tasty. It provides 11 calories per 100 g (3½ oz).

SPROUTING BEANS

We are all familiar with the Chinese bean sprout. This is often soya bean or moong bean. All beans can be made to sprout, and supermarkets now sell a mixture. Here the mixture is chick peas, green moong, Chinese red beans, sunflower seeds and soya beans. A recipe appears on page 166.

SNAKE GOURD

One of nature's oddities, the snake gourd (not to be confused with the snake squash of the Orient which is yellow, squat and curled-up, with a thin tail) grows hanging down from its indigenous Indian tree until at maturity, it is long and thin and up to a metre (40 in) in length. The picture indicates why it is known locally as the snake gourd. Cook as for drumsticks. The snake gourd provides 20 calories per 100 g (3½ oz).

SPINACH

The dark green leaf of an herbaceous plant, this delicious vegetable gets its unique flavour from its oxalic acid content. Thought to have originated in Iran, it is very popular in the subcontinent. Thorough rinsing is important to remove gritty soil. It should then be lightly cooked, not boiled to death. Indeed, baby spinach leaves can be stir-fried straight into the pot after washing. Spinach is an excellent source of fibre and is also good for iron and potassium. Boiled, it provides 30 calories per 100 g (3½ oz).

TINDOORA

The tindoora resembles a gooseberry in colour, markings and size, though not in shape (it is oval) nor taste. It is a tiny member of the marrow family and has a similar limited amount of flavour, but like courgette, its outer case is also edible. It has no English name, though in Bengali it is also known as *potol*. Cook whole until tender by boiling or currying. The tindoora provides 15 calories per 100 g (3½ oz).

TOMATO

Belonging to the nightshade family (as do the aubergine and potato), the tomato is a juicy fruit, normally round (though some species grow oval or pear-shaped). When ripe it is mostly scarlet, though there are some orange and green varieties available. For decades flavour has been sacrificed by the large sellers. Recently things have started to improve and there are interesting tasty types available such as plum tomatoes and cherry tomatoes. Canned tomatoes (normally the plum variety) are an excellent product, which can be substituted for, or combined with, the real thing. High in water content, and good for vitamin C, raw tomatoes provide 14 calories per 100 g (3½ oz).

storing fresh vegetables

resh produce should be stored at a
ol temperature. Remember that all
uits and vegetables contain a lot of
ater – leaves and soft fruit contain the
ost, roots and tubers the least. Thus
aves and soft fruit will keep for the
ortest time. After a day or two they
ilt and discolour, or shrivel because
eir internal water content has
creased.

The refrigerator and the commercial
ill cabinet are useful for some items
it not for others. Also it is essential
at the refrigerator's temperature
oes not go below 32°F (0°C) – freezing
oint. If it does the water in the
roduce will freeze and it will lose its
olecular structure upon thawing. The
mperature within the fridge is cooler
the top. You can buy a small
expensive device which sits inside
our refrigerator to keep a check on the
mperature.

Some fresh items keep better outside
e fridge. Tomatoes, courgettes,
arrow and gourds require 53–55°F
2–13°C). If the temperature drops
low this the vegetables are prone to
pid deterioration. Assuming this does
t occur and that the humidity is high
ough, all these items will keep well
r up to 14 days.

apsicum peppers, chillies, beans, peas
pod, and aubergine prefer a
mperature of between 43–48°F
–9°C) and will last in the fridge for
out 10–14 days, but will quickly
teriorate if the temperature is lower
an that.

nions, shallots, ginger, and garlic
ep best at 35–41°F (2–5°C) out of the
idge. If they were sound to start with,
ey can last for months. Keep them
t of direct sunlight (but not in the
rk) or else they may sprout leaves.

Lettuce, leeks, broccoli, cauliflower,
cabbage, radishes, celery and carrots
keep best at around 34°F (1°C) in high
humidity in the fridge, when they will
keep for up to an average of 10 days.
However, these vegetables lose vitamin
C and sugar (which turns to starch) the
longer they are stored, so fresh is best.

Potatoes, yam, sweet potatoes,
horseradish and ginger like 39–41°F
(4–5°C). Potatoes prefer the dark (to
prevent sprouting) where they too will
last for months.

Vegetables which grow in the high-
altitude Balti lands are very similar to
those which grow in temperate Britain.
The exotic hot temperature tropical
specials which grow on the plains are
not traditional in Baltistan. However,
some will be encountered at the Balti
house, including gourds, okra,
aubergine – and very good they are too,
either singly or in combination with
other ingredients.

colours in vegetables

Carotene is the yellow pigmentation
predominant in, amongst others,
carrots, mangoes, pumpkins, red
potatoes, swedes, melons and peach.
(It is also present in seafood, causing it
to go pink when cooked – see page 124.)
It converts to vitamin A in the body.
Chlorophyll gives vegetables their green
colour. This rapidly goes dull as most
green vegetables are cooked, though
the lighter and less prolonged the
cooking, the less colour is lost.

◆ Balti Tomato

AFTER MANY DECADES OF FOBBING US OFF WITH
THE TASTELESS TOMATO (STILL SADLY AVAILABLE),
OUR SUPPLIERS HAVE FINALLY DISCOVERED THAT
THE PUBLIC LIKE TOMATOES WITH REAL FLAVOUR.
THEY MAY COST MORE, BUT SEEK THEM OUT.
VARIETIES SUCH AS CANARIES, PLUM TOMATOES OR
CHERRY TOMATOES (ESPECIALLY THE MINIATURE
VERSION) MAKE GOOD BALTI SUBJECTS. TOMATOES
CAN BE ADDED TO ANY BALTI DISHES AS REQUIRED,
BUT HERE IS A BALTI RECIPE FOR THE TOMATO AS A
TASTY ACCOMPANIMENT IN ITS OWN RIGHT.
TOMATOES NEED NO PRE-COOKING. SIMPLY CHOP
THEM UP AND ADD TO YOUR COOKING.

serves 2 (see page 138)

300 g (11 oz) tomatoes, washed and
    weighed after removing stalks, or canned
    tomatoes, strained
3 tablespoons ghee or corn oil
$^2/_3$ teaspoons white cummin seeds
$^1/_2$ teaspoon fennel seeds
$^1/_3$ teaspoon coriander seeds
2 teaspoons Balti masala paste (see page 39)
3 teaspoons fresh garlic, finely chopped
1 teaspoon fresh ginger, finely chopped
4 tablespoons onion, finely chopped
3 or 4 fresh spinach leaves, chopped
2 teaspoons tomato purée
1 tablespoon tomato ketchup
1 tablespoon dried fenugreek leaf
2 tablespoons fresh coriander leaves, finely
    chopped
3 or 4 mint leaves, chopped
2 teaspoons garam masala (see page 41)
salt to taste

◆◆◆◆◆◆◆◆◆◆◆◆◆◆◆◆◆◆◆◆◆◆◆◆◆◆◆◆◆◆◆◆◆

1 Heat the ghee or oil in your Balti pan
or wok until quite hot. Stir-fry the seeds
for 30 seconds, then add the garam
masala, garlic and ginger together and
stir-fry for a further 30 seconds.
2 Add the onion and stir-fry for 2 or 3
minutes. Add the tomatoes, spinach,
tomato purée and ketchup and the dried
fenugreek and stir well and bring to the
sizzle. When hot and sizzling (after
about 3 or 4 minutes) add the fresh
leaves, garam masala and salt to taste.
Serve hot.

◆ Balti Sag

SAG OR SPINACH IS ONE OF THE MOST POPULAR BALTI AND CURRY VEGETABLES. BABY FRESH SPINACH IS NOW READILY AVAILABLE IN PACKETS CLEANED, TRIMMED AND OF VERY HIGH QUALITY. SHREDDED SPINACH CAN ALSO BE USED AS A HERB (IN SMALL QUANTITIES) TO ENHANCE ANY BALTI DISH. THERE IS NO NEED TO PRE-COOK THE SPINACH (UNLESS YOU WANT IT MUSHY). THIS METHOD RETAINS COLOUR, FLAVOUR AND CRUNCHINESS, YET COOKS THE SPINACH SUFFICIENTLY.

serves 2 (see page 138)

300 g (11 oz) fresh spinach leaves with the pithy part of the stalk removed
3 tablespoons ghee or vegetable oil
1 teaspoon white cummin seeds
1/2 teaspoon mustard seeds
3 teaspoons fresh garlic, finely chopped
4 tablespoons onion, finely chopped
3 tablespoons fresh coriander leaves
2 teaspoons Balti garam masala (see page 41)
salt to taste

◆◆◆◆◆◆◆◆◆◆◆◆◆◆◆◆◆◆◆◆◆◆◆◆◆◆◆

1 Heat the ghee or oil in your Balti pan or wok until quite hot. Stir-fry the seeds for 30 seconds, then add the garlic and stir-fry for a further 30 seconds.
2 Add the onion and stir-fry for 2 or 3 minutes. Add the spinach and stir with just enough water to make things mobile. As it softens down repeat the watering process until the spinach is nicely soft and sizzling (5 minutes should be plenty of time).
3 Add the fresh coriander leaves, garam masala and salt to taste. Serve hot.

◆ Paneer

PANEER IS THE ONLY FORM OF CHEESE MADE IN INDIA. IT IS REALLY SIMPLE TO MAKE BY HEATING AND CURDLING MILK, AND THEN SEPARATING THE SOLIDS. IT IS USED IN CURRIES AND SWEETMEATS (SEE INDEX), EITHER CRUMBLED OR IN ITS DENSER CUBED FORM. IT GOES HARD AND RUBBERY IF KEPT OVERNIGHT SO IT SHOULD ALWAYS BE FRESHLY MADE.

makes about 225 g (8 oz) paneer

2 litres (3½ pints) full-cream milk
freshly squeezed juice of 1 or 2 lemons

◆◆◆◆◆◆◆◆◆◆◆◆◆◆◆◆◆◆◆◆◆◆◆◆◆◆◆

1 Bring the milk just up to boiling point. Careful it doesn't boil over!
2 Take it off the heat and add lemon juice until the milk starts to separate. Stir to assist the separation.
3 Using a clean tea-towel and a large sieve, strain off the liquid (the whey). Relative to the solids (the curds), there is always a lot of whey, and whilst you can use some for stock or soup, you will probably discard most of it.
4 Fold the tea-towel over the curds, and form them into a flat disc which must now be compressed. The easiest way to do this is to fill a saucepan with water and place it, with a weight on its lid, on top of the disc.
5 For crumbled paneer, remove the weight after 15–20 minutes and crumble the paneer as shown. For cubes, leave the weight in place for at least an hour, maybe two, then the disc can be cut into cubes or chip shapes.

◆ Chana Dhal

CHANA OR GRAM LENTIL IS AN IMPORTANT LENTIL WHICH ORIGINATED IN THE HIMALAYAS AND IS WIDELY USED IN BALTI COOKING. IT IS A BRIGHT YELLOW SPLIT LENTIL, RESEMBLING THE YELLOW SPLIT PEA, ALTHOUGH IT IS SMALLER AND HAS A RATHER DIFFERENT FLAVOUR. CHANA'S TEXTURE IS SOFT AND SLIGHTLY NUTTY, AND IT IS THIS LENTIL WHICH IS USED TO MAKE GRAM FLOUR (BESAN).

serves 4 as an accompaniment

125 g (4½ oz) gram lentils (chana), split and polished
2 tablespoons butter, ghee or vegetable oil
2 teaspoons Balti masala paste (see page 39)
1 teaspoon green masala paste (see page 45)
2 tablespoons fresh chopped coriander leaves
aromatic salt to taste (see page 43)

◆◆◆◆◆◆◆◆◆◆◆◆◆◆◆◆◆◆◆◆◆◆◆◆◆◆◆

1 Pick through, wash and soak the lentils for at least 6 hours (see note on page 163).
2 Bring 2 pints (1.2 litres) water to the boil.
3 Give the lentils a final hot rinse and place them in the boiling water, stirring after a few minutes to ensure they are not sticking.
4 Reduce the heat to a gentle simmer. Leave the lentils to cook for 45 minutes. Skin off any scum during this time. Test that they are tender (if not continue) then drain.
5 Stir in the pastes and salt to taste.

Balti Sag with Sweetcorn and Crumbly Paneer

◆ Tarka Dhal

There are many small lentils and beans which make excellent dhal. The most readily available and the fastest to cook is the red lentil in its split and polished form. Dried, it is actually orange in colour and cooks into a gorgeous yellow purée. The Balti paste provides spicing, and the tarka is the caramelised frying of the garlic and onion, explained on page 45.

serves 4 as an accompaniment

125 g (4½ oz) red lentils (masoor) split and polished
2 tablespoons butter ghee or vegetable oil
250 g (9 oz) onion, finely chopped
4–6 garlic cloves, finely chopped
1 tablespoon Balti masala paste (see page 39)
2 tablespoons fresh chopped coriander leaves
aromatic salt to taste (see page 43)

◆◆◆◆◆◆◆◆◆◆◆◆◆◆◆◆◆◆◆◆◆◆◆◆◆◆◆

1 Pick through, wash and soak the lentils for about 20 minutes (see note on page 163)
2 Bring twice the volume of water of the soaked lentils to the boil.
3 Give the lentils a final hot rinse and place them in the boiling water.
4 Stir after a few minutes to ensure the lentils are not sticking.
5 Reduce the heat to achieve a gentle simmer. Leave the lentils to cook for about 30 minutes, stirring from time to time and skimming off any scum as it forms. Keep an eye on the water content. It should absorb precisely. If it looks too dry add some water.
6 During stage 5, heat the ghee or oil, and stir-fry the garlic and the onion to a tarka (see page 45).
7 Add the tarka and the remaining ingredients, including salt to taste, to the lentils, and mix well.

◆ Moong Dhal

Another small lentil, moong dhal, has green skin and is creamy yellow in its split and polished form. Here it is cooked in its split form, but you can use whole moong or polished moong if you prefer, with slight adjustments to cooking times (longer for whole, shorter for polished).

serves 4 as an accompaniment

125 g (4½ oz) green lentils (moong), split but not polished
2 tablespoons butter ghee or vegetable oil
4–6 garlic cloves, finely chopped
1 teaspoon green masala paste (see page 45)
1 teaspoon Balti masala paste (see page 39)
2 tablespoons fresh chopped coriander leaves
aromatic salt to taste (see page 43)

◆◆◆◆◆◆◆◆◆◆◆◆◆◆◆◆◆◆◆◆◆◆◆◆◆◆◆

1 Pick through, wash and soak the lentils for about an hour (see note on page 163).
2 Bring twice the volume of water of the soaked lentils to the boil.
3 Give the lentils a final hot rinse and place them in the boiling water.
4 Stir after a few minutes to ensure the lentils are not sticking.
5 Reduce the heat to achieve a gentle simmer. Leave the lentils to cook for about 30 minutes, stirring from time to time and skimming off any scum as it forms. Keep an eye on the water content. It should absorb precisely. If it looks too dry add some water.
6 During stage 5, heat the ghee or oil, and stir-fry the garlic for 30 seconds. Add the pastes and continue stir-frying for a further minute.
7 Add the stir-fry items to the lentils with the leaves. Salt to taste, and mix well.

PULSES

Lentils, dried beans and dried peas are called legumes or pulses, and have been dried since mankind first began civilised farming. In their dried form, they can be stored for years and traditionally provided high-quality nutrition over hard winters and non-growing periods. They provide a very high level of protein, (and fully replace meat in this aspect, for the vegetarian). They also provide sugars and starch, and are low in fat. They are good for calcium, and contain some iron and other minerals. Most pulses contain a toxin called lectin, normally eliminated during cooking. The red kidney bean is the exception, and needs pre-soaking to assist the process.

Balti people have long since relied on pulses, as have all the peoples of the subcontinent. They are a delicious and manifestly important ingredient in Balti dishes. Many packs of dried lentils and beans come in 500 g (1.1 lb) size which provides enough for around 10–12 portions. Cook in amounts of around 125 g (4½ oz), and freeze any excess in large yoghurt pots. Lentils and beans are available in cans, the net weight usually being 400 g (14 oz) including liquid. You can save considerable time using these products, although it costs a little more than the home-cooked equivalent. The liquid can be used in stock.

The pulse family is large, but for our purposes, we need only four lentil types, two beans and chickpeas.

lentils

| Chana Dhal | Black urid | Green Moong | Masoor |

lentils are pulses. Specifically, they are various types of small bean. When ripe, the pods are picked, opened and discarded, and small seeds which remain are dried in the sun. The seeds generally grow in two halves and are contained within an outer skin. They can be cooked as such, or simply split into two, and left with the skin on. More fibre comes from lentils with skin on, but a further refinement is available with factory polishing to remove the skin, known as split and polished lentils. In all these forms, many types of lentil, or dhal, are to this day a major staple in India. Here are four useful types which dried provide 300 calories per 100 g (3½ oz):

MASOOR DHAL
Dark green skins, orange seeds. Of all the lentils which make excellent dhal, the most readily available, and the fastest to cook is the red lentil in its split and polished form.

MOONG DHAL
Green skins and creamy yellow seed. Makes a pleasant creamy dhal.

URID DHAL
Black skins and white seed. Whole urid makes a nutritious dhal.

CHANA DHAL
Gram Lentil
Yellow skin and seed. An important

lentil which originated in the Himalayas and is widely used in Balti cooking. It resembles the yellow split pea in colour and size and it is this lentil which is used to make gram flour (besan).

chickpeas and dried beans

Red kidney beans

Lobia beans

KABLI CHANA
Buff skin, paler buff seed. A member of the pea family, the dried chickpea is a rock-hard sphere about 8 mm (⅝ in) in diameter. After prolonged soaking it cooks to a firm yet tender texture, giving good colour and visual interest as well as a fine taste. Dried chickpeas provide 320 calories per 100 g (3½ oz).

LOBIA BEANS
These attractive white beans are also known as cowpeas or black-eye beans,

because of their tiny black eye-shaped marks. They are high in nutrients. They lose their whiteness somewhat during cooking, but this makes them no less attractive. Dried lobia beans provide 325 calories per 100 g (3½ oz).

RED KIDNEY BEANS
An immensely popular dry bean, it obtains its name from its shape and its reddish-purple colour. Particular attention must be paid to removing the toxins (lectins) in the bean, which is simple: soak them for 24 hours, then rinse well prior to boiling. Dried red kidney beans provide 270 calories per 100 g (3½ oz).

cooking pulses

1 Always pick through the pulses by spreading them out on a table in batches and examining them. Small stones, even large pieces of grit are not uncommonly found. This is because the villagers still dry their pulses on the ground, or on flat roofs.

2 For the same reason a good rinse in cold water is essential.

3 Soak the pulses (timings vary according to type) to draw out the toxin lectin, and to soften them and therefore shorten cooking time.

4 Cooking can be in a saucepan or in the microwave. As they absorb water, the pulses will expand by up to twice their dry size. Use a saucepan large enough to allow for this.

◆ Kabli Chana Dhal

The dried chickpea, or Kabli Chana, a rock-hard sphere about 8 mm (⅝ inch) in diameter, is the largest member of the lentil family. After prolonged soaking it cooks to a firm yet tender texture, giving good colour and visual interest as well as a fine taste.

serves 4 as an accompaniment

125 g (4½ oz) chickpeas (kabli chana)
2 teaspoons Balti masala paste (see page 39)
1 teaspoons tandoori paste (see page 40)
110 g onion thinly sliced
1 tablespoon dried mint (optional)
6 tablespoons Greek yoghurt
2 tablespoons fresh chopped coriander leaves
aromatic salt to taste (see page 43)

◆◆◆◆◆◆◆◆◆◆◆◆◆◆◆◆◆◆◆◆◆◆◆◆◆◆◆

1 Pick through, wash and soak the chickpeas for at least 12 hours (see note on page 163).
2 Bring 2 pints (1.2 litres) water to the boil.
3 Give the chickpeas a final hot rinse and place them in the boiling water, stirring after a few minutes to ensure they are not sticking.
4 Reduce the heat to a gentle simmer. Leave the chickpeas to cook for 45 minutes. Skim off any scum during this. Test that they are tender (if not continue) then drain.
5 Add the remaining ingredients to the chickpeas, including salt to taste, and simmer until everything is hot and amalgamated.

◆ Urid Maahn Dhal

Whole black lentils are called urid. In this classic Kashmiri and Balti recipe, urid is enhanced with ginger, tomato and Balti spices. It is so nutritious that it can be eaten on its own, or with plain boiled rice or chapatti.

serves 4

300 g (10 oz) dried whole urid dhal (black lentils)
750 ml (1¼ pints) fragrant stock (see page 43) or water
4 tablespoons butter ghee or vegetable oil
½ teaspoon coriander seeds
½ teaspoon white cummin seeds
2 or 3 cloves finely chopped fresh garlic
5 cm (2 in) cube finely shredded fresh ginger
3 or 4 tablespoons finely chopped onion
8 to 12 cherry tomatoes quartered
1 tablespoon tomato ketchup
2 tablespoons finely chopped fresh coriander leaves
1 tablespoons finely chopped mint leaves
2 tablespoons finely chopped basil leaves
1 tablespoon Balti garam masala (see page 41)
aromatic salt to taste (see page 43)

◆◆◆◆◆◆◆◆◆◆◆◆◆◆◆◆◆◆◆◆◆◆◆◆◆◆◆◆

1 Soak the black lentils for 12 hours or overnight in a covered bowl, containing at least three times the volume of water to the lentils. They will shed some skins, and change colour a bit.
2 To cook, bring the measured amount of stock or water to the boil. Drain the black lentils, rinse them then add them to the boiling water.
3 Once they are boiling, reduce the heat until a gentle simmer is achieved.
4 Simmer for 40–50 minutes, stirring from time to time, until the black lentils are tender.
5 Whilst the black lentils are simmering, heat the ghee or oil in your Balti pan or wok until quite hot.
6 Stir-fry the seeds for 30 seconds, add the garlic and stir-fry for a further 30 seconds. Add the ginger and stir-fry for further 30 seconds, then add the onions and continue to stir-fry for 4 or 5 minutes more.
7 Add the garam masala, tomatoes and tomato ketchup and just enough water to make things mobile.
8 When hot and sizzling (after about 3 or 4 minutes) add the fresh leaves.
9 When the lentils reach the stage where they are tender enough to eat, drain off the excess water (if any) returning the black lentils to their pan.
10 Add the stir-fry items into the lentil pot. Stir well and simmer for a few more minutes. Salt to taste.

Maahn Rajma
Simply add some cooked or canned kidney beans to the Urid Maahn Dhal, for an authentic recipe variation.

Maahn Mattar
Add some thawed frozen peas to the Urid Maahn Dhal, for another authentic recipe variation.

Green Maahn Dhal
Use 300 g (10 oz) whole green moong dhal in place of the urid dhal. The remainder of the recipe is the same. Some red kidney beans can be added if you wish.

Green Maahn Dhal

◆ Lobia Beans

ALSO KNOWN AS COWPEAS, THESE WHITE BEANS WITH A TINY BLACK 'EYE' ARE ATTRACTIVE AND HIGH IN NUTRIENTS. YOU CAN USE CANNED BEANS FOR THIS. THE CONTENTS YIELD SLIGHTLY MORE, AND YOU CAN STRAIN AND USE SOME OR ALL OF THE BRINE IN THE COOKING. SIMPLY BRISKLY STIR-FRY TILL HOT, THEN COMPLETE STAGE 5.

serves 4 as an accompaniment

125g (4½ oz) lobia beans
3oz (75g) onion, thinly sliced
1 teaspoon Balti garam masala (see page 41)
2 tablespoons fresh chopped coriander
    leaves
aromatic salt to taste (see page 43)
2 teaspoons chilli powder (optional)

◆◆◆◆◆◆◆◆◆◆◆◆◆◆◆◆◆◆◆◆◆◆◆◆◆◆◆◆◆

1 Pick through, wash and soak the lobia beans for at least 12 hours (see note on page 163).
2 Bring 2 pints (1.2 litres) water to the boil.
3 Give the lobia beans a final hot rinse and place them in the boiling water, stirring after a few minutes to ensure they are not sticking.
4 Reduce the heat to a gentle simmer. Leave the lobia beans to cook for 45 minutes to one hour. Skim off any scum during this. Test that they are tender (if not continue) then drain.
5 Add the remaining ingredients to the beans, including salt to taste.

◆ Kidney Beans Rajma

THE IMMENSELY POPULAR RED KIDNEY BEAN (RAJMA) GETS ITS NAME FROM ITS SHAPE AND ITS REDDISH-PURPLE COLOUR. IT IS IMPORTANT TO SOAK THEM FOR 24 HOURS AND BOIL THEM TO REMOVE THE LECTIN, A TOXIN IN THE BEAN. YOU CAN USE CANNED RED KIDNEY BEANS IF YOU PREFER. SIMPLY DRAIN AND RINSE THEM (DISCARDING THE LIQUID). OMIT STAGES 1 TO 4 AND 9, ADDING THE CANNED BEANS INTO THE STIR-FRY.

serves 4 as an accompaniment

250 g (9 oz) dried rajma (red kidney) beans
750 ml (1¼ pints) fragrant stock (see page
    43) or water
4 tablespoons ghee or corn oil
5 cm (2 in) cube finely shredded fresh ginger
½ teaspoon green peppercorns, crushed
½ teaspoon panch phoran (see page 43)
85g (3 oz) onion, thinly sliced
1 red pepper, cut into diamonds
1 red chilli, chopped
2 teaspoons Balti masala paste (see page 39)
1 teaspoons tandoori paste (see page 40)
2 tablespoons fresh chopped coriander
    leaves
1 teaspoon Balti garam masala (see page 41)
75 g (3 oz) green peas, thawed (optional)
aromatic salt to taste (see page 43)
2 teaspoons chilli powder (optional)

◆◆◆◆◆◆◆◆◆◆◆◆◆◆◆◆◆◆◆◆◆◆◆◆◆◆◆◆◆

1 Pick through, wash and soak the kidney beans for up to 24 hours (see note on page 163).
2 To cook, bring the measured amount of stock or water to the boil.
3 Give the beans a final hot rinse and place them in the boiling water, stirring after a few minutes to ensure they are not sticking.
4 Reduce the heat to a gentle simmer. Leave the beans to cook for 45 minutes. Skim off any scum during this. Test that they are tender (if not continue) then drain.
5 Whilst the beans are simmering, heat the ghee or oil in your Balti pan or wok

until quite hot.
6 Stir-fry the ginger, peppercorns and panch phoran for 30 seconds, then add the onion, red pepper and chilli, and continue to stir-fry for 4 or 5 minutes more.
7 Add the pastes and just enough wate to make things mobile.
8 When hot and sizzling add the fresh leaves, and the garam masala, and the peas if required.
9 When the beans are tender enough eat, drain off the excess water (if any) returning the beans to their pan.
10 Add the stir-fry items into the pan. Stir well and simmer for a few more minutes. Salt to taste, and add chilli powder if required.

◆ Sprouting Beans

THE MIXTURE POPULARLY SOLD IN PACKETS (SEE PICTURE ON PAGE 158), CONTAINS WHOLE GREEN MOONG DHAL SEED, CHICKPEA, CHINESE RED BEANS, SUNFLOWER SEEDS AND SOYA BEANS. IT CA BE EATEN AS A SALAD, BUT TRY IT LIGHTLY COOK AS A BALTI STIR-FRY.

serves 4 as an accompaniment

125 g (4½ oz) mixed sprouting beans
2 or 3 cloves garlic, sliced
2.5 cm (1 in) cube ginger shredded
1 to 3 red and/or green chilli, chopped
    (optional)
1 teaspoon Balti garam masala (see page 4
2 tablespoons fresh chopped coriander
    leaves
aromatic salt to taste (see page 43)

◆◆◆◆◆◆◆◆◆◆◆◆◆◆◆◆◆◆◆◆◆◆◆◆◆◆◆◆◆

1 Blanch the beans, or microwave then to soften them just a little.
2 Heat the oil and stir-fry the garlic an ginger for 30 seconds.
3 Add the beans and optional chilli, an continue to stir-fry until they are hot.
4 Add the remaining ingredients, including salt to taste.

some vegetable combination dishes

If you are serving a meal composed of vegetable dishes only, then a choice of three or four of the preceding dishes, served with rice, and/or bread and chutneys makes a superb meal. Even hardened meat-eaters cannot fail to be impressed with the quality of Balti curried vegetables. If you are looking for one or two vegetable dishes to accompany meat, poultry or fish dishes, you can, of course, choose from the preceding recipes. Alternatively, you may wish to mix vegetables together in a single dish. Here I give a number of traditional combinations.

As with the single vegetable recipes, I am giving portion sizes that will satisfy four people when each dish is served with two or three others. The same size portion will be adequate for two diners, if one other dish is served, or for one person with the dish on its own.

Rather than reproduce earlier recipes again here, I have shown how you can adjust them to use the vegetable combinations of your choice by adjusting the total weight of the vegetables. For example, for the Balti Sag Aloo recipe, you can follow the Balti Bombay Potato recipe on page 141, halving the potato quantity and adding the equivalent weight of spinach. You can add spices to recipes to suit your taste, as well. If the recipe calls for three vegetables but you want to use two, simply adjust the quantities so that the total vegetable weight remains the same. And there are some vegetables you can add to any combination recipes, in small amounts, including bell peppers, celery, mangetout, mushroom, canned sweetcorn, spring onion and tomato, and fresh chillies.

All the recipes are easy to make and you can invent your own combinations, as you wish. There are some more elaborate vegetable combination dishes in the next chapter.

◆ Balti Sag Aloo

A COMBINATION OF SPINACH AND POTATO.

Serves 2 as an accompaniment dish

EITHER: Follow the recipe for Balti Bombay Potato on page 141, making the following changes. Halve the potato quantity and add 175 g (6 oz) chopped and trimmed spinach leaves at stage 2. Stir-fry for a bit longer. Continue with stage 3.
OR: Follow the recipe for Balti Sag on page 161, making the following changes.
Halve the spinach quantity. Add cooked potato in its place, towards the end of stage 3, allowing enough time for it to become hot.

◆ Balti Methi Sag Aloo

A COMBINATION OF SPINACH AND POTATO WITH THE ADDITION OF SAVOURY FENUGREEK.

Serves 2 as an accompaniment

Simply add 1 to 2 teaspoons of dried fenugreek leaves (methi) to either of the above conversions as soon as the intitial stir-fry is completed.

◆ Balti Sag Paneer

A COMBINATION OF SPINACH AND INDIAN CHEESE.

Serves 2 as an accompaniment

Follow the recipe for Balti Sag on page 161, making the following changes. Halve the spinach quantity. Add the paneer in its place towards the end of stage 3, allowing enough time for it to heat through.

◆ Balti Mattar Paneer

A COMBINATION OF PEAS AND INDIAN CHEESE.

Serves 2 as an accompaniment

Follow the recipe for Balti Pea on page 155, making the following changes. Halve the pea quantity. Add the paneer in its place towards the end of stage 3, allowing enough time for it to heat through.

◆ Balti Bindi Aloo

A COMBINATION OF OKRA AND POTATO.

Serves 2 as an accompaniment

Follow the recipe for Balti Bombay Potato on page 141, making the following changes. Halve the potato quantity and add 175 g (6 oz) okra at stage 2. Stir-fry for a few minutes. Continue with stage 3.

◆ Balti Kabli Chana Aloo

A COMBINATION OF COOKED CHICKPEA AND POTATO.

Serves 2 as an accompaniment dish

EITHER: Follow the recipe for Balti Bombay Potato on page 141, making the following changes. Halve the potato quantity and add 175 g (6 oz) canned (strained) chickpeas at stage 2. Stir-fry for a few minutes. Continue with stage 3.
OR: Follow the Kabli Chana recipe on page 164 and add cooked potato at stage 5.

Specials

One difference between serving Balti and ordinary curry, is that curries are served in separate bowls, whereas Balti curries are all mixed up in one bowl. In the previous chapter, I discussed the concept of mixing vegetables together to make interesting combinations. This concept can be taken a step further with the addition of other ingredients, a practice that has become an art form in certain Balti Houses. One of my favourites comes from Birmingham's aptly named 'I Am The King of Balti' restaurant, whose menu states 'If you can't find your favourite combination on our menu, our chef will be delighted to cook it especially for you.' With over sixty Balti dishes on their menu you'd think that the possibilities would be exhausted; of course in reality the permutations are almost infinite.

Some traditional Balti House combinations are straightforward. You could have Balti meat with mushroom, for example, or Balti meat with Mushroom and Dhal, or even Balti Meat with Mushroom, Dhal and Spinach. But that's not all. Other combinations have names like wartime code, all, of course, well-known to Balti aficionados. Balti Mt-Spi-Cha-Chi-Aub is a very popular dish. Decoded it becomes Balti meat with spinach, chana, chickpeas and aubergine. Alternatively, there is Balti Chk-Chi-Car-Cha-Spi-Aub – chicken, chickpeas,.carrot, chana, spinach and aubergine. Equal amounts of meat, chicken and prawns become Balti Tropical. To make Balti Tropical Plus, add Keema. Balti Tropical Vegetable combines any six vegetables of your choice, while Exotica is Tropical adorned with fruits such as banana and mango. And to cap it all Balti Exhaustion mixes Balti Tropical with Balti Tropical Plus and it contains just about anything and everything. I hope you'll have fun making up inventive combinations of your choice.

◆ Balti Exhaustion Dish

SEVERAL BALTI HOUSES SERVE THIS AS IS THE ULTIMATE COMBINATION DISH. IT CONTAINS ANYTHING AND EVERYTHING. THE 'EXHAUSTION' WILL COME AS A RESULT OF EATING IT, SAY THE BALTI HOUSES. ACTUALLY IT IS VERY POPULAR, AND IS A GREAT WAY FOR YOU TO USE UP LEFTOVERS. ALTERNATIVELY SERVE IT AS THE MAIN DISH AT A PARTY. THAT'S HOW I'VE PORTIONED IT HERE (FOR EIGHT PEOPLE), ALTHOUGH YOU COULD SERVE IT TO LESS PEOPLE AND FREEZE THE SURPLUS. REMEMBER TOO, YOU CAN USE ABSOLUTELY ANY INGREDIENTS; THIS IS JUST MY OWN SUGGESTION.

serves 8 (as a substantial main course)

1 quantity of Balti Tropical Plus (see page 171)
1 quantity of Balti Tropical Vegetables (see right)
2 teaspoons Balti garam masala (see page 41)
2 tablespoons fresh coriander leaves, chopped
aromatic salt to taste (see page 43)
GARNISH
flaked almonds, toasted
a swirl of single cream

◆◆◆◆◆◆◆◆◆◆◆◆◆◆◆◆◆◆◆◆◆◆◆◆◆◆◆◆

1 Cook the two tropical dishes according to their respective recipes and combine in a Balti pan or wok, bringing to the simmer.
2 Add garam masala, leaves and salt to taste. Simmer for a few minutes longer to amalgamate flavours, adding minute amounts of water as needed to keep things mobile.
3 Garnish and serve. If you have any leftovers from this large amount they can be frozen provided everything was fresh (not frozen) first time around.

Previous pages: Balti Exhaustion Dish

◆ Balti Cha-Chi-Spi-Dhal-Bhaji

THIS IS BALTI RESTAURANT SPEAK FOR CHANA, CHICKPEA, SPINACH AND DHAL.

serves 4 (as a substantial main course)

EITHER
2 tablespoons ghee or vegetable oil
3–6 garlic cloves, finely chopped
225 g (8 oz) onion, very finely chopped
1–2 tablespoons Balti masala paste (see page 39)
OR
250 g (9 oz) Balti masala gravy with masala paste added (see page 42)

around 10 heaped tablespoons cooked chana dhal (see page 161)
around 10 heaped tablespoons cooked kabli chana (see page 164)
3–6 tablespoons cooked tarka dhal if available
175 g (6 oz) mixed frozen vegetables, thawed
200 g (9 oz) fresh spinach leaf
Balti garam masala (see page 41)
2 tablespoons fresh coriander leaves, chopped
aromatic salt to taste (see page 43)

◆◆◆◆◆◆◆◆◆◆◆◆◆◆◆◆◆◆◆◆◆◆◆◆◆◆◆◆

EITHER
1 Heat the ghee or oil in the Balti pan or wok. Stir-fry the garlic for 30 seconds. Add the onions and continue stir-frying for at least 5 minutes.
OR
1 Bring the gravy to the simmer.
2 Add the chana, dhal and mixed vegetables and gently stir to the simmer.
3 Add the spinach, the garam masala, and fresh coriander. Add a little water if needed. When simmering, salt to taste and serve.

◆ Balti Tropical Vegetables

TROPICAL IS A BALTI RESTAURATEUR'S NAME FOR SPECIAL COMBINATION DISH USUALLY CONTAINING EQUAL AMOUNTS OF ANY SIX VEGETABLES OF YO CHOICE. HERE IS AN EXAMPLE, USING A LEAF, A BEAN, A LEGUME, A ROOT, A FRUIT VEGETABLE AND A SQUASH (I.E. CAULIFLOWER, GREEN BEANS RED KIDNEY BEANS, PARSNIP, TOMATO AND MARROW). THIS PARTICULAR COMBINATION GIVES A GOOD VARIETY OF COLOUR AND TEXTURE.

serves 4 (as a substantial main course)

EITHER
2 tablespoons ghee or vegetable oil
3–6 garlic cloves, finely chopped
225 g (8 oz) onion, very finely chopped
1–2 tablespoons Balti masala paste (see page 39)
OR
250 g (9 oz) Balti masala gravy with masala paste added (see page 42)
6–8 tablespoons cooked red kidney beans (see page 163)
150 g (5½ oz) green beans, cooked
10–12 smallish cooked cauliflower florets
1 parsnip, cooked and diced
6 cherry tomatoes, halved
300 g (11 oz) gourd squash or marrow, cooked
2 teaspoons Balti garam masala (see page 4
2 tablespoons fresh coriander leaves, chopped
aromatic salt to taste (see page 43)

◆◆◆◆◆◆◆◆◆◆◆◆◆◆◆◆◆◆◆◆◆◆◆◆◆◆◆◆◆

EITHER
1 Heat the ghee or oil in the Balti pan or wok. Stir-fry the garlic for 30 seconds Add the onions and continue stir-frying for at least 5 minutes.
OR
1 Bring the gravy to the simmer.
2 Add the beans, florets, parsnip, tomatoes and gourd and gently stir to the simmer.
3 Add the garam masala and fresh coriander. Add a little water if needed. When simmering, salt to taste and serve

combination dishes with meat, poultry and seafood

Unique to the Balti house are dishes which combine the above, and of course you can add any combination of vegetables too. For different flavours you can use any of the meat recipes between pages 58 and 81, the chicken recipes between pages 82 and 107, and any of the seafood recipes between pages 108 and 131.

◆ Balti Meat and Chicken

VERY POPULAR AT THE BALTI HOUSE – EQUAL AMOUNTS OF BALTI MEAT AND BALTI CHICKEN. YOU CAN USE ANY MEAT AND ANY CHICKEN RECIPE TOGETHER. USE THE QUANTITY MADE IN EACH RECIPE CHOSEN.

serves 4 (as a substantial main course)

1 quantity of any cooked Balti Meat recipe between pages 58 and 81
1 quantity of any cooked Balti Chicken between pages 82 and 107
1 or 2 teaspoons Balti garam masala (see page 41)
2 tablespoons fresh coriander leaves, chopped
aromatic salt to taste (see page 43)

◆◆◆◆◆◆◆◆◆◆◆◆◆◆◆◆◆◆◆◆◆◆◆◆◆◆◆◆◆◆

1 Cook the meat and the chicken according to their respective recipes and combine in a Balti pan or wok, bringing to the simmer.
2 Add the garam masala, coriander and salt to taste. Simmer for a few minutes longer to amalgamate flavours, adding minute amounts of water if needed to keep things mobile.
3 If you have any leftovers from this large amount, they can be frozen, provided everything was fresh (not frozen) first time around.

Balti Meat, Chicken and Mushrooms
Simply add chopped raw mushrooms at the beginning of stage 2 of the above.

◆ Balti Tropical

WE MET BALTI TROPICAL VEGETABLES ON PAGE 156. THE NON-VEGETARIAN VERSION HAS EQUAL AMOUNTS OF BALTI MEAT, BALTI CHICKEN AND PRAWNS. IT SOUNDS FAIRLY BIZARRE BUT IT WORKS WELL. THE NAME IS COMMONLY USED IN THE BALTI HOUSE ALTHOUGH NO ONE CAN TELL ME QUITE WHY IT IS "TROPICAL"!

serves 4 (as a substantial main course)

1 quantity of any cooked Balti Meat recipe between pages 58 and 81
1 quantity of any cooked Balti Chicken between pages 82 and 107
175 g (6 oz) peeled prawns in brine, and their liquid
1 or 2 teaspoons Balti garam masala (see page 41)
2 tablespoons fresh coriander leaves, chopped
aromatic salt to taste (see page 43)

◆◆◆◆◆◆◆◆◆◆◆◆◆◆◆◆◆◆◆◆◆◆◆◆◆◆◆◆◆◆

1 Cook the meat and the chicken according to their respective recipes and combine in a Balti pan or wok, bringing to the simmer.
2 Add the prawns and leaves, garam masala and salt to taste. Simmer for a few minutes longer to amalgamate flavours, adding minute amounts of the prawn liquid as needed to keep things mobile.
3 If you have any leftovers from this large amount, they can be frozen, provided everything was fresh (not frozen) first time around.

Balti Tropical Plus
The 'plus' here refers to the addition of Balti Keema to Balti Tropical above.

Use a full quantity of Keema (see pages 66 and 94), adding it at the beginning of stage 2.

◆ Balti Mt-Spi-Cha-Chi-Aub

WE MET A VEGETABLE VARIATION OF THIS DISH ON PAGE 156. BIRMINGHAM'S POPULAR ADIL'S BALTI HOUSE IS CREDITED WITH INVENTING THE CONCEPT. SIMPLY ADD MEAT AND YOU HAVE ANOTHER VERY POPULAR DISH. DE-CODED IT MEANS BALTI MEAT WITH SPINACH, CHANA, CHICKPEAS AND AUBERGINE.

serves 4 (as a substantial main course)

1 quantity of any cooked Balti Meat recipe between pages 58 and 81
1 quantity of cooked Balti Cha-Spi-Dhal-Chi recipe (see page 156)
2 teaspoons Balti garam masala (see page 41)
2 tablespoons fresh coriander leaves, chopped
aromatic salt to taste (see page 43)

◆◆◆◆◆◆◆◆◆◆◆◆◆◆◆◆◆◆◆◆◆◆◆◆◆◆◆◆

1 Cook the meat and the Cha-Spi-Dhal-Chi according to their respective recipes and combine in a Balti pan or wok, bringing to the simmer.
2 Add the garam masala, leaves and salt to taste. Simmer for a few minutes longer to amalgamate flavours, adding minute amounts of water as needed to keep things mobile.
3 If you have any leftovers from this large amount, they can be frozen, provided everything was fresh (not frozen) first time around.

◆ Balti Exotica

DREAMED UP BY ONE OF THE MORE ADVENTUROUS BALTI HOUSE OWNERS THIS RECIPE HAS A BASE OF COOKED BALTI MEAT, AND/OR POULTRY AND/OR FISH OR SHELLFISH. YOU CAN DREAM UP YOUR OWN TROPICAL 'ADDITIVES'. THE ADDITION OF NUTS, COCONUT, MANGO, BANANA AND KIWI FRUIT TO THE BALTI BASE GRAVY IS WHAT TURNS 'TROPICAL' INTO 'EXOTICA', PRODUCING A DISH WHICH IS NOT TOO SWEET.

serves 4 (as a substantial main course)

1 quantity of any cooked Balti Meat recipe between pages 58 and 81
1 quantity of any cooked Balti Chicken between pages 82 and 107
175 g (6 oz) peeled prawns in brine, and their liquid
2 tablespoon tandoori paste (see page 40)
2 tablespoons peanuts
3 tablespoons fresh coconut flesh, cut into chippings
1 fresh mango, cubed
2 firm bananas, cut into rings
2 teaspoons Balti garam masala (see page 41)
2 tablespoons fresh coriander leaves, chopped
aromatic salt to taste (see page 43)
GARNISH
kiwi fruit, peeled and sliced
fresh coriander leaves

◆◆◆◆◆◆◆◆◆◆◆◆◆◆◆◆◆◆◆◆◆◆◆◆◆◆◆◆◆

1 Cook the meat and the chicken according to their respective recipes and combine in a Balti pan or wok, bringing to the simmer.
2 Add the prawns and tandoori paste. Simmer for a few minutes longer to amalgamate flavours, adding minute amounts of the prawn liquid as needed to keep things mobile.
3 Add the peanuts, coconut, mango, bananas, garam masala and fresh coriander. Add a little water if needed. When simmering, salt to taste. Garnish with the kiwi fruit and whole leaves and serve.

◆ Balti Karachi

BALTI MEAT WITH KEEMA CHICKEN AND SAG, TOPPED WITH CRUMBLED EGG.

serves 4 (as a substantial main course)

1 quantity of Balti Meat (see page 63)
1 quantity of Balti Keema Chicken (see page 94)
2 teaspoons Balti garam masala (see page 41)
1 tablespoon dried fenugreek
6 tablespoon fresh baby spinach leaves, shredded
2 tablespoons fresh coriander leaves, chopped
aromatic salt to taste (see page 43)
GARNISH
hardboiled egg, crumbled

◆◆◆◆◆◆◆◆◆◆◆◆◆◆◆◆◆◆◆◆◆◆◆◆◆◆◆◆

1 Cook the Balti Meat and Keema Chicken according to their respective recipes and combine in a Balti pan or wok, bringing to the simmer.
2 Add the garam masala, fenugreek, leaves and salt to taste. Simmer for a few minutes longer to amalgamate flavours, adding minute amounts of water as needed to keep things mobile.
3 Garnish with the egg and serve. If you have any leftovers from this large amount, they can be frozen provided everything was fresh (not frozen) first

Balti Exotica

balti specials

The following special dishes can be made with any main ingredient

◆ Balti Zeera

THIS TASTY STIR-FRY IS ENHANCED WITH BLACK AND WHITE CUMMIN SEEDS (ZEERA). ITS SWEET TASTE IS SAID TO BE INFLUENCED BY CHINESE TRAVELLERS TO THE BALTI DISTRICT. FOR THE MAIN INGREDIENT, CHOOSE EITHER MEAT, CHICKEN, OR SHELLFISH.

serves 4

1 quantity of cooked Basic Balti Meat (see page 63) or chicken (see page 84) or seafood (see page 110)
2 tablespoons butter ghee
2–3 garlic cloves, finely chopped
400 g (14 oz) canned plum tomatoes
175 ml (6 fl oz) double cream
2 teaspoons white granulated sugar
12 fresh tangerine segments, chopped
2 teaspoons Balti garam masala (see page 41)
1 tablespoon fresh mint leaves, chopped
2 tablespoons fresh coriander leaves, chopped
aromatic salt to taste (see page 43)
SPICES
1 teaspoon white cummin seeds
1/2 teaspoon black cummin seeds
1/2 teaspoon wild onion seeds

◆◆◆◆◆◆◆◆◆◆◆◆◆◆◆◆◆◆◆◆◆◆◆◆◆◆◆◆◆

1 Cook your choice of Balti meat, chicken or fish according to its recipe.
2 Heat the ghee in the Balti pan or wok. Stir-fry the spices for 30 seconds then add the garlic and stir-fry for a further 30 seconds.
3 Strain the tomatoes, reserving the juice for drinking or other cooking. Add these, with the sugar and cream to the pan and bring to the simmer.
4 Combine this mixture with the cooked curry from stage 1, and bring it to the simmer.
5 Add the tangerine segments, garam masala, leaves and salt to taste. Simmer

for a few minutes longer to amalgamate flavours, adding minute amounts of water as needed to keep things mobile. Simmer until it is cooked to your liking.

◆ Balti Moghul

THE GREAT MOGHUL EMPERORS GAINED ACCESS TO THE SUBCONTINENT THROUGH THE KHYBER PASS. LATER THEY MADE KASHMIR THEIR COOL SUMMER HOME, AND KASHMIR IS THE HOME OF THE BALTI RESTAURATEURS. NOT FOR THE CALORIE COUNTER, THIS RECIPE IS RICH IN GHEE, CREAM AND AROMATICS. FOR THE MAIN INGREDIENT, CHOOSE EITHER MEAT, CHICKEN, OR SHELLFISH.

serves 4

1 quantity of cooked Basic Balti meat (see page 63) or chicken (see page 84) or seafood (see page 110)
100 g (3½ oz) raw cashew nuts
150 ml (5 fl oz) single cream
4 tablespoons Greek yoghurt
2 tablespoons butter ghee
2–3 garlic cloves, finely chopped
20 strands saffron
1–2 teaspoons Balti garam masala (see page 41)
2 tablespoons fresh coriander leaves, chopped
aromatic salt to taste (see page 43)
SPICES
2 brown cardamoms
2 star anise
1 teaspoon aniseed
1 teaspoon sesame seeds
GARNISH
flaked almonds, toasted
fresh coriander leaves

◆◆◆◆◆◆◆◆◆◆◆◆◆◆◆◆◆◆◆◆◆◆◆◆◆◆◆◆◆

1 Cook the Balti meat, chicken or fish recipe of your choice.
2 Mix the nuts, cream and yoghurt in the blender and grind to a fine pourable

paste. Add a little water if needed.
3 Heat the ghee in the Balti pan or wok. Stir-fry the spices for 30 seconds then add the garlic and stir-fry for a further 30 seconds. Add and stir-fry the paste for a further couple of minutes.
4 Add the saffron and enough water to keep things loose. Bring to the simmer.
5 Combine this mixture with the cooked curry from stage 1, and bring it to the simmer.
6 Add the garam masala, leaves and salt to taste. Simmer for a few minutes longer to amalgamate flavours, adding minute amounts of the water as needed to keep things mobile. Simmer until it is cooked to your liking.
7 Garnish and serve.

Balti Tropical Vegetables (see page 156 for recipe)

◆ Balti Murgh Skardu

THE CAPITAL OF BALTISTAN IS THE TOWN OF SKARDU. IT HAS A POPULATION OF A FEW THOUSAND, PLENTY OF HYBRID MILKING COWS, DZUOS (A CROSS BETWEEN A YAK AND A BUFFALO), A POLO GROUND, A FORTRESS, THE RIVER INDUS AND ONCE, A ROYAL FAMILY. IT HAS A FEW CHEAP HOTELS AND RESTAURANTS. THIS DISH WITH ITS AROMATIC SPICES AND CREAM IS TYPICAL OF THE TASTES OF BALTISTAN. FOR THE MAIN INGREDIENT, CHOOSE EITHER MEAT, CHICKEN, OR SHELLFISH.

serves 4

1 quantity of cooked Basic Balti Meat (see page 63) or chicken (see page 84) or seafood (see page 110)
2 tablespoons butter ghee
2–3 garlic cloves, finely chopped
175 ml (6 fl oz) double cream
2 teaspoons white granulated sugar
2 teaspoons Balti garam masala (see page 41)
2 tablespoons fresh coriander leaves, chopped
aromatic salt to taste (see page 43)
SPICES
1 teaspoon sesame seeds
1 teaspoon white poppy seeds
1/2 teaspoon fennel seeds
1/2 teaspoon lovage seeds
2–3 brown/black cardamom seeds
5 cm (2 in) piece cassia bark

1 Cook your choice of Balti meat, chicken or fish according to its respective recipe.
2 Heat the ghee in the Balti pan or wok. Stir-fry the spices for 30 seconds then add the garlic and stir-fry for a further 30 seconds.
3 Add the cream and sugar and enough water to keep things loose. Bring to the simmer.
4 Combine this mixture with the cooked curry from stage 1, and bring it to the simmer.

Balti Chk-Chi-Car-Cha-Spi-Aub

5 Add the garam masala, leaves and salt to taste. Simmer for a few minutes longer to amalgamate flavours, adding minute amounts of the water as needed to keep things mobile. Simmer until it is cooked to your liking.

◆ Balti Chk-Chi-Car-Cha-Spi-Aub

TRANSLATED THIS IS CHICKEN, CHICKPEAS, CARROT, CHANA, SPINACH AND AUBERGINE.

serves 4 (as a substantial main course)

1 quantity of any cooked Balti Chicken recipe between pages 82 and 107
1 quantity of cooked Balti Cha-Spi-Dhal-Chi recipe (see page 156)
1 carrot, cut into rings and blanched
6–8 cubes of aubergine, cooked
2 tablespoons red pepper, diced and blanched
1–2 chopped fresh red chillies, optional
2 teaspoons Balti garam masala (see page 41)
2 tablespoons fresh coriander leaves, chopped
aromatic salt to taste (see page 43)

1 Cook the meat and the Cha-Spi-Dhal-Chi according to their respective recipes and combine in a Balti pan or wok, bringing to the simmer.
2 Add the carrot, aubergine, red pepper, chillies, garam masala, leaves and salt to taste. Simmer for a few minutes longer to amalgamate flavours, adding minute amounts of the water as needed to keep things mobile.
3 If you have any leftovers from this large amount, they can be frozen, provided everything was fresh (not frozen) first time around.

◆ Jashasha Hunza Baltit

A 600-YEAR-OLD FORT GUARDS THE HILLY TOWN OF HUNZA BALTIT. BUILT IN THE TIBETAN STYLE, THIS AGED BUILDING IS A REMINDER THAT ONCE, A BRANCH OF THE SILK ROUTE RAN THROUGH HERE, LINKING CHINA TO INDIA. THIS DISH IS A REMINDER OF THE CHINO-TIBETAN ROOTS OF BALTI COOKING. FOR THE MAIN INGREDIENT, CHOOSE EITHER MEAT, CHICKEN, OR SHELLFISH.

serves 4

1 quantity of cooked Basic Balti Meat (see page 63) or chicken (see page 84) or seafood (see page 110)
2 tablespoons butter ghee
2–3 garlic cloves, finely chopped
8 oz (225 g) cooked beetroot (not bottled and vinegared), peeled and cut into shreds
1 tablespoon black molasses sugar
1 teaspoon soy sauce
2 teaspoons Balti garam masala (see page 41)
2 tablespoons fresh coriander leaves, chopped
aromatic salt to taste (see page 43)
SPICES
1 teaspoon fennel seeds
2–3 star anise
5 cm (2 in) piece cassia bark
4–6 cloves

1 Cook the Balti meat, chicken or fish according to its respective recipe.
2 Heat the ghee in the Balti pan or wok. Stir-fry the spices for 30 seconds then add the garlic and stir-fry for a further 30 seconds.
3 Add the beetroot, sugar and soy sauce and enough water to keep things loose. Bring to the simmer.
4 Combine this mixture with the cooked curry from stage 1, and bring it to the simmer.
5 Add the garam masala, leaves and salt to taste. Simmer for a few minutes longer to amalgamate flavours, adding minute amounts of the water as needed to keep things mobile. Simmer until it is cooked to your liking.

Side Orders

Just as the restaurateurs at the Balti house do, I have grouped together certain items, which are as important to the meal as the main dish. The main Balti staple is bread – naan bread being the most commonly encountered. The traditional and correct way to eat Balti (as with all Indian food), is to break off a piece of bread, and holding it in the right hand, use it to scoop a small amount of food directly from the bowl. Cutlery plays no part in the operation.

Rice does not grow in the mountainous region of Baltistan. The best Basmati rice in the world grows in the Himalayan foothills, not many miles away, and although it is not traditionally eaten with Balti, there is no reason at all why those who believe that curry and rice go together shouldn't have rice with their Balti curry.

Chutney comes directly from the ancient Hindi word, chatnee, and is defined in Hobson Jobson (an Anglo-Indian glossary, published in 1886) as a 'strong relish, made of a number of condiments and fruits, etc, the merits of which are now well known in England'. The authors were referring, of course, to Sweet Mango Chutney, factory-bottled by such luminaries as Mr J. A. Sharwood, a Victorian Raj merchant. Chutneys are today even better known, and more popular than ever. They can be split onto two types: one which is cooked and preserved, often in a sugar syrup, such as the mango chutney referred to above; the other is freshly prepared and must be eaten the same day. Raitas are always fresh, simple mixtures with yoghurt. Pickles are always cooked in oil with little or no sugar, and are usually spicy and salty, and they keep in the bottle. No Balti meal is complete without a selection of four or more of these fresh and bottled items. Finally, I have included a small selection of desserts which will round off your meal.

rice with balti

Plain Rice by Boiling

Use the smaller quantity for smaller appetites, and the larger for healthier appetites.

225–350 g (8–12 oz) basmati rice
1.25–1.75 litres (2–3 pints) water

1 Pick through the rice to remove grit and impurities.
2 Boil the water. It is not necessary to salt it.
3 Rinse the rice briskly with fresh cold water until most of the starch is washed off. Run boiling kettle water through the rice for its final rinse. Strain it, and add it immediately to the boiling water, put the lid on and start timing.
4 When the water returns to the boil, remove the lid, and stir frequently. After 6 minutes, remove and taste a little.
5 If the centre of a grain is no longer brittle, but still has a good al-denté bite to it, remove from the heat and drain. It should seem slightly undercooked.
6 Shake off excess water. Transfer the rice to a warmed serving dish. Place it into a warming drawer for at least half an hour to dry and separate. Stir gently once during this time to loosen the rice.

Plain Rice by Absorption

Cooking rice by a pre-measured ratio of rice to water, which is all absorbed into the rice, is undoubtedly the best way to do it. Provided that you use basmati rice, the finished grains are longer, thinner and much more fragrant and flavourful than they are after boiling.

The method is easy, but many cookbooks make it sound far too complicated. Instructions invariably state that you must use tightly lidded pots and precise water quantities and heat levels, and never lift the lid during the boilng process. However, I lift the lid, I might stir the rice, and I've even used

Previous pages: Kashmiri Rice

the absorption method without a lid. Also, if I've erred on the side of too little water, I've added a bit during 'the boil'. Too much water is an insoluble problem. It's all rule-breaking stuff but it still seems to work.

Another factor always omitted in other books, is the time factor. They all say or imply that rice must be served as soon as it is cooked, and that there is no margin of error in the time and method. In reality, the longer you give the rice to absorb the water/steam, after cooking, the fluffier and more fragrant it will be. So it can be cooked well in advance of its being required for serving because, after the initial 'boil' and few minutes actual cooking, the rice is quite sticky, and it needs to relax. After 30 minutes it can be served and is fluffy, but it can be kept in a warm place for much longer – improving in fluffiness all the time. This is the way the restaurants do it. They cook in bulk using up to 5 kg (11 lb) rice (around 80 portions) at a time in huge aluminium saucepans. They follow this recipe exactly (the timings do not change, no matter how much rice is being cooked). They cook their rice at the end of the lunch session, put it in a very low oven and by the time they open for business in the evening it's perfect. (And, kept warm in the oven, it lasts the whole evening.)

Cooking rice by absorbtion does need practice, but after one or two attempts you'll be able to do it without thinking. Here are some tips:
1 Choose a pan, preferably with a lid, which can be used both on the stove and in the oven. Until you have had lots of practice, always use the same pan, so that you become familiar with it.
2 Keep a good eye on the clock. The timing of the boil is important or you'll burn the bottom of the rice.
3 Use basmati rice.
4 If you intend to let the rice cool down for serving later, or the next day, or to

freeze it, do not put it in the warmer. It is better slightly undercooked for these purposes.
5 300 g (10 oz) of dry rice and 600 ml (20 fl oz) is about 1 part rice to 2 parts water. This 1:2 (300:600) ratio is easy to remember, but do step up or down the quantities as required in proportion.

For small appetites use 225 g (8 oz) rice to 450 ml (16 fl oz) water
For large appetites use 350 g (12 oz) rice to 700 ml (24 fl oz) water

Here is my foolproof method, using a quantity for 'average' appetites.

serves 4

300 g (10 oz) basmati rice
600 ml (20 fl oz) water
1 tablespoon butter ghee

1 Soak the rice in cold water for at least 10 minutes, at most 20 minutes.
2 Rinse the rice until the water is more or less clear, then strain.
3 Measure the water and bring it to the boil.
4 Choose a saucepan or a casserole pot with a lid, with a capacity of at least twice the volume of the strained rice.
5 Heat the ghee in the saucepan or pot.
6 Add the rice and stir-fry, ensuring the oil coats the rice, as it heats up.
7 Add the boiled water and stir in well.
8 As soon as it starts bubbling put the lid on the pan and reduce the heat to under half. Leave for 6 minutes, but turn the heat off after all the water has disappeared, which will probably be after about 3 minutes or so.
9 Inspect after 6 minutes: if the liquid has not been absorbed, replace the lid and leave for 2 minutes; if and when it has, stir the rice well, ensuring that it is not sticking to the bottom. Now taste. It should not be brittle in the middle. If it is, add a little more water and return to

igh heat.

10 Place the saucepan or casserole, lid
on, in a warming drawer or oven
preheated to its very lowest setting (no
higher than 100°C/210°F/Gas ⅛). You can
serve the rice at once, but the longer
you leave it, the more the grains will
separate. Thirty minutes is fine, but it
can be left for up to 90 minutes.

Colouring Rice

There is no doubt that colouring your
rice adds greatly to its appearance.
There are two very ancient traditional
methods, using the natural colourings,
turmeric and saffron. The modern
method uses dyes.

Turmeric

To get your grains evenly coloured,
ranging from orange to pale yellow, the
turmeric must be added to the boiling
water. The less turmeric you use the
paler the colour.

Saffron

This must be added after any frying, or
else its fragrance will be destroyed.
'Bury' the saffron strands in cooked rice
and leave the rice unstirred for 30
minutes or more. Mix in well just before
serving.

Multi-coloured Rice

To achieve the different shaded/coloured
rice effect you see in restaurants, you
have to use food colouring. The best
colour is sunset yellow, and to achieve it,
simply sprinkle a tiny fraction of a
teaspoon on top of the rice before it
goes in the warmer. Do not stir
immediately; allow the colouring
10 minutes to soak into the rice and
then stir. You'll get a mixture of
coloured grains from deep to pale
yellow mixed in with white and very
attractive it looks too. If you wish to, you
can go completely multi-coloured with
yellow, red and green.

▶ THE INGREDIENTS FILE

food colouring

Authenic tandooris and tikkas in India
have always been cooked with natural
colours. Red is achieved using paprika
or chilli. Oil is coloured deep red using
certain roots. Yellow derives from
saffron and turmeric. You can use
anatto seed powder for yellow and
beetroot powder for red, but though
natural, neither is heat-stable, so they
change colour, becoming browner, when
cooked.

NOTE: the very bright red and orange
food that we are accustomed to at the
tandoori house, is an invention of the
restaurateur. It is achieved by using
tartrazine food dyes. Made from coal
tar, they are said to have 'side-effects',
particularly on children, and these
include allergic reactions, asthma
attacks and hyperactivity. These dyes
are also present, of course, in numerous
factory-produced foods, such as ready
meals, confectionery, sauces, and baked
products. The food tastes no different
with or without them, but if you wish
to have vibrant-coloured tandoori and
rice dishes, purchase them in powdered
form, and remember, they are
extremely concentrated, so use just the
tiniest amount.

Pullao Rice by Absorption

You can omit some of these spices if you
don't have them to hand. If you don't
like chewy spices omit or remove the
cloves, bay, cassia and so on. Saffron can
be optionally added, after the rice has
been stir-fried.

25–30 strands of saffron (optional)
SPICES
4 green cardamoms
4 cloves
5 cm (2 in) piece casia bark
2 bay leaves
1 teaspoon fennel seeds
½ teaspoon black cummin seeds
1 brown cardamom
2 star anise

1 Follow the recipe for cooking rice by
absorption (see page 00) adding the
spices at stage 5, stir- frying it for 30
seconds. Proceed with the rest of the
recipe.

Flavouring Plain Rice

The following recipes are spicings for
plain rice, cooked either way, which are
quick to do.

Quick Pullao Rice

Note: in this case, the turmeric can be
optionally omitted, or it can be boiled as
the rice boils to give an overall
colouring.

serves 4

1 quantity plain rice, cooked (see pages
    180–181)
½ teaspoon turmeric (see above)
1 tablespoon butter ghee
1 tablespoon coconut milk powder
1 tablespoon ground almonds
a pinch food colouring powder, sunset
yellow (optional)
SPICES
1 teaspoon fennel seeds
1 teaspoon black cummin seeds

1 Simply stir-fry everything together in
a large Balti pan or wok, until hot
enough to serve. Stir carefully so as not
to break the rice grains.

Lemon Rice

Note: in this case, the turmeric must be boiled with the rice water to give an overall colouring.

serves 4

1 quantity plain rice, cooked (see pages 180–181)
½ teaspoon turmeric
2 teaspoons mustard blend oil
2 tablespoons fried cashew nuts
1 tablespoon coconut milk powder
2 lemons, freshly squeezed
SPICES
1 teaspoon mustard seeds
1 teaspoon sesame seeds
6 curry leaves, fresh or dry

1 Simply stir-fry everything together in a large Balti pan or wok, until hot enough to serve. Stir carefully so as not to break the rice grains.

Chilli Rice

This can be as hot as you like.

serves 4

1 quantity plain rice, cooked (see pages 180–181)
2 teaspoons sunflower oil
SPICES
1 teaspoon mustard seeds
6–8 dried red chillies
1 teaspoon chilli powder

1 Simply stir-fry everything together in a large Balti pan or wok, until hot enough to serve. Stir carefully so as not to break the rice grains.

Nutty Rice

Nuts and rice go well together.

serves: 4

1 quantity plain rice, cooked (see pages 180–181)
110 g (4 oz) onion tarka (see page 45)
1 tablespoon cashew nuts, fried
1 tablespoon almonds, fried
1 teaspoon Balti garam masala (see page 41)

1 Simply stir-fry everything together in a large Balti pan or wok, until hot enough to serve. Stir carefully so as not

◆ Kashmiri Mushroom Rice

MUSHROOMS ABSORB EXCESS MOISTURE IN THE RICE AND PROVIDE A GOOD COLOUR CONTRAST.

serves 4

1 quantity pullao rice, cooked (see page 181)
6–8 mushrooms – any type, chopped

◆◆◆◆◆◆◆◆◆◆◆◆◆◆◆◆◆◆◆◆◆◆◆◆◆◆◆◆◆◆◆

1 Simply stir-fry everything together in a large Balti pan or wok, until hot enough to serve. Stir carefully so as not to break the rice grains.

◆ Balti Biriani

AT THE BALTI RESTAURANT, RICE AND CURRIED CHICKEN ARE STIR-FRIED TOGETHER AND SERVED HIGHLY GARNISHED WITH A SIDE DISH OF CURRY GRAVY. CHICKEN CHUNKS FROM ANY OF THE CHICKEN RECIPES IN THIS BOOK WILL DO. OR, OF COURSE, YOU CAN USE CHUNKS OF MEAT, SEAFOOD, OR VEGETABLES FROM ANY OF THE RECIPES, AND IN ANY COMBINATION. HAVE FUN!

serves 4

1 or 2 teaspoons butter ghee
6 tablespoons onion tarka (see page 45)
6–8 chunks cooked Balti Bhoona Chicken (see page 84)
450 g (1 lb) cooked pullao rice (see page 181)
450 g (1 lb) Balti masala gravy (see page 42)
2 teaspoons Balti garam masala (see page 41)
aromatic salt to taste (see page 43)
GARNISH
cucumber
shredded salad leaves
onion rings
nuts, fried or toasted
baby cherry tomatoes
sultanas
desiccated coconut
strips of omelette

◆◆◆◆◆◆◆◆◆◆◆◆◆◆◆◆◆◆◆◆◆◆◆◆◆◆◆◆◆◆◆

1 Heat the ghee or oil in a large Balti pan or wok. Add the tarka with the Bhoona , and stir-fry until simmering, then add the rice. Mix well, stirring gently so as not to break the rice grains.
2 Add a few tablespoons of the masala gravy and the garam masala.
3 Salt to taste and serve when hot, or keep in a warmer until you are ready.
4 Optionally garnish, restaurant-style, with any or all of the suggestions above. Divide the remaining Balti gravy into four individual bowls, and serve alongside the Biriani.

Balti Biriani

RICE

Chawal

Rice (*Oryza Sativa*) was domesticated in south India 9,000 years ago, and grown in heavily irrigated 'paddy' fields. The plant is a slender grass, whose grains form thin 'ears'. The Tamils called this grain arisi, derived from their word 'to separate', referring to the process of splitting the grain from the husk to produce brown rice (not to be confused with the Parsee dish of the same name). This must be further hulled to remove its brown bran, thus producing the familiar white polished grain.

Today there are over 7,000 varieties of rice and it is the staple of over two-thirds of the world's population. Paramount in Indian cooking is Basmati, which grows mainly in the foothills of the Himalayas, the best of which is from Derha Dun. Basmati rice has an unparalleled flavour. Once cooked, it elongates enormously to create fluffy, superb-textured grains, especially if the grain is aged. And a great tip is to lay down Basmati rice, like fine wine. Keep it in an air-tight container for one or more years (ten is not unheard of). Watch out for dirty rice (washed in muddy rivers) and cheap brands with broken grain or grit. Remember, as with most things, you get what you pay for.

WHEAT

Ata or aata or atta

Wheat is a grass plant which grows in temperate areas. Its grain seeds grow in clusters or 'ears'. When ripe, the ears are harvested and the grain is separated from the chaff by threshing. The all-important wheat grain, or kernel, is composed of starch and proteins called gluten. The harder the grain, the more gluten it contains. Endosperm makes up 83 per cent of the grain, and it makes white flour; 14 per cent is bran, 2 per cent is the wheatgerm and the remaining 1 per cent is the exterior of the grain, full of vitamins and minerals.

The job of the miller is to separate these components and make different types of flour. The process is complex. Grain is sorted to remove unwanted items then soaked and dried to harden it. Then it is 'winnowed' or cracked open between grooved rollers. Sieving separates the endosperm. Larger pieces are air-blasted to separate the remaining bran then re-winnowed. Now called semolina, the endosperm is ground again, this time through fine rollers, and it is now plain white flour. The number of stages depends on the grade and fineness of flour required. It is often bleached by the miller to make it whiter. The addition of a rising agent creates self-raising flour. Strong white flour is milled from one of the hard varieties of wheat grain, which has more gluten and thus creates a more elastic dough, good for Indian bread.

The separated bran is ground separately and blended into the white flour, producing coarser, browner wholemeal flour. The Indian version of this, *ata*, is similar to British wholemeal flour but is finer ground from a harder, more glutinous grain. Wheatgerm can be added to whole flour making it a protein wheatmeal flour, or it is sold as a product in its own right.

MILLET AND GRAM

Bajra and Besan

Wheat is not the only bread-making staple used in India. Millet (*bajra*) is grown primarily in north and west India for flour. Long, thin, delicate corn ears are grown to about 15 cm x 1 cm and contain thousands of tiny seeds, the millet itself. The seeds are a warm, stone-grey with a hint of yellow. Its flour is finely ground into a silvery-grey flour which is widely available. It can be substituted for all the wheat flour recipes in this book. Bengalis, in the north-east of India, adore gram flour (besan) so much that one of its names is Bengal Gram. It is the only flour to use in pakoras or onion bhaji and is made, not from chick peas, as some cookery writers insist, but from chana dhal, which gives the flour its gorgeous, blonde colour and its unique flavour.

breads with balti

Dough Making

Before we get down to the individual breads, it is important to study basic dough-making techniques. Once you have mastered the method, you will confidently produce perfect bread. The principal secret lies in the first kneading, or mixing of the basic ingredients, flour and water. This requires patient and steady mixing either by hand or by machine, transforming the tacky mass of flour and water into a dough. It should be elastic without being sticky and should feel pliable, springy and soft to handle.

Leavened Bread

If a raising agent is kneaded into the dough, and it is kept warm, it ferments, causing the dough to aerate with tiny bubbles, and rise. This is called leavening. Fresh yeast, though rarely used at the restaurant, is the most effective raising agent, though it gives a slightly sour taste. Yeast powder is weaker, but acts faster. Yoghurt does work, but it must be home-made; factory-made culture is too weak. Self-raising flour with bicarbonate of soda is a common restaurant mixture. Milk is said to make the dough tastier, with or without water, and sugar can be added to make it sweeter.

◆ Plain Naan

AT THE RESTAURANT, AND IN THE RUGGED LANDS OF THE NORTH-WEST FRONTIER, THEY COOK FLAT DISCS OF LEAVENED BREAD IN THE CLAY OVEN CALLED THE TANDOOR LITERALLY BY STICKING A DISC INSIDE THE TANDOOR NECK. GRAVITY MAKES THEM GO TEAR-SHAPED. AT HOME WE MUST 'CHEAT' BY PRE-SHAPING THEM, AND COOKING THEM UNDER THE GRILL. KALONJI AND/OR SESAME SEEDS ARE TRADITIONALLY ADDED TO THE DOUGH. ATA (WHOLEMEAL) FLOUR MAKES AN INTERESTING ALTERNATIVE NAAN.

makes 4

450 g (1 lb) strong white flour
25 g (1 oz) fresh yeast
warm water
2 teaspoons sesame seeds
½ teaspoon wild onion seeds
lukewarm water
1 tablespoon melted ghee

◆◆◆◆◆◆◆◆◆◆◆◆◆◆◆◆◆◆◆◆◆◆◆◆◆◆◆◆◆◆

1 Dissolve the fresh yeast in a small bowl containing a little lukewarm water.
2 Choose a large ceramic or glass bowl at room temperature, and put in the flour.
3 Make a well in the centre and pour in the yeast and sufficient warm water to combine the mixture into a lump.
4 Turn the lump out on to a floured board, add the seeds and knead with the heel of your hand.
5 Return the dough to the bowl and leave in a warm, draught-free place to ferment and rise. (This is called proving.) This can take an hour or so, during which time the dough should have doubled in size. It should be bubbly, stringy and elastic, as shown in the photograph on page 178.
6 Turn out the dough and knock back to its original size by re-kneading it.
7 Divide the dough into four equal parts.
8 On a floured work surface, roll out

each piece into a teardrop shape at least 5 mm (¼ in) thick.
9 Preheat the grill to three-quarters heat, cover the rack pan with foil, put the naan on to it, and set it in the midway position.
10 Watch it cook (it can easily burn). As soon as the first one develops brown patches, remove it from the grill.
11 Turn it over and brush the uncooked side with a little melted ghee. Return it to the grill and cook until it is sizzling, then remove.
12 Repeat with the other three naans, then serve at once.

◆ Karak Naan

ALSO CALLED KHARRI, JANDALA, FAMILY NAAN, OR ELEPHANT EAR, THIS IS NAAN MADE AS LARGE AS YOU CAN. AT SOME BIRMINGHAM BALTI HOUSES, WHERE THEY COMPETE TO PRODUCE THE LARGEST KARAKS, THEY CAN BE 90 CM (36 IN) IN LENGTH.

makes 2

450 g (1 lb) strong white flour
25 g (1 oz) fresh yeast
warm water

◆◆◆◆◆◆◆◆◆◆◆◆◆◆◆◆◆◆◆◆◆◆◆◆◆◆◆◆◆◆

1 Follow the Plain Naan recipe from stages 1–6.
2 Divide the dough into two equal parts not four. You will need a large baking sheet, and it will be hard to handle.
3 Cook as normal, following the rest of the Plain Naan recipe. If it will not fit in one go, grill one half then rotate it and grill the other half. Turn it over and repeat.

◆ Peshawari Naan

THIS IS MADE SWEET AND RICH BY ADDING
SULTANAS AND ALMOND FLAKES TO THE DOUGH.

makes 4

450 g (1 lb) strong white flour
25 g (1 oz) fresh yeast
warm water
2–3 tablespoons almonds, flaked
1–2 tablespoons sultanas
2 tablespoons ghee, melted

◆◆◆◆◆◆◆◆◆◆◆◆◆◆◆◆◆◆◆◆◆◆◆◆◆◆◆◆

1 Follow the Plain Naan recipe to the
end of stage 2.
2 Roll each part out into discs about 7.5
cm (3 in) in diameter. Place almonds and
sultanas in the centre of each. Pick up
the outside of each disc and bring it
together in the centre, over the fruit and
nuts and press firmly, making a 'patty'.
Flour the patties and roll out to 20 cm
(8 in) diameter.
3 Complete using the Plain Naan recipe.

◆ Keema Naan

THE EASIEST WAY TO MAKE THIS IS TO MAKE ANY
KEEMA (SEE INDEX) AND ADD IT TO THE DOUGH.
AMONG OTHER STUFFED NAAN TYPES, ARE
KULCHA (ONION; SEE RIGHT), AND ANANAS
(PINEAPPLE), BHARE (STUFFED WITH ANYTHING,
E.G. MASHED POTATO, VEGETABLES OR EGG, FOR
EXAMPLE), AND LASSAN (GARLIC).

makes 4

450 g (1 lb) strong white flour
25 g (1 oz) fresh yeast
warm water
175 g (6 oz) Balti Keema curry (see page 00)
3–4 tablespoons ghee

◆◆◆◆◆◆◆◆◆◆◆◆◆◆◆◆◆◆◆◆◆◆◆◆◆◆◆◆

1 Follow the Plain Naan recipe (see
page 185) to the end of stage 2.
2 Roll each part out to discs of about

7.5 cm (3 in) in diameter. Place some of
the keema in the centre of each. Pick up
the outside of each disc and bring it
together in the centre, over the keema
and press firmly, making a 'patty'. Flour
each patty and roll out to 20 cm (8 in) in
diameter.
3 Complete using the Plain Naan recipe.

◆ Kulcha Naan

makes 4

1 batch leavened dough (see page 185)
1 tablespoon ghee
½ teaspoon white cummin seeds
4 tablespoons fried onions

◆◆◆◆◆◆◆◆◆◆◆◆◆◆◆◆◆◆◆◆◆◆◆◆◆◆◆◆

1 Follow the previous recipe replacing
the keema with the seeds and onion.

◆ Ananas Naan

makes 4

1 batch leavened dough (see page 185)
100g (4oz) pineapple chunks, fresh or
  canned, drained and coarsely chopped
3 to 4 tablespoons ghee

◆◆◆◆◆◆◆◆◆◆◆◆◆◆◆◆◆◆◆◆◆◆◆◆◆◆◆◆

1 Follow the Peshawari Naan recipe (see
left) replacing the almonds and sultanas
with the pineapple.

◆ Chupattis

THESE DRY UNLEAVENED BREAD DISCS HAVE BEEN
MADE IN THE SUBCONTINENT FOR THOUSANDS OF
YEARS, FROM A SIMPLE MIX OF FLOUR AND WATER.
THE FLOUR IS UNLEAVENED, I.E. THE DOUGH HAS
NO RAISING AGENT, SO CANNOT FERMENT TO
BECOME AERATED. INDIAN WHOLEMEAL FLOUR
(ATA), IS FROM HARDER, MORE GLUTINOUS GRAIN
THAN THOSE OF THE WEST, AND IS FINER GROUND,
CREATING A MORE ELASTIC DOUGH. A DISK OF ATA
DOUGH IS ROLLED THIN TO ABOUT 15 CM (6 IN) IN
DIAMETER. IT IS DRY-COOKED IN A TAVA, A FLAT
GRIDDLE PAN, OR EVEN DIRECTLY ON TO THE
FLAME. IT COOKS FAST, PUFFING UP SLIGHTLY AND
OBTAINING DISTINCTIVE SCORCH MARKS. TO BE
ENJOYED AT ITS BEST, IT SHOULD BE SERVED AT
ONCE, THOUGH, AS WITH ALL INDIAN BREADS, IT
CAN BE REHEATED OR EVEN FROZEN.

makes 8

450 g (1 lb) fine wholemeal or ata flour
warm water

◆◆◆◆◆◆◆◆◆◆◆◆◆◆◆◆◆◆◆◆◆◆◆◆◆◆◆◆

1 Choose a large ceramic or glass bowl
and put in the flour.
2 Add warm water little by little and
work it into the flour with your fingers.
Soon it will become a lump.
3 Remove it from the bowl and knead it
with your hands on a floured board until
the lump is cohesive and well combined.
4 Return it to the bowl and leave it to
rest for 10 minutes.
5 Briefly knead it once more. Divide the
dough into eight equal parts and shape
each one into a ball.
6 On a floured board, roll each ball into
a thin disc about 15 cm (6 in) in
diameter.
7 Heat a tava or heavy frying pan until
very hot. Place one chupatti on to the
tava, and turn to cook the other side
after a minute or two.
8 Repeat with the other chupattis. Serve
immediately.

raitas

Raitas are fresh, simple mixtures of yoghurt with one or more other ingredients.

◆ Red Balti Raita

225 g (8 oz) natural Greek yoghurt
1 teaspoon tandoori masala paste (see
    page 40)
½ teaspoon chilli powder (optional)
½ teaspoon garam masala (optional)

◆◆◆◆◆◆◆◆◆◆◆◆◆◆◆◆◆◆◆◆◆◆◆◆◆◆◆◆◆◆◆

1 Mix together the ingredients. Serve
chilled.

RAITA VARIATIONS
Almost anything savoury can be mixed
into the Plain or Balti Raitas above. Here
are some suggestions:

Cucumber Raita: Add cucumber cut into
matchsticks, or make a decorative
display on a flat plate.

Mixed Raita: Add cucumber, onion,
tomato and fresh coriander, chopped.

Hot Raita: 1 teaspoon each chilli powder
and chopped fresh red and/or green
chillies.

◆ Green Balti Raita

225g (8oz) natural Greek yoghurt
2 tablespoons very finely chopped fresh mint
1 teaspoon very finely chopped fresh green
    chilli
2 teaspoons bottled vinegared mint
½ teaspoon salt
½ teaspoon chilli powder (optional)
½ teaspoon garam masala
½ teaspoon white sugar
¼ teaspoon mango powder
a little green food colouring (optional)

◆◆◆◆◆◆◆◆◆◆◆◆◆◆◆◆◆◆◆◆◆◆◆◆◆◆◆◆◆◆◆

1 Mix together the ingredients. Serve
chilled.

◆ Yellow Tandoori Raita:

225 g (8 oz) natural Greek yoghurt
2 tablespoons finely chopped mint
100 ml (3½ fl oz) mango juice
2 tablespoons pineapple juice
1 tablespoon sugar
1 whole fresh green chilli, finely chopped
1 teaspoon finely chopped ginger
1 teaspoon very finely chopped garlic
½ teaspoon salt
¼ teaspoon yellow food colouring

◆◆◆◆◆◆◆◆◆◆◆◆◆◆◆◆◆◆◆◆◆◆◆◆◆◆◆◆◆◆◆

1 Mix together. Cover and allow to
marinate in the fridge for at least 24
hours.

fresh chutneys

◆ Simple Cachumber Salad

1 large red or white onion, thinly sliced
2 green chillis, thinly sliced
½ red pepper, finely chopped
1 cherry tomato, thinly sliced
1 tablespoon freshly chopped coriander
aromatic salt to taste (see page 43)

◆◆◆◆◆◆◆◆◆◆◆◆◆◆◆◆◆◆◆◆◆◆◆◆◆◆◆◆◆◆◆

1 Combine everything in a bowl, adding
salt to taste. Cover and chill for up to 24
hours.

◆ Orange Chutney

½ white onion, thinly sliced
½ orange capsicum, thinly sliced
2 or 3 orange segments, chopped
a sprig of parsley or coriander
1 teaspoon lemon juice
¼ teasoon paprika

◆◆◆◆◆◆◆◆◆◆◆◆◆◆◆◆◆◆◆◆◆◆◆◆◆◆◆◆◆◆◆

1 Combine everything in a bowl, add
salt to taste. Cover and chill for up to 24
hours.

Green Mint Chutney: 1 teaspoon sugar,
1 teaspoon bottled vinegared mint, ¼
teaspoon mango powder, a little green
food colouring (optional).

◆ Fresh Chilli Purée

UNCOMPROMISINGLY HOT!

450 g (1 lb) fresh green chillies, de-stalked
1 bunch coriander leaves, stalks removed
300 ml (½ pint) clear distilled malt vinegar

◆◆◆◆◆◆◆◆◆◆◆◆◆◆◆◆◆◆◆◆◆◆◆◆◆◆◆◆◆◆◆

1 Combine all the ingredients in a food
processor and grind to a purée. You may
need a little more vinegar. Stored in a
screw-top jar, this will last indefinitely.

bottled chutney and pickles

There are several types of bottled Indian chutneys and pickles which go with Balti curries. The most common are mango chutney, lime pickle, mango pickle, brinjal (aubergine) pickle, chilli pickle and mixed pickle (usually containing lime, mango and some chilli). They are all quite hot (some are marked 'hot' and contain extra chilli) and sour, and once you acquire a taste for them, you will wonder how you ever managed without! They keep indefinitely in their lidded jars.

◆ Mango Chutney

MANGO CHUTNEY IS ONE OF THE MOST FAMOUS PRODUCT OF THE CURRY LANDS, BUT THE LOCALS DON'T LIKE IT VERY MUCH, FINDING IT TOO SWEET. BUT AT THE BALTI HOUSE IT IS STILL NUMBER ONE, ESPECIALLY SERVED WITH PAPADOMS.

Mango chutney is made by simmering ripe, de-seeded, chopped mangoes in water, with sugar, a little vinegar and a few spices until the mangoes have cooked and softened into a brown syrup. You could bottle your own but there are so many ready-made brands available, you may decide it's not worth the considerable mess and effort involved. The quality varies from one brand to the next, so try a few until you find the one you like. Some add chilli powder to produce hot mango chutney, which is a russet-red colour. It will keep indefinitely in a lidded jar.

◆ Dominique's Sweet and Hot Tomato Chutney

A SIMPLE AND DELIGHTFUL HOME-MADE CHUTNEY WHICH LASTS INDEFINITELY ONCE BOTTLED.

Makes 600 g (1lb 4oz) chutney

150 ml (5 fl oz) water
225 g (8 oz) sugar
450 g (1lb) tomatoes, chopped
12 garlic cloves, finely chopped
2–3 bay leaves
150 ml (5 fl oz) distilled white vinegar
1½ teaspons nigella seeds
1½ teaspoon chilli powder

1 Place the water and sugar in a 1.4 litre (2¼ pint) non-stick saucepan, and heat gently until the sugar is completely dissolved.
2 Raise the heat, add all the remaining ingredients and bring to the boil.
3 Lower the heat to achieve a gently rolling simmer. It will appear watery, but will reduce. If you prefer, you can remove the tomato skins after about 20 minutes. Stir regularly, making sure it doesn't stick to the bottom of the pan while the mixture reduces.
4 Remove the pan from the heat, cool and spoon into warmed jars; cover and label.

◆ Lemon, Lime, Mango, Aubergine or Chilli Pickle

IT IS NOT AT ALL DIFFICULT TO MAKE YOUR OWN PICKLE.

Makes: about 900 g (2 lbs) pickle

450 g (1lb) lemons, limes, green mango, aubergines or chillies weighed after stage 1
900 ml (1½ pints) vinegar
1 tablespoon salt
1 tablespoon sugar
450 ml (¾ pint) vegetable oil
10 large garlic cloves, chopped
2 tablespoons Balti masala paste (see page 39)

1 If you are using lemons or limes, quarter them. Remove the pit from mangoes and chop them. Destalk and chop aubergines or chillies.
2 Put the vinegar, salt and sugar into a large pan and heat to a simmer. Add the fruit or vegetable of your choice and simmer, stirring occasionally, for about 30 minutes, during which time the vinegar reduces.
3 Heat 3 tablespoons of the oil in a wok. Stir-fry the garlic and masala paste for a couple of minutes.
4 Add this stir-fry to the saucepan with most of the remaining oil and cook gently until the vinegar boils out and the oil comes to the top. Put aside to cool slightly.
5 Wash and lightly warm some screw top jars in oven to ensure they are dry.
6 Heat the remaining oil. Fill the jars with the pickle, pouring some of the hot oil on top to seal it. Cover with greaseproof paper and put on caps. Leave for at least 1 month.

CHEF'S TIP
When you have a spoonful or two left in some old pickle or chutney bottles, mix all the remnants together and rebottle. Depending on what you use, you'll get a different pickle every time.

desserts

◆ Sugared Almonds

THESE ARE DELICIOUS ON THEIR OWN OR AS A GARNISH FOR SWEET DISHES.

200 g (7 oz) whole almonds, shelled
6 tablespoons butter ghee
icing sugar

◆◆◆◆◆◆◆◆◆◆◆◆◆◆◆◆◆◆◆◆◆◆◆◆◆◆

1 Heat the ghee in your wok, and stir-fry the nuts for 5 minutes.
2 Drain (reserving the ghee for other uses). Coat in icing sugar. Store in a airtight container until needed.

◆ Nutty Sweet Rice

THIS IS AN INTERESTING WAY TO USE UP LEFTOVER PLAIN RICE.

serves 4

350 g (12 oz) cooked plain rice
2 tablespoons butter ghee
2 tablespoons chopped almonds
2 tablespoons chopped walnuts
2 tablespoons chopped pistachio nuts
6 green cardamom pods, cut open
6 tablespoons clear honey

◆◆◆◆◆◆◆◆◆◆◆◆◆◆◆◆◆◆◆◆◆◆◆◆◆◆

1 Heat the ghee in a non-stick pan. Stir-fry the nuts and cardamom pods for about 1 minute then add half the honey and continue to stir-fry for a further 30 seconds.
2 Add the rice, and carefully stir-fry (so as not the break the grains) until hot right through.
3 Drizzle on the remaining honey and serve hot or chilled with Greek yoghurt.

◆ Mango Syllabub

A REALLY SIMPLE DESSERT USING THE QUEEN OF INDIAN FRUIT.

serves 4

2–3 ripe mangoes
225 g (8 oz) natural Greek yoghurt
200 ml (7 fl oz) double cream
sugar to taste

◆◆◆◆◆◆◆◆◆◆◆◆◆◆◆◆◆◆◆◆◆◆◆◆◆◆

1 De-pit the mangoes (see page 44). Peel off the skin, and mash the flesh.
2 Mix the flesh with the yoghurt, cream and sugar.

◆ Kesari Shrikhand

THIS IS A SAFFRON YOGHURT SYLLABUB WHICH IS INCREDIBLY EASY TO MAKE AND ALMOST INSTANT. IT IS LIGHT AND SWEETISH AND, BEING THICK IN TEXTURE, IT IS FUN AND ELEGANT TO SERVE IT IN STEMMED WINE GLASSES FOR A MORE ELABORATE OCCASION. YOU CAN REDUCE THE STRAIN OF ENTERTAINING BY PUTTING THE MIXTURE INTO THE GLASSES EARLY ON AND STORING THEM IN THE FRIDGE UNTIL YOU ARE READY TO SERVE.

550 g (1¼ lb) natural yoghurt, strained (best for taste and texture)
150 ml (5 fl oz) double or Cornish cream
2 tablespoons ground almonds
3 tablespoons sugar (adjust to taste)
1 teaspoon ground green cardamoms
6–10 saffron strands
GARNISH
freshly grated nutmeg
pistachio nuts, chopped

◆◆◆◆◆◆◆◆◆◆◆◆◆◆◆◆◆◆◆◆◆◆◆◆◆◆

1 Simply beat all the ingredients together.
2 After placing into serving bowls or glasses, garnish and serve.

◆ Sevian

A CREAMY, SWEET VERMICELLI PUDDING. INDIA HAS ENJOYED SWEET VERMICELLI SPICED WITH CARDAMOM FOR CENTURIES.

serves 4

250 g (9 oz) dried vermicelli
200 ml (7 fl oz) milk
200 g (7 oz) sweetened condensed milk
1½ teaspoons seeds from green cardamoms
4 tablespoons pure butter ghee
1 tablespoon golden sultanas
1 tablespoon molasses or brown sugar
GARNISH
sugared almonds (see left)

◆◆◆◆◆◆◆◆◆◆◆◆◆◆◆◆◆◆◆◆◆◆◆◆◆◆

1 In a non-stick pan, bring the milk to the simmer, and add the condensed milk, and the cardamom seeds, and keep it at a rolling simmer.
2 Heat the ghee in your wok. Add the vermicelli, and stir-fry until golden (about 2–3 minutes). Add the milk, sultanas and the molasses or sugar, and simmer the noodles until they are as al-denté as you wish.
3 Garnish with sugared almonds and serve at once.

Mango Hedgehog
See page 44.

Kesari Shrikhand

◆ Baltistan Fruit Bowl

A LUXURIOUS EXOTIC FRUIT SALAD, ENHANCED WITH A TOUCH OF ALCOHOL.

serves 4

your own choice of fruit (some suggestions include: pineapple, melon, apple, pear, seedless grapes, tangerine, plum, cherries, currants, berries)
½ teaspoon green cardamom seeds, ground
175 ml (6 fl oz) apricot brandy
400 g (14 oz) can peaches in syrup
sugar to taste

◆◆◆◆◆◆◆◆◆◆◆◆◆◆◆◆◆◆◆◆◆◆◆◆◆◆◆◆

1 Decide visually on an overall quantity of fruit i.e. however much looks right for the number of people you'll be serving.
2 Prepare the fruit by cutting away husks, stalks and seeds/stones.
3 Cut the fruit into the shapes you require.
4 Combine the fresh fruit with the cardamom, apricot brandy and the canned peaches and their syrup and add sugar to taste.
5 Serve chilled.

◆ Moira Banana

IN THE STATE OF GOA THERE IS A TOWN CALLED MOIRA. IT IS NOT A PLACE WHERE TOURISTS GO AND IS UNREMARKABLE IN MANY WAYS. BUT FROM THAT TOWN I COLLECTED THIS DELICIOUSLY SIMPLE RECIPE WHICH USES A PARTICULAR KIND OF LOCAL BANANA. THIS IS NOT EXPORTED BUT I HAVE FOUND THAT THE DISH WORKS WELL WITH ORDINARY BANANAS.

serves 4

2 tablespoons raisins
2 tablespoons sultanas
1 tablespoon chopped mixed nuts
2 tablespoons butter ghee
4 tablespoons brown sugar
2 tablespoons sherry or rum
4 large fresh bananas

◆◆◆◆◆◆◆◆◆◆◆◆◆◆◆◆◆◆◆◆◆◆◆◆◆◆◆◆

1 Grind the raisins, sultanas and nuts in a food processor with a little water.
2 Heat the ghee with an equal quantity of water. Add the sugar and stir well. When simmering add the raisins, sultanas and nuts. Simmer for a while so that it thickens a little. Add the sherry or rum then take off the heat.
3 Peel and chop up the bananas. Pour the hot sauce over them and serve at once.

◆ Banana Fritters

SIMPLE, EFFECTIVE AND A VERY POPULAR PUDDING.

serves 4

4 large ripe bananas
2 tablespoons custard powder
3 tablespoons coconut milk powder
1 egg
few drops vanilla essence
2 tablespoons caster sugar
100 ml (3½ fl oz) vegetable oil
icing sugar for dusting
lemon or lime wedges

◆◆◆◆◆◆◆◆◆◆◆◆◆◆◆◆◆◆◆◆◆◆◆◆◆◆◆◆

1 Peel and mash the bananas.
2 Mix together the custard and coconut powders, the egg and the vanilla essence. Add the sugar and the mashed banana. Add just enough water to make a stiff mixture which should drop off the spoon with a little resistance.
3 Heat about 3 tablespoons oil in a frying pan and spoon a dollop of mixture into the pan, flattening it with the back of the spoon to form a disc shape.
4 After about 20 seconds, make sure the fritter is loose on the pan.
5 Repeat with the rest of the mixture, until the pan is full but not crammed.
6 Turn the fritters over in the order they went in. Add oil as needed.
7 The size of your dollop will determine how many fritters you make, and the size of your pan will dictate how many you can cook in one go. Cook until slight blackening occurs on each side.
8 As the fritters come out of the pan, dust with icing sugar and keep warm until you are ready to serve them. They are lovely served with lemon or lime wedges.

The Balti World

The northernmost part of the 'subcontinent' is literally on the 'roof of the world'. It is called Baltistan, and is in Pakistani Kashmir in the area they call the Upper Northern Territories. Covering an area of 10,000 square miles and with a population of under one million, Baltistan is sandwiched between the world's highest mountain ranges – the Himalayas, the Karakorams and the Hindu Kush. Pakistan's highest mountain K2, at 27,900 feet, is just one of many mountains peaking over 23,000 feet. The average valley height is 9,000 feet. Winters are severe and the area is literally cut off from the rest of the world for months on end. Air pressure is low, oxygen is short and water boils at 70°C because of the altitude.

It is one of the most elusive, toughest places on earth to survive. Yet people have lived there for many centuries. In fact Baltistan's valleys are extremely fertile, assisted by the mighty River Indus, which flows through Baltistan on its way from Tibet to the Arabian Sea near Pakistan's second city, Karachi. Called the 'Father of Rivers', the Indus flows for 3,300 km (2,560 miles) and has always been of major importance to the region. Some thousand miles south of Baltistan, it is the reason that the plains of Pakistan are so extremely fertile. Two thousand years ago, a branch of the Spice Route came through Baltistan's lone mountain pass, connecting China and India in lucrative two-way trade.

Baltistan's spring and summer are delightful and at times the temperature can peak at 35°C. Autumn is mild, until the winds get going. The valleys are very fertile and produce grows quite rapidly in the summer enabling the people of Baltistan to be virtually self-sufficient in terms of food. They grow rice, wheat, barley, maize and millet, and fresh fruit such as apples, apricots, blackberries, gooseberries, peaches, pears, pears, prunes, and walnuts are prolific in season. Vegetables grown include asparagus, beans, carrots, lentils, onions, peas, potatoes, radish, turnips, watercress and ten varieties of mushrooms. As much as possible is dried and stored for the long winter.

Dairy products are popular and come from the female ox (the Dri). Meat comes from yak, and buffalo of Chinese origin; a hybrid is called the Dzo and its young, the a-ko, are popular for meat. Goats also provide meat and milk. Fresh-water fishing is good from the River Indus and its many tributaries, and large and small game, flighted and non-flighted, is widespread and plentiful. Until recently there were no restrictions on hunting the ibex, lynx, markhar and musk deer so it is not surprising that these have now become extremely

rare. The snow leopard is also hunted – it is regarded as a pest and it is quite prolific. Game birds small and large are also prolific, the most popular of which is partridge (chi kor). Domestic chickens are valuable and relatively expensive.

Little changed in Baltistan and Kashmir for hundreds of years, but inevitably, some of its more enterprising people looked towards the West to take the main chance, and it came during the 1960s when Britain actively sought to reinforce its labour force with immigrants from the subcontinent. Other Asians had come to Britain before them and settled in Southall, Wembley, Brick Lane, Glasgow, Leicester, and other major cities. At that time there was no Asian community in Birmingham. Indeed there were precious few Indian restaurants in Birmingham. For some reason, these early Kashmiris settled on a run-down part of Birmingham in which to make their new lives. They chose to live in the suburb of Moseley, a couple of miles south-east of New Street station, an area, along with neighbouring Sparkbrook and Sparkhill, now known as the home of Balti. No one could have foreseen how the simple food of the new local community would soon become so popular with native Britain.

By the time the brothers Mohammed and Ashraf Arif arrived, the community was beginning to put down roots. Coming from a restaurant background, they started the now celebrated Adil's Balti House in 1976, located at 148 Stoney Lane, right in the heart of Moseley. Today in this area alone there are no fewer than 40 Balti Houses ranging from tiny cosy unlicensed one-man-band establishments to luxurious empires with a huge complement of staff and a massive turnover of customers.

Whether the first Balti house was the Paris (see page 11) or Adil's probably matters little. Arif's restaurant opened a year or two after the Paris, but he is adamant that Balti was his idea. 'My grandfather ran a restaurant in Kashmir called Adil meaning "Justice",' he said. 'Customers there picked their own raw ingredients and watched the entire cooking process. Apart from that, in all other respects, the cooking at our Adil's restaurant is identical.' Ashraf learned to cook there and in 1969, the brothers came to England to join their father, who by now worked in a restaurant in Bradford. When they settled in Birmingham, the idea to set up a new Adil's seemed obvious. Adil's restaurant soon became popular and a second branch opened near by on the same street.

Adil's, like the Paris, was, in effect, a curry transport café. Furnishings were basic. Formica chairs and tables were bolted to the floor. It stayed open from 10 a.m. to 3 a.m. daily and you paid on ordering. It offered a wide choice of dishes – Balti Meat, Balti Chicken, Balti Prawns, Balti Vegetables, Balti Dhals; all could be ordered in any combination. Balti Meat with Peas, or Balti Chicken with Carrots, or Balti Prawns with Chickpeas or Balti Meat with Chicken or Balti Prawns with Meat were just some examples on the original menu. As the restaurateurs were Pakistani Kashmiri Moslems, alcohol was not served and the Balti House not licensed.

During the 1980s, new Balti Houses began to open around the Midlands. Things became more sophisticated and menus were longer, with some restaurants offering over 60 Balti dishes. Although it has been redecorated recently, Adil's remains a typical simple Balti house. It is still unlicensed, (but there is, conveniently, an off-licence next door!). It is very busy and enormously popular. Glass tops cover the menus on each table. Animated conversation is punctuated by the regular clatter and hiss of steel Balti pans being served by the energetic staff. A peep into the kitchen reveals a hive of activity and a monster stock of Balti pans, waiting alongside the gas stoves and tandoori ovens. Tantalising smells impregnate all areas.

A visit to this area is fascinating. Not only are there the legendary Balti houses themselves, there are all types of Asian stores which seem to be open all hours. A visit to a grocers such as Azad's Supermarket on Stoney Lane is typical. The experience begins outside with sacks of onions and potatoes, and piles of fruit and vegetables inviting you to come inside for more. And when you do step in, the gorgeous smell of spices wafting in the air is enough to make you drool. Fresh exotic fruit and vegetables are piled up in their bins. Row upon row of spices make you want to start cooking there and then, and packets of rice and lentils range from small 500 g packs to 10 kg sacks. There also seem to be more pickles and chutneys here than in the whole of Pakistan, with brands you've never heard of. At the Milan Sweet Centre across the road you can re-energise yourself with a spicy snack or an Indian sweetmeat. Or call into Adil's for a snack. It's next door to Azad's. Such venues are dotted all around the area, along with Halal butchers, sari shops, and specialist music and video shops. On Stratford Road, just down from the Royal Naim, is Gopils. This is the biggest and best Indo-Pakistani utensils arts and crafts shop in Britain. As well as brass, copper and stainless steel Balti serving pans, there are ethnic vases and urns, ornaments, and knick-knacks, wall hangings, and jewellery. Venture further in, and you come across a caterer's dream: nests of Balti pans of all types jostle for floor space amidst saucepans big enough to feed the five thousand. Stainless steel, aluminium, cast iron, and even non-sticks are all there, and a bigger assortment you'll never see.

Plans are afoot by Birmingham Council to create a kind of Chinatown in the area, its name yet to be decided. Baltitown does not somehow have the same ring to it; Baltistan might be a better choice. After all 'stan' means country, and Balti – well everyone knows what that is. One sceptic has suggested Balti Disney but such bureaucratic intervention does not meet with everyone's approval.

Balti aficionados do not like change. They like the place and its food just as it is now, and they cannot get enough of it. Their leader is Andy Munro, who works full-time for local government, but seems to spend all the rest of his time eating thinking and dreaming Balti. Join him and his friends and you'll find yourself immersed in Balti legends and endless arguments about which was the first Balti house and which is the best. They talk of the 'Balti triangle' being that area within

Brum's mystical eastern suburbs, centred around Sparkbrook where Balti began. They refer to Balti naan breads as being as light as, and the same shape as, a duvet. One almost expects them to refer to their tog weight. They argue as to which venue cooks the largest naan. They call Stoney Lane the 'Balti Run', and Lye near Wolverhampton the 'Balti capital of the Black country'. They refer to Birmingham's Bristol Street as 'Spice Alley', which must not, of course be confused with 'Spice Avenue' a new up-market Balti house in the middle of the Balti triangle which Munro reckons, 'is rather like discovering the New York Hilton in Beirut', where they even 'flaboyed' (sic Spice Avenue) the Balti specials in brandy at a 'predictably five star price'! A murmur of discontent rumbles round the aficionados; there is genuine concern that going 'up-market' is likely to change the nature of Balti, not to mention its low price. Munro says:

'A Balti house should be unpretentious but clean. Dress can be as informal or a formal as you wish. Booking should not be necessary. The food should be inexpensive, starter and main course with bread being under £7. The diner should have an unrestricted amount of choice of combinations of 'mix n' match' ingredients. One Balti should be quite sufficient as a portion. The food should be freshly cooked. Spices should have 'street credibility' – they should be subtle, not pungently hot. It should take no more than 15 minutes to serve. The food should come to the table in sizzling black Balti pans. Cutlery should not be expected. Use naan bread in the right hand to scoop

up the food and wipe the bowl clean. The Balti house should be unlicensed and they should not object to, nor charge for diners bringing in their own alcohol.'

Other curiosities they discuss include The Falcon (called as you might guess the Baltese Falcon by the local Balti-philes), and 'Balti Towers', at which there is no sign of Basil except in the spices. The extremists even boast that they breakfast on Balti (at the Minar, Sparkbrook which opens at 9 a.m. on Sundays). Several Balti houses, among them the Royal Naim, open all day and every day. Adil's has pioneered such coded delights as Balti Mt-Spi-Cha-Chi-Aub, meaning, Balti meat with spinach, chana dhal, chickpeas and aubergine. Another favourite is Balti Tropical which is a combination of Balti meat, chicken and prawns. At the Sanam in Tipton one dish is called the '240 Watts Balti Special', because, according to the restaurant's owner, 'it is a light meal'. At Lye's Central they serve 'The Balti Chicken and the Egg'. The ultimate mix is called 'The Exhaustion Balti Dish', made by at least two Balti houses – Azim's and the

Royal Watan. I asked a waiter why it was called 'Exhaustion'. 'Simple,' he replied in a perfect Kashmiri Brum accent, 'it will exhaust you eating it! '

A few years ago, I was asked by the BBC to suggest a good curry venue for a late night chat show. I suggested Balti at Adil's and a complete outside broadcast was set up on the first floor of the restaurant. I arrived before the show with Ron Atkinson, then manager of Aston Villa football team (footbalti team?) and his wife. A total hush fell upon the large restaurant as we came in, then a resounding cheer went up from the customers. Ron was clearly popular. He beamed and nodded like the pope and we picked our way through to the stairs. Ron seemed oblivious to the fact that his immaculately turned out winter-tanned wife looked rather out of place in her expensive frock and jewels. He didn't see her expression freeze as she spotted the state of the toilet and the oil drums on the staircase up to our room. Yes, some Balti houses are a bit basic!

She cheered up considerably when Steve Nalon arrived and kept us in stitches with his impersonations of the Archer's Jack Woolley and Margaret Thatcher. Other guests included an Indian actress, Labour Politician Keith Vaz and a Liberal Baroness. The chat show began. Conversation flowed and the food came and went. It was, of course, delicious. The BBC had brought in a couple of cases of Cobra Indian Lager which went down well. Mrs. Atkinson confessed that she didn't like curry but this Balti meal was so good, she would eat it on another occasion. Mrs. Atkinson was a convert.

Keeping Balti

By definition Balti should be freshly cooked. However, we are bound to get surplus items or 'left-overs' which it would be ridiculous to throw away.

Always use a refrigerator to store cooked Balti, and ensure that the food is cold before refrigerating. Putting warm food into the fridge raises the temperature inside the fridge while the heat exchange motor struggles to bring the temperature back down. This can cause food already in the fridge to go off. It is preferable to use refrigerated Balti dishes within 24 hours, bearing in mind that their texture and flavour will change. Meat and poultry will appear slightly blander, because the spices have marinated into the ingredients. Vegetables will go softer.

Provided that you know that the raw ingredients used to cook the Balti dish were absolutely fresh, not pre-frozen, and were cooked immediately after purchase, and cooled rapidly after cooking, covered and placed in the fridge as soon as it became cold, then it is safe to store the dish in the fridge for up to 48 hours. Even so 48 hours is a long time even in a fridge. Freezing is a much safer method of storing.

Portions

Appetites vary enormously, and a 'huge' plateful to one person may leave another person hungry.

When I entertain or supply food for paying customers, I always provide enormous helpings. It is far better to have fully satisfied diners, than the other way around. You know the signs of the still-hungry diner: the available food disappears very quickly, then the diner looks furtively around, whites of the eyes indicating the preliminary signs of panic. Some restaurants, it seems, are unable to learn the signs. I've seen portions so skimpy that an anorexic teenager would pass out, rice layered so thin on the salver that you can see more

salver than rice. So serve generously and enjoy your diners' enjoyment. I can live with 'should-never-have-eaten-so-much' complaints. They're not meant in any case.

So what is a generous portion?.

My average serving per person is 175 g (6 oz) net weight of the principal ingredient before cooking. The average Balti dish will include a further 50 g (2 oz) of flavouring and thickening ingredients (spices, garlic, ginger, onion, tomatoes, pepper and so on).

A Balti meal is fun with a number of main dishes. The more people who are eating the meal, the easier this is. With four people you might serve one meat, one poultry, one fish/shellfish, and two vegetable dishes, plus rice, bread and chutneys. For each person allow approx. 50 g (2 oz) (uncooked weight) of each of these dishes plus 50 to 75 g (2 to 3 oz) extra. Allow 50 g (2 oz) dry uncooked rice per person for a smaller portion, 75 g (3 oz) for larger appetites. For lentils, allow 25 g (1 oz) uncooked weight, minimum per person.

If all this sounds complicated it isn't really. As always common sense should prevail.

As much of the enjoyment of Balti eating is to 'mix-and-match' combinations of items, I have adopted a portions formula in this book which should help you. All meat, chicken and fish/shellfish recipes are given as four-portion servings. Vegetables, on the other hand, are given as single-portion servings. Some items which you may wish to use a lot of – meat, lentils, etc. – are also given in 'bulk' ten-portion recipes. Using some fresh and freezing the rest will save you time, smells and multiple washing up.

SERVING AND DINING

As you have already seen in the introduction on page 10 and as every Balti-maniac well knows, most of the fun

of Balti is in the serving and dining.

Traditionally, the various dishes should come to the table in a blackened, well-used Balti pot – the two-handled wok-like pan described on page 15. A smarter alternative is a chromium-plated version. These dishes come in a variety of sizes.

For preference, at home, I like to issue the diner with a Balti pan to eat out of, ideally 25–27.5 cm (10–11 in) diameter. The food itself can be served in similar sized pans or smaller versions of around 12.5 cm (5 in) diameter for individual portions. Put the pans on dinner plates and/or side plates. Willow pattern is favourite at the Balti house but any type will do.

Bread can be served in a huge Balti pan of around 35 cm (14 in) diameter, while chutneys look great in tiny ones of around 7.5 cm (3 in).

As for eating Balti, the traditional way in the Balti lands and at the Balti house is to use no cutlery. The chupatti or naan is the traditional 'implement'. Break off a smallish wedge and using your right hand only, scoop up the food with the bread and pop it all into your mouth. After a while it becomes quite easy and not at all messy. Leave enough bread to do the traditional wipe up of the dish at the end! For the faint-hearted, a fork and dessertspoon are the only acceptable items of cutlery. A finger bowl and ample napkins are mandatory! And plenty of finger lickin' is expected!

Alcohol and Beverages

The traditional beverages to accompany Balti are water, fruit juices, cordials, and lhassi (yoghurt with water, crushed ice, spices and salt or sugar).

Lager is still the most popular drink, with over 55 per cent of diners preferring it.

Some robust dry red, white and rosé wines also go well with Balti cooking. Sparkling whites or rosés and, of course, champagne, cannot be beaten.

Glossary

This is a comprehensive glossary and includes some items not mentioned in this book as well as those that are, in order that it can be used as a general reference work. It may be worth checking the index for words that do not appear here, to see if they can be found elsewhere in the book.

The 'Indian' words are mostly Hindi and some Urdu. The English spelling is 'standard' but can vary as the words have been transliterated.

A
Achar Pickle
Adrak Ginger
Ajwain or Ajowain Lovage seeds
Akni Spicy consommé-like stock. Also called *yakni*
Alloo Potato
Am Mango
Am chur Mango powder
Anardana Pomegranate
Aniseed *Saunf*. Small deliciously flavoured seeds resembling fennel seeds
Areca Betel nut
Asafoetida *Hing*. A rather smelly spice
Aserio Small, red-brown seeds with a slight aniseed flavour used for medical purposes
Ata or Atta Chupatti flour. Fine wholemeal flour used in most Indian breads. (English wholemeal is a suitable alternative.)

B
Badain Star anise
Badam Almond
Balti Balti dishes first appeared in the UK in the Midlands. Cubes of meat, chicken, fish or vegetables are marinated, then charcoal-grilled, then simmered in a sauce and usually served in a karahi or Balti pan.
Baragar The process of frying whole spices in hot oil
Basil Used only in religous applications in Indian cooking, but widely used in Thai cooking
Basmati The best type of long-grain rice
Bay leaf *Tej Pattia*. Aromatic spice
Besan *See* Gram flour
Bhajee or Bhaji Dryish, mild vegetable curry
Bhajia Deep-fried fritter, usually onion
Bhare Stuffed
Bhoona or Bhuna The process of cooking the spice paste in hot oil. A Bhoona curry is usually dry and cooked in coconut.
Bhunana Roast
Bhindi Okra or ladies' fingers
Biriani Traditionally rice baked with meat or vegetable filling with saffron, served with edible silver foil. The restaurant interpretation is a fried rice artificially coloured, with filling added.
Blachan *See* Shrimp Paste
Black salt *Kala namak*. A type of salt, dark grey in colour. Its taste, of sea water, is relished in India but not, I find, in the West
Bombay Duck A crispy deep-fried fish starter or accompaniment to a curry
Bombay Potato Small whole potatoes in curry and tomato sauce
Boti Kebab Marinated cubes of lamb cooked in a tandoor oven
Brinjal Aubergine
Burfi or Barfi An Indian fudge-like sweetmeat made from reduced condensed milk, in various flavours

C
Cardamom *Elaichi*. One of the most aromatic and expensive spices
Cashew nuts *Kaju*
Cassia bark Aromatic spice, related to cinnamon
Cayenne pepper A blend of chilli powder from Latin America
Ceylon Curry Usually cooked with coconut, lemon and chilli
Chana Type of lentil. *See* Dhal
Charoli Sweetish, pink-coloured, irregularly shaped seeds for which there is no English translation. Ideal in desserts. Sunflower seeds are a good alternative.
Chawal Rice
Chilgoze or Nioze Small, long, creamy nuts with brown shells used in cooking or eaten raw
Chilli *Mirch*. The hottest spice.
Chirongi or Charauli Small rounded nuts resembling Egyptian lentils. Used in puddings or pullaos.
Chor magaz Melon seeds. Used as a thickener.
Chupatti A dry 15 cm (6 in) disc of unleavened bread. Normally griddle-cooked, it should be served piping hot. Spelling varies (e.g. Chuppati, Chapati, and so on).
Chutneys A relish made with fruits and spices. The most common ones are onion, mango and tandoori. There are dozens of others which rarely appear on the standard menu. *See also* Sambals
Cinnamon *Dalchini*. One of the most aromatic spices.
Cloves *Lavang*. Expensive and fragrant spice.
Coriander *Dhania*. One of the most important spices in Indian cookery. The leaves of the plant can be used fresh and the seeds whole or ground.
Cummin or Cumin *Jeera*. There are two types of seed: white and black. The white seeds are very important in Indian cookery. The black seeds (*kala jeera*) are nice in pullao rice and certain vegetable dishes. Both can be used whole or ground.
Curry The only word in this glossary to have no direct translation into any of the subcontinent's 15 or so languages. The word was coined by the British in India centuries ago. Possible contenders for the origin of the word are karahi or *karai* (Hindi), a wok-like frying pan used all over India to prepare masalas (spice mixtures); *kurhi*, a soup-like dish made with spices, gram flour dumplings and

buttermilk; *kari*, a spicy Tamil sauce; *turkuri*, a seasoned sauce or stew; *kari phulia*, neem or curry leaves; *kudhi* or *hadhi*, a yoghurt soup; or *koresh*, an aromatic Iranian stew

Curry lands India is the main curry land with 900 million, mainly Hindu, people. Other curry lands are her Moslem neighbours to the west – Pakistan, Afghanistan, and, to a lesser extent, Iran, where the roots of some Indian food are. To the north lie Nepal and Bhutan whilst Moslem Bangladesh lies to the east. India's south-eastern curry-land neighbours include the predominantly Buddhist Burma and Thailand, whilst multinational Malaysia and Singapore, with huge, mainly Moslem Indian populations, are also curry lands. The tiny island of Sri Lanka has a very distinctive curry style and one must not forget significant pockets of curry-eating Asians in Africa and the Caribbean. The total number of people whose 'staple' diet is curry exceeds 1 billion – 25 per cent of the world's population.

Curry leaves Neem leaves or *kari phulia*. Small leaves a bit like bay leaves, used for flavouring.

Cus cus See poppy seed

D

Dahi Yoghurt

Dalchini or Darchim Cinnamon

Degchi, Dekchi or Degh Brass or metal saucepan without handles also called *pateeli* or *batlio*

Dhal Lentils. There are over 60 types of lentils in the subcontinent, some of which are very obscure. Like peas, they grow into a hard sphere measuring between 1 cm (½ in) (chickpeas) and 3 mm (⅛ in) (urid). They are cooked whole or split with skin, or split with the skin polished off. Lentils are a rich source of protein and when cooked with spices are extremely tasty. The common types are chana (resembling yellow split peas, used to make gram flour/besan); kabli chana (chickpeas); massoor (the most familiar orangey-red lentil which has a green skin); moong (green-skinned

lentil, used also to make bean sprouts); toor or toovar (dark yellow and very oily); and urid (black skin, white lentil).

Dhania Coriander

Dhansak Traditional Parsee dish cooked in a purée of lentils, aubergine, tomato and spinach. Some restaurants also add pineapple pieces.

Dill Heart

Dopiaza Traditional meat dish. *Do* means two and *Piaza* means onion. It gets its name because onions appear twice in the cooking process

Doroo Celery

Dosa or Dosai A South Indian pancake made from rice and lentil flour. Usually served with a filling

Dum Steam cooking. Long before the West invented the pressure cooker, India had her own method which still exists today. A pot with a close-fitting lid is sealed with a ring of dough. The ingredients are then cooked in their own steam under some pressure.

E

Ekuri Spiced scrambled eggs

Elaichi Cardamom

F

Fennel *Sunf* or *soonf*. A small green seed which is very aromatic, and has an aniseed taste.

Fenugreek *Methi*. The seeds of this important spice are used in fresh or dried form. They are very savoury and are used in many northern Indian dishes.

Fish sauce This is the runny liquid strained from fermented anchovies, and is a very important flavouring-agent.

Five-Spice Powder Combination of five sweet and aromatic spices used in Chinese and Malay cooking. Usually ground. A typical combination would be equal parts of cinnamon, cloves, fennel seeds, star anise and Szechuan pepper.

Foogath Lightly cooked vegetable dish

G

Gajar Carrot

Galangal or Galingale A tuber related to ginger which comes in varieties known as greater or lesser. It has a more peppery taste than ginger (which can be substituted). It is used in Thai cooking where it is called *kha*, and in Indonesian (*laos*) and Malay (*kenkur*). It is available in the UK in fresh form (rare), dried or powdered.

Garam masala Literally 'hot mixture'. This refers to a blend of spices much loved in northern Indian cookery. The Curry Club garam masala contains nine spices.

Ghee Clarified butter or margarine much used in north Indian cookery

Ginger *Adrak* (fresh), *sont* (dried), a rhizome which can be used fresh, dried or powdered

Gobi or Phoolgobi Cauliflower

Goor or Gur Jaggery (palm sugar) or molasses

Gosht Lamb, mutton or goat

Gram flour Besan. Finely ground flour, pale blond in colour, made from chana (see Dhal). Used to make Pakoras and to thicken curries

Galub jaman An Indian dessert. Small 2.5 cm (1 in) diameter balls of flour and milk powder, deep-fried to golden and served cold in syrup. Cake-like texture

Gurda Kidney. Gurda kebab is marinated kidneys skewered and cooked in the tandoor

H

Halva Sweets made from syrup and vegetables or fruit with a thicker texture than Turkish delight. Served cold in small squares. It is translucent and comes in bright colours depending on ingredient used, e.g. orange (carrot), green (pistachio), red (mango), etc. Sometimes garnished with edible silver foil

Handi Earthenware cooking pot

Hasina kebab Pieces of chicken breast, lamb or beef marinated in spices and then skewered and barbecued with onion, capsicum pepper, and tomato. Of Turkish origin

Hindi Hindi is the official language of India. Although there are 14 or so other languages in India, only Hindi translations have been used in this glossary.

Hing Asafoetida

Hooper Kind of rice noodle found in Sri Lanka

Huldi Turmeric

I

Idli Rice and lentil flour cake (South Indian) served with light curry sauce.

Imli Tamarind

Isgubul Vegetable seed

J

Jaifal or Taifal Nutmeg

Jaggery *See* Goor

Jalfrezi Sautéed or stir-fried meat or chicken dish, often with lightly cooked onion, garlic, ginger, green bell pepper and chilli.

Jalebi An Indian dessert, comprising flour, milk powder and yoghurt batter pushed through a narrow funnel into deep-frying oil to produce crispy golden rings. Served cold or hot in syrup.

Javatri Mace

Jeera or Zeera Cummin

Jinga Prawns

K

Kabli chana Chickpeas. *See* Dhal

Kdhai Yoghurt soup

Kaju Cashew nut

Kala jeera Black cummin seeds

Kala namak Black salt

Kaleji Liver

Kalonji Wild onion seeds

Karahi (or *Karai, korai*) The Indian equivalent of the wok.

Karela Small, dark green, knobbly vegetable of the gourd family

Kashmir chicken Whole chicken stuffed with minced meat

Kashmir curry A restaurateurs' creation – a sweetish curry often using lychees

Katori Small serving bowls designed to go on a thali (tray)

Kebab Skewered food cooked over charcoal. A process over 4,000 years old which probably originated in Turkey where 'kebab' means 'cooked meat'. (*See* Boti, Shami and Sheek kebabs.)

Kecap manis Indonesian version of soy sauce, but sweeter and slightly sticky. Soy sauce can be substituted, although it is more salty.

Keema Minced meat curry

Kewra Screwpine water. An extract of the flower of the tropical screwpine tree. It is a fragrant clear liquid used to flavour sweets. It is a cheap substitute for rose water

Khir Technique for making a sort of cream, whereby milk is cooked with cucumber and puréed

Khurzi Lamb or chicken, whole with spicy stuffing and/or coating, also called Kashi

Kish mish Sultanas

Kofta Minced meat or vegetable balls in batter, deep-fried, and then cooked in a curry sauce

Kokum (or Cocum) A variety of plum, pitted and dried. Prune-like and very sour.

Korma To most restaurants this just means a mild curry. Traditionally it is very rich: meat, chicken or vegetables are cooked in cream, yoghurt and nuts, and are fragrantly spiced with saffron and aromatic spices. Actually korma is a frying method and it is possible to find very hot kormas

Koya Reducing milk to a thick sticky solid. Used for sweet-making

Kulcha Small leavened bread. It can be stuffed with mildly spiced mashed potato and baked in the tandoor

Kulfi Indian ice cream. Traditionally it comes in vanilla, pistachio or mango flavours

Kus Kus *See* poppy seeds

L

Lasan Garlic

Lassi (or Lhassi) A refreshing drink made from yoghurt and crushed ice. The savoury version is lhassi namkeen and the sweet version is lhassi meethi

Lavang Cloves

Lemon grass A fragrant-leafed plant which imparts a subtle lemony flavour to cooking. Use ground powder (made from the bulbs) as a substitute

Lentils See Dhal

Lilva A small oval-shaped bean which grows in a pod like the European pea

Lime Leaves Markrut or citrus leaves. Used in Thai cooking, fresh or dried, to give a distinctive aromatic flavour

Loochees A type of bread made in Bengal using white flour

Lovage *Ajwain* or *ajowain*. Slightly bitter round seeds

M

Mace *Javitri*. The outer part of the nutmeg

Macchi or Macchli Fish

Madras You will not find a traditional recipe for Madras curry as this is another restaurateurs' invention. But the people of South India do eat hot curries; someone must have christened his hot curry 'Madras' and the name stuck

Makhani A traditional dish. Tandoori chicken is cooked in a ghee and tomato sauce

Makke Cornflour

Makrut or Markut Citrus or lime leaf

Malai Cream

Malaya The curries of Malaya are traditionally cooked with plenty of coconut, chilli and ginger. In the Indian restaurant, however, they are usually mild and contain pineapple and other fruit

Mamra Puffed basmati rice

Mango Powder *Am chur*. A very sour flavouring agent

Masala A mixture of spices which are cooked with a particular dish. Any curry powder is therefore a masala. There are many spelling variations – massala, massalla, musala, mosola, massalam, etc.

Massoor Red lentils. *See* Dhal

Mattar Green peas

Meethi Sweet

Melon seeds *Chor magaz*

Methi Fenugreek

Mirch Pepper or chilli

Moglai or Moghlai Cooking in the style of the Moghul emperors whose chefs took Indian cookery to the heights of gourmet cusine three centuries ago. Few restaurateurs who offer Moglai dishes come anywhere near this excellence.

Mollee Fish dishes cooked in coconut and chilli

Mooli Large white radish

Moong Type of lentil. *See* Dhal

Mulligatawny A Tamil sauce (*molegoo* – pepper, *tunny* – water) which has become well known as a British soup

Murgh Chicken

Murgh Masala(m) A speciality dish of whole chicken, marinated in yoghurt and spices for 24 hours then stuffed and roasted. *See also* Khurzi

Mustard seeds Small black seeds which become sweetish when fried

N

Namak Salt

Nam Pla Fish sauce

Naan (or Nan) Leavened bread baked in the tandoor. It is teardrop shaped and about 20–25 cm (8–10 in) long. It must be served fresh and hot

Naan, Keema Naan bread stuffed with a thin layer of minced meat curry then baked in the tandoor

Naan, Peshwari Naan bread stuffed with almonds and/or cashews and/or raisins. Baked in the tandoor

Nargis Kebab Indian scotch eggs. Spiced minced meat wrapped around a hardboiled egg, then deep-fried

Naryal Coconut

Neem Curry leaf

Nga-Pi Shrimp paste. Concentrated block of compressed shrimp, vital as a flavouring in Thai, Burmese and Malayan cooking in particular.

Nga-Pya Fish sauce

Nigella Wild onion seeds

Nimboo Lime (lemon)

Nutmeg *Jaifal*

O

Okra *Bindi*. A pulpy vegetable also known as ladies' fingers

P

Pan (or Paan) Betal leaf folded around a stuffing – lime paste or various spices (*see* Supair) and eaten after a meal as a digestive

Pakoras To all intents and purposes the same as the bhajia

Palak (or Sag) Spinach

Panch phoran Five seeds (*see page* 43)

Paneer Cheese made from cows' or buffalos' milk which can be fried and curried

Papadom Thin lentil flour wafers. When cooked (deep-fried or baked) they expand to about 20 cm (8 in). They must be crackling, crisp and warm when served. They come plain or spiced with lentils, pepper, garlic or chilli. There are many spelling variations, including popadom, pappadom, etc.

Paprika Mild red ground pepper made from red bell peppers. It is used mainly for its red colour.

Paratha A deep-fried bread

Pasanda Meat, usually lamb, beaten and cooked in one piece

Patia Parsee curry with a thick, dark brown, sweet and sour sauce

Patna A long-grained rice

Pepper *Mirch*. Has for centuries been India's most important spice. Peppercorns are a heat agent and can be used whole or ground

Phall (or Phal) A very hot curry (the hottest), invented by restaurateurs

Piaz (Peeaz or Pyaz) Onion

Pickle Pungent, hot pickled vegetables or meat essential to an Indian meal. Most common are lime, mango and chilli

Pistachio nut *Pista magaz*. A fleshy, tasty but expensive nut which can be used fresh (the greener the better) or salted. Goes well in savoury or sweet dishes such as biriani or pista kulfi (ice cream)

Poppy seeds *Cus cus* or *Kus Kus*. White seeds used in chicken curries, blue seeds used to decorate bread. (Not to be confused with the Moroccan national dish cous-cous, made from steamed semolina.)

Prawn butterfly *Jinga prai patia*. Prawn marinated in spices and fried in butter

Prawn puri Prawns in a hot sauce served on puri bread

Pullao Rice and meat or vegetables cooked together in a pan until tender (*see also* Biriani)

Pullao rice The restaurant name for fried rice coloured yellow with spices

Pulses Dried peas and beans, including lentils

Puri A deep-fried unleavened bread about 10 cm (4 in) in diameter. It puffs up when cooked and should be served at once

R

Rai Mustard seeds

Raita A cooling chutney of yoghurt and vegetables which accompanies the main meal

Rajma Red kidney beans

Rasgulla Walnut-sized balls of semolina and cream cheese cooked in syrup (literally meaning 'juicy balls')

Rashmi kebab Kebab minced meat inside a net-like omelette casing

Rasmalai Rasgullas cooked in cream and served cold

Ratin jot Alkanet root. It is used as a deep red dye for make-up, clothing and food

Rhogan Josh (or Gosht) Literally it means red juice meat, or lamb in red gravy. It is a traditional northern Indian dish, in which lamb is marinated in yoghurt, then cooked with ghee, spices and tomato. It should be creamy and spicy but not too hot. There are spelling variations – rogon, roghan, rugon, rugin, etc.; jush, joosh, jesh, etc.; gooosht, goose, gost, etc.

Rose water *Ruh gulab*. A clear essence extracted from rose petals to give a fragrance to sweets. *See* Kewra

Roti Bread

Ruh gulab Rose water essence

S

Sabzi generic term for vegetables

Saffron *Kesar* or *zafron*. The world's most expensive spice, used to give food a delicate aroma and yellow colouring

Sag or Saag Spinach

Salt *Namak*

Sambal A Malayan term denoting a side dish accompanying the meal. Sometimes referred to on the Indian menu

Sambar A South Indian vegetable curry made largely from lentils

Samosa The celebrated triangular deep-fried meat or vegetable patty served as a starter or snack

Sarson ka sag Mustard leaves (spinach-like)

Saunf or Souf Aniseed

Seeng Drumstick. A bean-like variety of gourd which looks exactly like a drumstick

Sennl Allspice

Sesame seed *Til*. Widely used in Indian cooking

Shami kebab Round minced meat rissoles

Shashlik Cubes of skewered lamb

Sheek or Seekh kebab Spiced minced meat shaped on a skewer and grilled or barbecued. Also called shish kebab, shish meaning skewer in Turkis. See Kebab

Sonf Fennel seeds

Sont (or Sonth) Dry ginger

Subcontinent Term used to describe India, Pakistan, Bangladesh, Nepal, Burma and Sri Lanka as a group

Supari Mixture of seeds and sweeteners for chewing after a meal. Usually includes aniseed or fennel, shredded betal nut, sugar balls, marrow seeds, and so on.

T

Taipal or Jaiphal Nutmeg

Tamarind *Imli*. A date-like fruit used as chutney, and in cooking as a souring agent

Tandoori A style of charcoal cooking originating in north-west India (what is now Pakistan and the Punjab). Originally it was confined to chicken and lamb (see Boti Kebab), and naan bread. More recently it has been applied to lobster too. The meat is marinated in a reddened yoghurt sauce and placed in the tandoor

Tarka Garnishes of spices/onion

Tarka dhal Lentils garnished with fried spices

Tava (or Tawa) A heavy, almost flat, circular wooden-handled griddle pan used to cook Indian breads and to 'roast' spices. Also ideal for many cooking functions from frying eggs and omelettes to making pancakes.

Tej patia The leaf of the cassia bark tree. Resembles bay leaf which can be used in its place

Thali set A tray used to serve your meals in true authentic Indian fashion. Each diner's thali tray holds a number of katori dishes in which different curry dishes, rice and chutneys are placed. Breads and papadoms go on the tray itself

Tikka Skewered meat, chicken or seafood, marinated then barbecued or tandoori baked

Til Sesame seeds

Tindla A vegetable of the cucumber family

Tindaloo *See* Vindaloo

Toor (or Toovar) A type of lentil. *See* Dhal

Tukmeria (or Tulsi) Black seeds of a basil family plant. Look like poppy seeds.Used in drinks

Turmeric *Haldi* or *huldi*. A very important Indian spice, used to give the familiar yellow colour to curries. Use sparingly or it can cause bitterness

U

Udrak Ginger

Urid A type of lentil. *See* Dhal

V

Vark (or Varak) Edible silver or gold foil

Vindaloo A fiery hot dish from Goa. Traditionally it was pork marinated in vinegar with garlic. In the restaurant it has now come to mean simply a very hot dish. Also sometimes called bindaloo or tindaloo (even hotter).

Z

Zafron Saffron

Zeera Cummin

The Curry Club

Pat Chapman has always had a deep-rooted interest in spicy food in general, and in curry in particular. Having accumulated, over the years, a vast amount of information he felt could usefully be passed on to others, he conceived the idea of forming an organisation for this specific purpose.

Since its foundation in January 1982, the Curry Club has built up a membership of several thousand, among them a marchioness, some lords and ladies, knights a-plenty, a captain of industry or two, generals, admirals and air marshals (not to mention a sprinkling of ex-colonels), actresses, politicians, rock stars, sportsmen and even an airline, a former Royal Navy warship, and a hotel chain.

The club has 15 members whose name is Curry or Curries, 20 called Rice and several with the name Spice or Spicier, Cook, Fry, Frier or Fryer and one Boiling. We have a Puri (a restaurant owner), a Paratha and a Nan, a good many Mills and Millers, one Dal and a Lentil, an Oiler, a Gee (but no Ghee), a Cummin and a Butter but no Marj (several Marjories though, and a Marjoram and a Minty). We also have several Longs and Shorts, Thins and Broads, one Fatt and one Wide, and a Chilley and a Coole.

There are Curry Club members on every continent including a good number of Asians, but by and large the membership is a typical cross-section of the Great British Public, ranging in age from teenage to dotage, and in occupation from refuse collectors to receivers, high-street traders to high-court judges and tax inspectors to taxi drivers. There are students and pensioners, millionaires and unemployed . . . thousands of people who have just one thing in common – a love of curry and spicy foods.

Members of the Curry Club regularly receive a bright and colourful magazine with features on curry and the curry lands. It includes news items, recipes, reports on restaurants, picture features, and contributions from members and professionals alike. The information is largely concerned with curry, but by popular demand it now includes regular input on other exotic and spicy cuisines such as those of Thailand, the spicy Americas, the Middle East and China. We produce a wide selection of publications, including the books listed at the front of this book.

Curry diners will be familiar with the Curry Club window sticker and restaurant quality certificate, which adorns the windows and walls of the

thousand best curry establishments. Curry Club members form the national network of reporters responsible for the selection of these restaurants, now published annually as the highly successful *Good Curry Guide*, with prestigious awards to the top restaurants.

Obtaining some of the ingredients required for curry cooking can sometimes be difficult, but the Curry Club makes it easy, with a comprehensive range of products, including spice mixes, chutneys, pickles, papadoms, sauces and curry pastes. These are available from major food stores and specialist delicatessens up and down the country. If they are not stocked by a retailer near you, try contacting the Club's associate, well-established and efficient mail-order service. Hundreds of items are in stock, including spices, pickles, pastes, dried foods, canned foods, gift items, publications and specialist kitchen and tableware.

On the social side, the Club holds residential weekend cookery courses and gourmet nights at selected restaurants. Top of the list is our regular Curry Club gourmet trip to India and other spicy countries; we take a small group of curry enthusiasts to the chosen country and visit the incredible sights, in between sampling the delicious food of each region.

If you would like more information about the Curry Club, write (enclosing a stamped, addressed envelope please) to: The Curry Club, PO Box 7, Haslemere, Surrey GU27 1EP.

The Store Cupboard

Here is a list of items you will need to make the recipes in this book, and its sister book, the *Curry Bible*, subdivided into those that are essential and those that are perhaps less so, as they appear in just one or two recipes. The list may look somewhat formidable but remember, once you have the items in stock they will last for some time. I have listed the minimum quantities you'll need in metric only, as given on most packaging these days.

Essential Whole Spices

Bay leaf	3 g
Cardamom, black or brown	30 g
Cardamom, green or white	30 g
Cassia bark	30 g
Chilli	11 g
Clove	20 g
Coriander seeds	60 g
Cummin seeds, white	25 g
Curry leaves, dried	2 g
Fennel seeds	27 g
Fenugreek leaf, dried	18 g
Mustard seeds	65 g
Peppercorn, black	47 g
Sesame seeds, white	57 g
Wild onion seeds (nigella)	47 g

Non-essential Whole Spices

Alkanet root	3 g
Allspice	50 g
Aniseed	25 g
Caraway seeds	25 g
Celery seeds	25 g
Cinnamon quill	6 pieces
Cummin seeds, black	25 g
Dill seeds	25 g
Fenugreek seeds	47 g
Ginger, dried	6 pieces
Lovage (ajwain) seeds	27 g
Mace	8 g
Nutmeg, whole	6 nuts
Panch phoran	30 g
Pomegranate seeds	30 g
Poppy seeds	52 g

Saffron stamens	0.5 g
Star anise	30 g

Essential Ground Spices

Black pepper	100 g
Chilli powder	100 g
Coriander	100 g
Cummin	100 g
Garam masala	50 g
Garlic powder and/or flakes	100 g
Ginger	100 g
Paprika	100 g
Turmeric	100 g

Non-essential Ground Spices

Asafoetida	50 g
Cardamom, green	25 g
Cassia bark	25 g
Clove	25 g
Galangal	20 g
Lemon grass	20 g
Mango powder	100 g
Salt, black	50 g

Essential Dried Foods

Basmati rice	2 kg
Coconut milk powder	100 g
Gram flour	1 kg
Jaggery	100 g

Non-essential Dried Foods

Food colouring powder, red E129	25 g
Natural red colouring (beetroot powder)	25 g
Food colouring powder, yellow E110	25 g
Natural yellow colouring (annatto)	25 g

Lentils and Pulses

Black-eyed beans (lobia)	500 g
Chana, split	500 g
Chickpeas	500 g
Massoor (red) lentils	500 g
Moong green, whole	500 g
Red kidney beans	500 g

Toor or tovar, split	500 g
Urid, whole black	500 g

Nuts (all shelled)

Almonds, ground	100 g
Almonds, flaked	100 g
Almonds, whole	50 g
Cashews, raw	100 g
Peanuts, raw	100 g
Pistachios, green	100 g

Miscellaneous

Papadoms, spiced and plain (pack)	300 g
Puffed rice (mamra)	100 g
Red kidney beans	500 g
Rice flour	500 g
Rose water, bottle	7 fl oz
Sev (gram flour snack)	200 g
Silver leaf (vark – edible)	6 sheets
Supari mixture	100 g
Tamarind block	300 g

Oils

Mustard blend	250 ml
Sesame	250 ml
Soya	250 ml
Sunflower	250 ml
Vegetable ghee	250 g

Canned items

Chickpeas	420g
Coconut milk	400g
Lobia beans	420g
Patra	420g
Plum tomatoes	420g
Red kidney beans	420g

Index